Praise for *De...*

"In this dynamic narrative, William H... strates that America's decision for in... inevitable. Hogeland's lively portrayal ... principal actors in the drama—Sam Adams, John Adams, Tom Paine, and a fascinating cast of lesser-known street radicals—is superb. As we follow his story, we come to appreciate anew the ways in which those nine weeks preceding independence would change not only America but also the world."

—Richard R. Beeman, professor of history, University of Pennsylvania, and author of *Plain, Honest Men: The Making of the American Constitution*

"In *Declaration*, William Hogeland, a talented historian with a strong narrative gift, tells the engrossing story of what he calls the 'nine tumultuous weeks' leading up to the Declaration of Independence. He does so with insight, verve and an eye for the telling detail. He brings to life not only the usual heroic figures from this period but also a supporting cast of scoundrels, idealists and cranks who might be called the Founding Foster-Parents."

—Aram Bakshian, Jr., *The Wall Street Journal*

"History writer William Hogeland here offers us an even more credible feel of being inside the bare-knuckled struggle that took place in Philadelphia in the supercharged nine weeks that led up to the issuance of the Declaration of Independence. . . . Even though we know the outcome in advance, there is a delicious suspense to this story."

—James Srodes, *The Washington Times*

"A vivid and thrilling account of the struggles that tipped the balance for independence in the weeks before the Declaration. . . . As with a good novel, I was sorry when it ended."

—Jesse Lemisch, professor emeritus of history, John Jay College of Criminal Justice, City University of New York

"Richly detailed. . . . In presenting a slow motion view of the Continental Congress in that crucial Philadelphia spring and summer, Hogeland allows us to see the same sort of nuances and imperfections as when our seats are just about on stage."

—Tony Lewis, *Providence Journal-Bulletin*

"Hogeland has written a fearless work of narrative history, one whose breakneck pace and wide-ranging lens perfectly mirror the palpable sense of urgency and momentousness in the streets and state rooms of Philadelphia during the summer of 1776."

—Scott Berg, author of *Grand Avenues: The Story of the French Visionary Who Designed Washington, D.C.*

"At times, in Hogeland's provocative telling, the debates and drama resemble our era's relentless political face-offs and stalemates, complete with overheated rhetoric, vicious ad hominem attacks, factional media amplification, endemic manipulation and subterfuge, and carefully hidden agendas. . . . How these, and other entwined political and social dramas, played out is the rich material of this feisty, vivid book."

—Gene Santoro, *American History*

ALSO BY WILLIAM HOGELAND

The Whiskey Rebellion: George Washington, Alexander Hamilton, and the
Frontier Rebels Who Challenged America's Newfound Sovereignty

Inventing American History

Declaration

The Nine Tumultuous Weeks
When America Became Independent
May 1–July 4, 1776

WILLIAM HOGELAND

Simon & Schuster Paperbacks
New York   London   Toronto   Sydney

Simon & Schuster Paperbacks
A Division of Simon & Schuster, Inc.
1230 Avenue of the Americas
New York, NY 10020

First Simon & Schuster trade paperback edition July 2011

SIMON & SCHUSTER PAPERBACKS and colophon are registered
trademarks of Simon & Schuster, Inc.

For information about special discounts for bulk purchases,
please contact Simon & Schuster Special Sales at
1-866-506-1949 or business@simonandschuster.com.

The Simon & Schuster Speakers Bureau can bring authors
to your live event. For more information or to book an event,
contact the Simon & Schuster Speakers Bureau at
1-866-248-3049 or visit our website at www.simonspeakers.com.

Designed by Nancy Singer

Manufactured in the United States of America

10 9 8 7 6 5 4 3 2 1

The Library of Congress has cataloged the hardcover edition as follows:

Hogeland, William.
    Declaration : the nine tumultuous weeks when America became independent,
May 1–July 4, 1776 / William Hogeland.
        p.   cm.
    Includes bibliographical references and index.
    1. United States—History—Revolution, 1775–1783—Causes.   2. United States.
Declaration of Independence.   3. United States. Continental Congress.   4. United
States—Politics and government—To 1775.   5. United States—Politics and
government—1775–1783.   6. Great Britain—Politics and government—1760–1789.
7. Revolutionaries—United States—History—18th century.   I. Title.
    E210.H686   2010
    973.3'11—dc22   2010003239
    ISBN-13: 978-1-4165-8409-4 (hardcover)
    ISBN-13: 978-1-4165-8410-0 (pbk)
    ISBN-13: 978-1-4165-8425-4 (ebook)

W.H.H.
1927–1996

B.M.W.
1900–1989

Who shall write the history of the American Revolution?
Who can write it?
Who will ever be able to write it?
—John Adams

All politics is local.
—Tip O'Neill

Contents

1 Cold Wind, Warm Election   1

2 Samuel Adams and the Secret Meeting   11

3 The Revolution Is Now Begun   35

4 The Farmer Immovable   51

5 The State House and the Street   73

6 *Der Alarm*   91

7 Blind Eyes   105

8 Black Silk   129

9 "They are not represented in this house"   143

10 Independence Days   159

Notes   189

Sources   247

Acknowledgments   259

Index   261

Declaration

1

Cold Wind, Warm Election

May 1, 1776

Voters kept arriving on Philadelphia's western outskirts. At the block of Chestnut Street between Fifth and Sixth streets, outside the door to the Pennsylvania State House, the men kicked up dust, a growing crowd of tricornered hats and winter-beaten coats. Soon they were trading insults and threats. It was Mayday of 1776, bright but cold, with a wind blowing from the Delaware River, and the polls had been open since ten in the morning for what one visitor predicted would be "the warmest election that ever was held in this city." The voters were choosing a new Pennsylvania government. The vote was expected to be close, the day tense and possibly even violent. The State House itself, assertively symmetrical in high Georgian style, spoke only of grace and stability. Cupolas adorned the bell tower, which drew gazes up and heads back as it pierced the sky. Big mechanical clocks celebrated Pennsylvania's leadership in science and technology. Words from Leviticus proclaimed liberty. In a light-suffused chamber on the ground floor one of the oldest deliberative bodies on the continent—one of the best respected in the English-speaking world—the Pennsylvania assembly, made laws.

But grace and stability hadn't been evident lately. The assemblymen had moved upstairs to a committee room. They were lending their regular room to the Continental Congress, a body of delegates representing the various American colonial governments. The body had gathered in Philadelphia in 1774 as the First Continental Congress to mount a formal, intercolonial resistance to trade and police policies of England. Colonial governments objected to those policies for violating liberties that Americans believed they were guaranteed by English law. Yet many colonists, in and out of government, objected to the colonies' joining in opposition. Some deemed colonial resistance outright sedition. Delegates to the First Congress had fought bitterly over how far and how assertively to protest and resist.

Things had grown dire since then. Delegates to the Second Congress, which convened in Philadelphia in the spring of 1775, were now responsible for operating a poor excuse for a military force, optimistically called the Continental Army, which had actually gone to war against the British Army. The shooting had started in April 1775, when British regiments occupying Boston, Massachusetts, where American resistance had been especially confrontational, marched in formation out of town and into the nearby countryside. At Lexington and Concord, country militias confronted those ranks of crack redcoats and the soldiers were sent running back to Boston, harried by guerilla musketmen. With the British troops shocked and humiliated by defeat, militias from elsewhere in New England, and then from the other colonies, hastened to Massachusetts to aid what became a colonial siege, keeping the British occupiers stuck in Boston. In Philadelphia, the Second Continental Congress gave firm support to Massachusetts by forming the Continental Army. The delegates sent George Washington, a Virginia militia colonel with few qualifications other than charisma and an impressive physique, up to Massachusetts to command the army and manage the siege.

Then, late in March, word had come to Philadelphia that the redcoats had burned their own forts and broken their own cannon, and had sailed their ships out of Boston Harbor. Things hadn't been entirely quiet since then. British ships had shelled and threatened coastal towns. Lord Dunmore, royal governor of Virginia, now operating from a British warship, offered slaves freedom if they'd rise up against their plantation masters. An American expedition to Quebec was in the process of failing. Only a few miles downriver from Philadelphia, two British men-of-war were tacking up and down the bay, patrolling the Delaware's mouth to stop the city's trade. But there had been no invasion.

Now that pause was over. The biggest armada in English history was forming, row on row of masts and sails mustering in the harbor at Halifax, Nova Scotia, and transport ships from England had been sighted on the high seas, carrying thousands of soldiers, best disciplined in the world, expert at shaking curtains of lead from ranked muskets. Then they would charge, a thicket of blades, to slice bashed-up opponents into piles of gore. British retribution had been a year in the planning. It wouldn't be mild.

⌒

So the voters outside the Pennsylvania State House this cold Mayday had reason to be frightened and testy and ready to push and shove.

The question they had to decide today, under pressures they could never have imagined before, was a terrible one:

Reconciliation with England? Or American independence?

Reconciliation had long been the watchword. The war against England was defensive: that was the position of the Continental Congress and the colonial governments it represented, as well as a fervent belief of many Americans, even patriots. Taking up arms had been justified, after years of Parliament's abuse, by British troops' outright military aggression in Massachusetts. The war was supposed to make England see reason and bring Parliament to terms that would restore American liberties. Many colonists, including outspoken American resisters, referred to England as "home" and considered themselves loyal inhabitants of a glorious nation and great empire. They sought nothing more from the war than a quick conclusion and a just reconciliation with the mother country.

But some Americans had a different desire, and it was shocking: American independence. The idea had hardly been spoken aloud until recently. Its boldest adherents were from Massachusetts, which had always taken extreme positions against England; certain well-connected Virginians supported independence, too. In every colonial government and in the Continental Congress, the "reconciliationists" opposed the "independents" with force. Reconciliationists condemned declaring independence as a mad, doomed scheme of Massachusetts extremists.

No colony had been more committed to achieving reconciliation with England than Pennsylvania. And Pennsylvania made its opposition to independence decisive. Already called the keystone, rich and big, the Congress's host, it was the most influential of the colonies. Philadelphia's port on the Delaware dominated American trade, and the city was considered the second most important and elegant in the empire. A geographical position between New England and the South made Pennsylvania not only economically powerful but also militarily strategic, capable of fatally dividing Massachusetts from Virginia. And Pennsylvania held political sway over Delaware, New Jersey, Maryland, and New York, which formed a solid middle-colony bloc for reconciliation. Those colonies instructed their delegates in the Congress to pursue peace with England and to vote against any measure that might so much as hint at an American declaration of independence. Thanks to Pennsylvania's leadership, no effort in the Congress to push for independence could succeed.

But all that might change today. The Pennsylvania assembly was scheduled to begin its new session on May 20 in the temporary committee room upstairs. This election was for new Pennsylvania assemblymen, and a ticket of assembly candidates had announced their support for American independence. If those independence candidates could win a majority in the Pennsylvania assembly, the colony would reverse its policy for reconciliation almost overnight. The assembly would vote to change instructions to Pennsylvania's delegates in the Congress. So great was Pennsylvania's influence that an independence assembly elected here today could swing the whole Congress toward declaring independence and making the war a revolutionary one.

Hence the ugly mood. American independence or reconciliation with England? In an election that might determine Americans' fate, there was no middle ground. The Continental Congress had taken an unaccustomed weekday recess, giving over the ground floor of the State House to receiving and recording Philadelphians' ballots. Up and down the coast, people on both sides of the question awaited the results with fear and hope. As Pennsylvania went today, so must go the country, and the country was so passionately divided, and the contest in Pennsylvania so close, that nobody could confidently predict the outcome.

~

Samuel Adams of Boston was not to be seen at the polls that Mayday. He'd done more than he hoped anyone would ever know to push the Pennsylvania election toward American independence. He made it his business to be anywhere but at the center of what he inspired.

He roomed with his second cousin John Adams near the Delaware River's loud docks. He'd arrived in the spring of 1775, shortly after the shooting war had broken out at Lexington and Concord, entering Philadelphia in dour triumph. Muffled churchbells tolled to show the colonies' support for his suffering Massachusetts. Most visitors were overwhelmed by the size, stink, and hustle of the busiest port in America and second-most-sophisticated city in the empire. Some marveled at the broad avenues on a rational grid. Not Samuel Adams. He found little to remark on and nothing to admire or approve in Philadelphia, in the province of Pennsylvania itself, or in the middle colonies as a whole. He'd been called out of his New England country, and out of Boston's narrow alleys and turning streets, by a duty to make things like today's election go a certain way. Where he saw frippery and pusillanimity, a saving change must come.

Of what was called middling height (fairly short) and middling build (somewhat stocky), at fifty-three Adams was past middle age, and physical vigor had never been the source of his success. He was shaken by an intermittent, full-body tremor that sometimes made him unable to write. He dressed not just plainly but shabbily. He hadn't even learned to ride until recently, and then only at the insistence of cousin John, his top deputy, thirteen years younger. John thought nobody as important as Samuel should go horseless and that riding

6

improved health. After some help in mounting, Samuel managed to stay on top all the way from Massachusetts to Philadelphia, enduring the burning and soreness that the saddle would cause any new rider, especially one his age. The Adamses had some flannel drawers made along the way to cushion the seat, and by the time they arrived in town, the younger Adams was confounded. The servants had been whispering that the elder Adams was the better rider.

Samuel Adams had will. And he had a calling. From his earliest days in back-room Boston politics he'd been working against royal elements in government and Parliamentary involvement in Massachusetts trade. For more than ten years he'd been openly harassing royal governors. In the Massachusetts legislature, he authored bills against British trade acts and petitions dissenting from the governors' enforcement efforts. In the newspapers, under many pen names, he extolled liberty and made vicious attacks both on royal administrators and on citizens who seemed weak in the patriot cause. In taverns, political clubs, and the Boston town meeting he made civic virtue identical with crowds' fierce street protests. In correspondence with officials in other colonies he fostered intercolonial resistance.

Samuel Adams had pushed Massachusetts toward the shooting at Lexington and Concord, and now he'd gone all the way. England was a irredeemable tyrant, he said, not to be bargained with. A complete break offered the only hope for virtue in Massachusetts and throughout America.

That was treason. The British called Adams a "Machiavel of chaos," among other things. They would hang him if they could, and his cousin John, too.

He had an official role in Philadelphia as a member of the Massachusetts delegation to the Continental Congress. Unofficially he was that delegation's boss, or tried his best to be. But his ultimate purpose, in defiance of the hangman, of Pennsylvania, of Congress, of his own delegation, and of anyone else, was to turn the war of defense into a war of offense, and turn America independent.

So he badly wanted pro-independence assemblymen elected in keystone Pennsylvania today. But he never took anything for granted. "We cannot make events," he'd advised an ally the night before this election. John Adams had a finer ear for a joke than his cousin, a bitterer one, too, and he might have laughed aloud: Who had ever been more audacious in making events than Samuel Adams? Samuel meant it. He didn't, in fact, make events. He improved on them. At home in Boston he could fix an election. Here he'd done all he could.

For all of his terrible urgency, Samuel Adams always seemed to remain in faith that the chance for irresistible action would soon reveal itself.

⁓

At the polls, violence broke out at about two that afternoon, when a man named Joseph Swift became irate at the presence of so many immigrants.

Before and after marking their ballots and handing them in at the Chestnut Street windows, voters came into the yard behind the State House, a high-walled expanse set with tall trees. Pale new leaves caught the wind while far below, the "independents" and the "reconciliationists" formed knots, glaring and gossiping and rubbing up against each other.

The immigrants who infuriated Joseph Swift were Germans. As a bloc they were known to favor independence. Not that Swift was a loyalist. Hated in most colonies, loyalists had fled to England or Canada or substantially lowered their profiles. Swift was a Pennsylvania patriot, a man about town of old stock, on the board of the biggest hospital and on the vestry of Christ Church, which was more than a century old and whose new steeple made it the tallest structure in the colonies. Men like him supported the Continental Congress and the Continental Army. They were risking their security and possibly their lives to restore liberties. The Germans—"Dutch," most Pennsylvanians called them—clung to a guttural language, strange food, and incomprehensible newspapers. Why should they be allowed to swing Pennsylvania toward Massachusetts madness, American independence?

In the yard, Swift got the Germans' attention and told them that, except for what he implied was the ludicrous technicality of their naturalization, they had no right to vote in Pennsylvania. (Immigrants from the mother country were natural by blood.) He drove the point home: Dutch had no more right to vote, he said for all to hear, than Negroes did. Or, he added, Indians.

Philadelphia's Germans had a well-deserved reputation for toughness. This bunch moved in on Swift. If he'd expected help, he'd made an error. Others in the crowd gathered to watch. As the Germans began pushing Swift around, his friends couldn't step in. Swift's bigotry might cause a full-scale riot. The independents, poll-watching and electioneering in the yard, would run through the streets to broadcast it and bring out more of their vote. Swift's friends started falling all over themselves apologizing to the Germans. The Germans turned on them, too.

In the brawl, Swift managed to shake himself free of the yard and run down Chestnut Street, Germans in pursuit. He fled along the walk against the route of voters, eastward toward the Delaware, arriving at the mansion of one of the city's wealthiest merchants. Breathless and shaken, Swift was taken in. His pursuers were left in the street.

The independents back at the State House took heart from that fracas. Their hope soared at about 6 P.M., when the sheriff closed the State House door with voters still arriving. Voting was concluded for the day, the sheriff shouted. It would resume at nine the next morning. But less genteel voters couldn't take time off during the workday. They had to vote before nine and after six. Closing the polls seemed to disenfranchise them. The voters started haranguing the sheriff. They demanded that the election continue. They refused to disperse.

The sheriff threw the door open. People flowed in. To the satisfaction of the independents, voting resumed on the authority of the voters themselves. Late that night, when at last the independents went to bed, they had reason to think they would awaken to a new day for America.

The election results told a different story.

On May 2, when the results started coming in, it became clear that voters had rejected the new ticket. They'd returned to the Pennsylvania assembly a majority of establishment lawmakers whose purpose was to ensure that Pennsylvania's delegates in the Continental Congress blocked any move for American independence.

The majority had spoken. Reconciliationists up and down the coast could look forward to an end of Boston extremism. The war would remain defensive, legitimate, restoring old rights and keeping America within the empire.

Samuel Adams had other ideas.

2

Samuel Adams and the
Secret Meeting

May 3

Two days after the independents' failure in the Pennsylvania election, three Philadelphians came to the rooms Samuel and John Adams shared near the Delaware waterfront. These men were frequent visitors. Samuel Adams had been plotting with them for months, often with John in attendance. Today had turned rainy and cold, and it was getting late, but they had to assess the disastrous election results. They needed a new way to bring about American independence.

They tried to leave no detailed account of their discussions. Samuel Adams closed some letters with "burn this." John saw him time and again throwing papers in the fire, or in warm weather, shredding and throwing them out the window. Samuel took few chances with leaving records for the British or for history.

The men in the Adamses' rooms were Thomas Young, James Cannon, and Christopher Marshall. None was a delegate to the Congress or a Pennsylvania assemblyman. With other less than reputable men like Thomas Paine, Timothy Matlack, and Benjamin Rush, they formed a group of outsiders. Aside from Paine, they were unknown to the rest of the country, and until recently Paine had been the most obscure of all. Yet they'd begun taking over Philadelphia city politics, as well as politics throughout Pennsylvania. Samuel Adams believed he could not bring about American independence without them.

Thomas Young was the most flamboyant. He was a doctor, an occupation by no means considered refined, and he hadn't gone to the medical college in Edinburgh, Scotland, where more genteel physicians were certified. Young grew up in the Hudson River valley of rural New York. That made him, in colonial terms, a westerner. Tall, virgin timber and stumpy farm plots, cut from fearsome mountains and foothills, could inspire unusual American minds to improvisation. At the age of six Thomas Young was reading, memorizing, and reciting philosophy and science. At seventeen he was apprenticing in medicine while teaching himself Latin, Greek, German, Dutch, and French, important to medical practice. He soon had a firm grasp on botany, the science by which drugs were made.

In colonial America, insiders ruled and backwoods brilliance like Young's rarely led to wealth. He was poor most of his life. Sometimes he had no taxable property at all. By 1776, committed to the secret Philadelphia coalition with Samuel Adams, he had a sickly wife and six children.

Yet in the 1750s, when still in his twenties, Thomas Young began treating poor farmers in the hilly country near Amenia, New York, and he began to have ideas. He'd named Amenia himself, out of his romance with the classics (the Latin word *amoena* means "pleasing to the eye"), although nobody would ever be sure of what he meant by it. He was a talker, deeply self-educated, and he could be funny. He played Mozart on the violin. He liked to repeat the searing thoughts of Voltaire, the famed philosophe. None of those accomplishments endeared him to local authorities, and in 1756 he was indicted for blasphemy. He'd been heard calling Jesus a knave and a fool—and then, in case anyone wasn't sure whom he had meant, he explained that this Jesus was the one people called the son of a virgin. Reason should be "the only oracle," Young put it in a long paper embracing Voltaire. Like Voltaire he could be unreasonable in pursuit of reason. He was forced to apologize publicly for his remarks about Jesus.

In the early 1760s he briefly had cash to invest, and he hoped to put it into some land far to the north, plots in the forbidding forests of the Green Mountains between New York and New Hampshire, an area that was not part of any colony. The plots were offered at low prices by a man whose claim was said to be derived directly from the Indians and certified by the crown. Thomas Young's idea was that these Green Mountain lands might be bought and improved by ordinary people. Everywhere in colonial America, merchants were sewing up land and industry, living high by collecting rents from tenants while lending them money at exorbitant interest rates. Merchants were often known, as a class, as "the creditors," their dependents as "the debtors." Foreclosure could be epidemic.

Young envisioned terminally indebted farmers and landless laborers forming townships in the Green Mountains. In hardworking, small-farm prosperity, they would live free of oppression by the greedy.

That idea was squashed by the government of New York, which

challenged the investors' claim. New York had been lobbied by what Thomas Young deemed a monopoly of those very merchants from whom he was hoping to free people, rich land-jobbers far better capitalized than he and his friends. Young got angry. When Ethan Allen, a young friend from nearby Salisbury, Connecticut, began buying and selling Green Mountain plots in defiance of New York and soliciting people from northwestern Connecticut to emigrate northward almost en masse, Young gave approval, counsel, and support. (In Salisbury, he'd schooled Allen in Voltaire.)

Young liked to name places. Advising Allen's supporters to name their new area, he proposed *Vermont,* from French *vert* and *mont*, after the Green Mountains. With Young's encouragement, Ethan Allen became the fearsome strongman of Vermont, a legendary outlaw, and he published Young's paper on the sacredness of reason under his own name as *Ethan Allen's Bible.*

And around Amenia, when tenant farmers began rioting against landlords, Young gave them support, too. In 1763, he published a startling pamphlet. Common people, not the rich, are the rightful repositories of liberty, Young wrote. Workers, he now believed, should enjoy not just equal but actually superior rights against land barons who loll around on the sweat and struggle of others. Government should give protection to all citizens and, if anything, favor the unprivileged. Or else government should be overturned.

The colonies were just then coming into conflict with the home government in England. The American language of rights and liberty might have seemed to offer hope for the sweeping social change that Young was proposing. Certainly there was plenty of crowd action, and Young sought it out. He began to move about the country. He brought his wife and growing family from town to town.

But he gave American patriots a problem, and he had a problem with them. His desire to place government in the hands of artisans, mechanics, small farmers, and laborers in no way accorded with the philosophy of the leaders who had begun resisting new British trade laws. Those leaders called themselves "Whigs." Merchants, land-owning gentlemen, politicians—the very kind that Thomas Young loathed—Whigs didn't look forward, like Young. They thought of themselves as embodying the oldest English traditions in govern-ment. They found precedent for American protests in the signing of Magna Carta in 1215 at Runnymede, when barons forced King John to accept limitations on royal power. In Article 52 of Magna Carta, the king agreed that he could not take property at will, by levying a tax, say, or just moving his retinue into someone's castle. He could take property only by consent of the property owner. Liberty, in the Whig view, meant security in property, and that required consent in government and legal restraints on power.

In Whig theory, such consent was best given through elected, representative bodies like the House of Lords and House of Com-mons, delegated to sit in Parliament at the king's court and represent the propertied interest there. Houses of Parliament were responsible for determining whether a king's demands for financing were well-justified and worthy of consent. American Whigs recalled with ex-citement the grand progress of representation in English government. In the Civil War of the 1640s, the monarch overreached so badly that Parliament felt justified in waging war on him and cutting off his head. American Whigs' favorite writers were still the Civil War "lib-erty" writers, the theorists James Harrington and Algernon Sidney and the poet John Milton. The story climaxed in the great settlement of 1689, when the last Stuart king was deposed and William and Mary acceded to the throne. In documents that Whigs revered—among them the Bill of Rights and the Act of Settlement—peace came to England through clearly articulated limits on royal power, "constitutionally," as Whigs liked to say. The king was "in Parliament," part of a government that properly balanced the interests of king, lords, and commons.

Liberty had triumphed. Yet in the Whig view, it was always at risk. English Whigs had long scorned "Tories," those whom they saw as enthralled by and dependent upon royal power, decadent throwbacks, Whigs thought, to Civil War royalists. In the 1760s and '70s, with the growing colonial resistance to England, American Whigs began to use the term *Tory* to refer to apologists for British policy, and to anyone else whose commitment to resisting that policy seemed less than complete.

For like their English forebears, American Whigs were championing representative government. The rights and powers of their colonial assemblies seemed under attack by British government. Parliament had levied taxes that the colonial representative bodies hadn't consented to. Americans saw themselves acting in the spirit of the Magna Carta, of Harrington and Sidney and Milton and what they called "the good, old cause."

The problem for Dr. Thomas Young, as he went from town to town making a loud case for giving power to poor and laboring people, was that representative government had never involved the participation of people like that. American objections to the policies of king and Parliament were based precisely on the Whig principle: an ineluctable connection between liberty and private property. American governments granted representation to those with property in excess of a certain value. Others did not qualify to vote. Because those who owned only enough property to qualify to vote might feel sympathy with those who didn't qualify at all, even more property was required to hold office. Political power was concentrated, to Whigs rightly and naturally, in property. Thomas Young's ideas made him few friends among Whig patriot gentlemen. They called him an incendiary, a scourge, a bawler, low-class.

His time in Boston, however, was well spent. Arriving there from Albany in 1766 with an upstart medical practice, Young caused his usual controversy. He was accused by an established doctor of causing a patient's death. In letters to newspapers, Young called the other doctor a blockhead, and Boston doctors called Young a quack. Boston's Sons of Liberty, dedicated to resisting both the royal element in Massachusetts government and Parliament's incursions on American rights, by no means a working-class club, included members like Dr. Joseph Warren, an established Whig physician. Dr. Warren had good reasons for disdaining Dr. Thomas Young.

Samuel Adams, however, a leader of the Sons, took a different view. He was running the Boston town meeting in opposition to British government. He assessed the new doctor. The two men differed sharply. Young was still spouting antireligious ideas, and Adams was an inveterate Calvinist. Young was preaching working-class democracy, tantamount to anarchy to Adams. But Young suggested putting any enemy of liberty to death, and while Adams might not have phrased it that way, he knew what Young meant. He placed Young in two town committees. As Adams expected, the doctor turned out to be a powerful organizer.

The Sons of Liberty needed working-class turnout in protests and riots, and Young helped them get it. Boston had Puritan roots. The town didn't sanction Christmas and Easter; it associated those holidays with rituals of the Roman Catholic church, which many colonists feared and loathed above all other institutions as a tyrannical perversion of Christianity, the Whore of Babylon. Instead Boston licensed an anti-Catholic holiday, Pope's Day. Called Guy Fawkes

Night in England, Pope's Day occurred on November 5, anniversary of a failed Catholic plan to blow up the houses of Parliament. Every year, Boston's laborers took to the streets to savage the pope of Rome as the Antichrist. It was a day of scabrous mockery and misrule. Boys lorded it over men. Poor people went from fine house to fine house demanding money from the prosperous, to be spent on all-day feasting and drinking. Two gangs, one from the South End and one from the North, performed military drills and held parades before separate reviewing stands. The parades featured garish costumes, with a huge pope in effigy and boys dancing in feathers as the pope's demon helpers while mock-threatening the crowd. Then the two gangs fought. The winning gang was entitled to burn the loser's pageant materials on a hill. The night ended with bonfires in the streets.

Thomas Young helped bring the North and South End gangs together in Stamp Act protests. The Sons of Liberty held political versions of Pope's Day, civic pageants viciously satirizing the effects of British intrusions. One event turned into a full-scale attack on the home of a stamp-tax official. Gangs entered his home and smashed things up.

Even Dr. Warren had to admit Dr. Young's effectiveness in the cause, but Warren and others like him would have been nervous, too. Was the crowd's target really British oppression? Or was it local wealth? Pope's Day misrule was extending itself into everyday politics. Patriot leadership didn't want society topsy-turvy, except on certain holidays. But Thomas Young did.

Samuel Adams wasn't afraid of losing control of Boston. His next plan would lead to the decisive accomplishment of Thomas Young's Massachusetts period, critical to Young's success, ten years later, in the secret Philadelphia coalition. Adams showed Young how a self-appointed network could seize political power. Typically, groups dissenting from an official policy communicated with one another to establish a unified opposition, outside government. Adams realized that such "committees of correspondence" could instead be formally created by town meetings—the local governing bodies throughout Massachusetts. The Massachusetts assembly was always in danger of being shut down by the royal governor. But the governor had no power to shut down town meetings. With Thomas Young doing the riding and talking around the colony, Adams used committees of correspondence to coordinate the separate town governments in a single, disciplined organization. Each committee of correspondence was supposedly responsible to the town that had created it. But schooled by Adams and Young, each committee pressed its town to adopt resolutions against the governor and Parliament. Those resolutions had the force of law. The town committees thus came to serve as a shadow legislature, encouraging Massachusetts toward the crisis of April 1775, the shooting war at Lexington and Concord.

Samuel Adams was characteristically quiet about his innovations in organizing, Dr. Young characteristically exultant. He said that he and Adams had made some heads reel. His loud enjoyment and bad reputation had consequences. In the early 1770s, when British soldiers were occupying Boston, some of them assaulted him. He got away, and with his growing family fled Boston for Newport. Hearing a rumor that he would be arrested there, in 1774 he escaped to Philadelphia. There he met James Cannon.

~~~

Of the idiosyncratic personalities in the secret meeting at the Adamses' on May 3, James Cannon was Dr. Young's temperamental opposite. He was the quiet one. But he was deadly effective. A mathematician by training, a teacher by trade and inclination, Cannon was at once analytic and creative. He'd been figuring out how to take the organizing that Young had learned in Massachusetts to a new extreme, for purposes far beyond resisting England.

Cannon and Young had education and poverty in common. Cannon was born in 1740 in Edinburgh. He came to Pennsylvania at twenty-three, earned his bachelor's degree from the Academy and College of Philadelphia, and began teaching math there in the early 1770s. Teaching was neither prestigious nor well-paying. Educated immigrants used the job as a springboard up and out. Some went on to became lawyers and merchants. Some even made fortunes. James Cannon was still teaching his courses at the college right up until his death in 1782. In the 1770s, teaching of another kind was helping him change Pennsylvania.

Cannon shared with Young the desire to transform workers' lives. Philadelphia was more than its broad streets, brick mansions, hectic docks and markets, thriving trade, and august government. Merchants, a small group of families, held more than half the city's wealth. They lived in showy splendor. But many of the rest were impoverished. Not far from the State House lived residents of the Bettering House, run by Quaker merchants. The idea behind it was not just to feed and clothe hungry, cold people, though it was emphatically not to give them political power. According to the Quaker merchants, paupers were victims of their own moral degradation. The idea was to "better" them. Before the founding of the Bettering House, the city had responsibility for relief, offering small supplies of food and firewood to help families get ahead at home. The Bettering House took responsibility off the city's hands. Families moved into the house, where they were separated by sex, preached to, and made to spin, weave, and dye cloth. Unemployment was growing. Low pay destroyed many families employed in the hardest kind of work. By the mid-1760s the number of paupers toiling in the Bettering House reached a record high.

In 1775, James Cannon co-founded an alternative: the United Company of Philadelphia for Promoting American Manufacturers, or the American Manufactory. Since local merchants had made agreements against importing British goods, and there was also a huge pool of unemployed workers, Cannon and his partners saw an opportunity to give ordinary people fair and steady employment by making affordable domestic cloth. The company was radical in both operation and purpose. It didn't give alms or lectures. Women spun at home, at will, around other responsibilities and brought work to the factory for dyeing and weaving. The board of directors was composed of artisans and lower-middle-class businessmen, well connected to the poor of all neighborhoods, religions, and ethnicities. Overhead was low, and families stayed together.

Here was Cannon's and Young's shared vision of the American future. Output at the American Manufactory grew quickly while that of the Bettering House kept falling. Meanwhile the factory became a headquarters for radical ideas about labor and politics.

Social differences between city and country had often been deemed decisive, but now James Cannon began to think otherwise. Like Young's New York, Pennsylvania had western backcountry, many days' ride from the capital. In the pine barrens and tortuous mountain passes, settlers' lives could be a bitter struggle. With predatory creditors making the foreclosure crisis perennial, more and more settlers were giving up dreams of ownership and working as day laborers on the farms and in the factories of their creditors.

Cannon began linking the slums to the backcountry. Poor and laboring people in colonial America, excluded from legitimate process, often rioted, as Young's Amenia neighbors did, for debt relief. They seized courts where debt cases were heard, boycotted sheriffs' auctions of foreclosed farms, and rescued debt prisoners. Such events were called in Latin *mobile vulgus,* for "a readily movable crowd," shortened to "mob." But crowds tended to act spasmodically. They organized to correct an immediate situation, then subsided.

Amid the growing conflict with England, crowds in Pennsylvania gained new purpose. As in other colonies, many Whig committees formed to enforce boycotts on British trade, draft petitions, and organize protests. In June 1774, Philadelphia artisans and mechanics— craftsmen and shopkeepers who had formed their own patriotic society—walked to the State House, twelve hundred strong. A committee of gentlemen was meeting there to work up a good Whig response to the worsening situation in Boston. The artisans forced their way in and interrupted the meeting. They denounced it. They refused to call it a Philadelphia committee and mocked it as an upper-class interest, "the Merchants Committee." They demanded it change its character and its name and begin acting in genuine public interest. To that end, they demanded their own participation.

This was a startling moment. Whig leadership everywhere was trying to keep the working class focused on liberty, on property and representative right, and not on social equality. But here in Philadelphia an organized working class was demanding participation in a new political process. Under pressure of that demand, Pennsylvania's patriot committees grew and changed. The Pennsylvania-wide Committee of Safety, created by the assembly and run by the usual elites, remained socially conservative, as did the Philadelphia County committee. But the city of Philadelphia's Committee of Inspection and Observation, charged at first with enforcing boycotts against England, and then with maintaining day-to-day order during a difficult period, began to play a decisive role both in resisting England and in influencing government across the colony. And it was the most susceptible to working-class influence. Called successively the Committee of Forty-Three, the Committee of Sixty-Six, the First One Hundred, and the Second One Hundred, and known colloquially as "the City Committee," it soon drew one third of its membership from artisans and small manufacturers.

The committee began demanding social change. It petitioned the assembly against laws artisans deemed unfair. It demanded assembly votes published in roll-call form, to make government accountable. It went so far as to demand public galleries in the assembly room. City Committee leadership was becoming, if not identical with, then at least intertwined with the American Manufactory and the artisan movement. The committee made recommendations to the assembly, which the supposedly higher and more official body often found hard to decline.

James Cannon wanted more. Artisans were elected to the committee, and in a few cases even to the assembly itself, but those were master craftsmen, with enough property to vote and hold office legally. The people hadn't yet smashed the connection between the right to vote and ownership of property. The opportunity for truly radical change came with the shootings at Lexington and Concord in the spring of 1775. Throughout Pennsylvania, militias began drilling, both official and unofficial. The ad hoc militias were known as "associators." Soon, with the battalions of regular provincial militia in Philadelphia, there were thirty-one companies of Philadelphia militia, as well as fifty-three battalions of associators spread across the countryside and backcountry.

In every militia unit, Cannon realized, rank-and-file soldiery came from the least privileged class, the unpropertied, the nonvoting.

Militia privates added up to thousands of men, and militia service was one area of official life in America that did enjoy a democratic process. Men elected some of their own officers. Musters were scenes of drinking, socializing, and public debate.

If that armed, trained force were to organize itself throughout the militia, turning Pennsylvania's military force into an institution dedicated to its own interest as a class, it would be literally irresistible. The protection of Pennsylvania depended on these men. If, as one, they demanded the vote regardless of the property qualification, how could they be denied?

By late 1775, Pennsylvania's lower-class white men, urban and rural, had transformed themselves politically. They were represented by the Committee of Privates, a cross-Pennsylvanian body elected by privates in every militia unit. A first in labor history, the Committee of Privates was also a school of class politics. It was managed in part by Cannon, who wrote many of its resolves and circular letters, and it was connected to the American Manufactory and the City Committee. Yet the Committee of Privates developed itself in a manner, the Privates themselves felt, that was reminiscent of the New Model Army, with which the English Puritan Oliver Cromwell had triumphed over royalist forces in the 1640s. Just as American Whigs had tales of Runnymede, where barons made King John sign the Magna Carta to guarantee security in property, and just as Whigs pored over books by the liberty writers Harrington, Sidney, and Milton, so did working-class democrats have their own history and fable. In the Putney debates, held in a church in Surrey, England, in 1647, soldiers known as Levellers had argued that they should be given the vote. A Leveller tailor named George Joyce, a cornet, lowest rank in Cromwell's army, led five hundred men on his own authority in agitating for fairness for his class. Folk tradition had it that Joyce personally arrested the king and stood beside the executioner when the royal neck was severed.

The Levellers failed. Cromwell was no democrat. But now, in Pennsylvania in 1776, unpropertied men with no former political experience—no vote!—were writing full-scale essays on radical politics. They petitioned both the assembly and the Congress for the right to choose even their brigadier generals. Their leaders sent letters to newspapers arguing for opening the franchise and against the accumulation of wealth. Some wanted to put a legal cap on property ownership.

There was discipline in their cause, imposed by intimidation. The City Committee and the Committee of Privates were tightly intertwined, the political and military wings of an insurgency. At the Manufactory, a man accused of questioning the City Committee's authority and the need for American independence was made to recant his view before a crowd. When Isaac Hunt, a lawyer, defended merchants accused of breaking the boycott on England, he was taken from his home, placed in a cart, and dragged about the city to militia fife and drum. At various places in town he renounced his error. In one way, these were traditional means of village regulation. In another way, something new was happening. The crowd, the militia privates, and the committee were becoming a police force both in the city and throughout Pennsylvania. If the American colonies declared independence, Pennsylvania would be in the hands of its artisans and laborers.

James Cannon, Thomas Young, and their friends were using a crisis with England to disconnect rights from property. The new government they envisioned for Pennsylvania would require American independence. But its real purpose was a revolution against class privilege in America.

～

The third comrade at the Adamses' on May 3, Christopher Marshall, was neither flamboyant and charismatic like Young nor analytical and effective like Cannon. The eldest, at sixty-five, Marshall owned an apothecary shop, an upper-artisan profession. Drugs were necessary and mysterious, the pharmacy at once a shop, a laboratory, and a haunted house. Counterintuitive reactions occurred in the pot still, known as an alembic, with two chambers connected by a tube known as a retort. They gave off strong smells.

Marshall could seem strange. Sometimes he was morose, sometimes judgmental. He was religious, which put him at odds with his comrade Thomas Young's rationalism, but it caused him trouble similar to Young's. Rumors about Marshall had to do with alchemy and forgery. Pharmacy was based on older arts involving efforts to transmute base metals into gold, as well as into materials that could pass for gold. Crystalline residues in alembics and retorts could resemble precious stones. At a time when money was metal, alchemy shared a history with counterfeiting. But Marshall was also a Quaker, and Quakers dominated Pennsylvania's business establishment. If Marshall's Quakerism had been of the usual kind, he might have been spared rude speculation.

Marshall, however, was evangelical. He harkened back to "enthusiasms," as they were called, which the Society of Friends prided itself on having outgrown. In the seventeenth century, Friends in England and Wales had arraigned the spiritlessness of established religion. They'd called for a new form of worship sparked by an inner light, not outward form. They went naked to condemn the degradation around them. They quaked when they prayed. In America as in England, Quakers had therefore been jailed and hounded. The exception was

Pennsylvania, a haven of religious freedom established by the famous Quaker William Penn. There, over generations, the Pennsylvania Society of Friends had moderated Quaker enthusiasms. Despised by many, Quakers were now largely tolerated as sober and effective businesspeople. Many were extraordinarily rich.

Christopher Marshall, by contrast, was an unreconstructed quaking Quaker. He shared Thomas Young's commitment to freedom of conscience, but Marshall looked away from the rationalism of the Enlightenment to find freedom in old, stubborn religious nonconformism. He was by no means alone in connecting working-class politics to evangelical feeling. In England, aspirations of laborers and the poor had long been closely connected to Christian conviction, and given certain teachings of Jesus, the connection was hardly surprising. But it was at odds with the established churches. Some of Marshall's political ideas lay in the seventeenth-century Puritan revolution against monarchy and high-church worship. Some lay in the Levellers' dissent from the Puritan leadership itself. And other religious groups joined the Levellers.

In the 1650s, Fifth Monarchy Men hoped to prepare Parliament for the second coming of Christ. They came from sects like the General and the Particular Baptists, who denied the efficacy of infant baptism, and from "Seventh-Day Men," who followed Jewish law by worshipping on Saturdays, and they envisioned an army of saints sailing to Europe and bringing the whole world to Christ by loving force of arms. Release debtors from prison, they urged, repeal regressive taxes, topple all power based on greed. Ranters hung around alehouses to rail against privilege and went naked in the streets to deny the sanctity of secular law. Diggers were the most practical. Amid famine in 1649, and then the worst winter in years, they moved onto public lands across England. Diggers dug. They grew crops in defiance of the law. They lived communally, rejecting private property. They believed they were following the primitive Christians and modeling perfected human society for the coming millennium.

In America, the Great Awakening of the 1750s inspired a sense that the millennium was imminent. Awakening preachers railed against the authority of what they called dead churches. People were converted from within, the preachers said, and the transforming reign of Christ would be marked by American society's transformation. The Awakening began as a youth movement, and as the fervor dissipated, its message remained strong mainly among laboring people in both cities and countryside. Rioters against predatory creditors often had evangelical inspiration, and James Cannon too was evangelical, although he believed in freedom of conscience for people like his ally Thomas Young. The American Manufactory project was in many ways a Great Awakening legacy.

The Philadelphia Monthly Meeting of the Society of Friends, however, made enthusiasts unwelcome. In 1751, it accused the apothecary Christopher Marshall of criminal and irreligious activities. He had, it said, been transmuting metals, and had become involved with criminal charlatans who now claimed he'd helped them make and pass counterfeit money. Marshall was found innocent of all charges. The meeting then said he'd brought dishonor on the Friends and it disowned him.

Thus by 1776 Christopher Marshall had spent twenty-five years as a kind of lapsed Quaker fundamentalist, innocent of shady experiments and criminal activities but not the sort of person establishment Quakers wanted to know. His spiritual journey had made him a universalist. He was coming to believe that a loving God would save all people and damn none. He read deeply in German and Swiss mystical traditions. He would soon help found a schismatic church called, with implicit attack on the Friends, "the Free Quaker Meeting." On the corner of Fifth and Arch streets, self-described "fighting Quakers" dissented from pacifism and linked the struggle with England to millennial hope and the vision of the early Quakers.

Marshall's shop had meanwhile became one of the biggest pharmacies in America. His sons were in charge, supplying the Continental Army with badly needed drugs for ill and wounded soldiers. They would go on to make their profession respectable. They wouldn't have been found at Samuel Adams's rooms on May 3. They wouldn't plot unexpected things for the Congress with which they were contracting. Marshall couldn't get along with them. He kept a diary, in which he recorded with bitter precision the abuse and disrespect he felt his sons and their wives heaped on him and his wife.

In that diary Marshall also defeated Samuel Adams's efforts to leave no paper trail. He carefully recorded his and his cohort's many meetings with the Adamses, from 1774 through 1776, in the secret effort to achieve American independence by transforming Pennsylvania's legislature.

By the time they arrived at the Adamses' that evening of May 3, Marshall, Cannon, and Young had been talking for almost two straight days about the failure of American independence in Pennsylvania's Mayday election. Having found one another a few years earlier, they'd made plans that were now coming to climaxes throughout the province. They had much in common, and they had differences. Marshall and Cannon were evangelical, like many working-class radicals with roots in the Awakening. Yet Marshall, for all his defiance and eccentricity, was a fundamentalist, with strict ideas about acceptable doctrine, whereas Cannon wanted religious freedom. Young, for his part, was acerbic on all matters religious.

They'd drunk a lot of coffee together. The drink's syrupy bitterness and heady, heart-thumping buzz were a fad among eighteenth-century intellectuals. With the American boycott on tea, the brew had patriotic connotations, too. Philadelphia merchants, assemblymen, delegates, and dissidents sat around the big urns at the London Coffee House and the Merchants Coffee House, where wine and sprits were also served. The radicals drank coffee at Marshall's pharmacy, and at his home, and at the American Manufactory. They'd spent months in an almost constant state of conversation.

On May 2, they'd met at Cannon's house, with their friends Thomas Paine and Timothy Matlack, to rue the lost election. Earlier today, they'd met again, this time at Marshall's, and talked about it some more. Then they'd gone to Thomas McKean's house. McKean enjoyed the social and political connections in Philadelphia that these radicals lacked. A Whig gentleman of forty-two, excited about liberty and rights, McKean was a rising Philadelphia lawyer. He represented Delaware in the Congress, where he chaired a committee of middle-colony delegates. Thin and tall, with a hawklike face, he was famously proud, some said brusque and overbearing. In his later years, he always carried a gold-knobbed stick.

McKean was just the kind of person, in fact, whose privilege Dr. Thomas Young and the others had been trying to end. And McKean, under normal circumstances, wouldn't have deemed Young and his friends fit company.

But circumstances weren't normal. In the Congress, McKean was impatiently on the Adamses' side of the independence question. He was one of the few upscale Whigs left on what had become the

30

radically downscale Philadelphia City Committee, which he helped legitimize. The very unlikeliness of McKean's alliance with these working-class radicals held the key to Samuel Adams's secret operations in Philadelphia. In a network of mutual need, this alliance had no basis but opportunity.

Adams knew how to foster such alliances, and he knew their value. In defeat, nothing could be more cohesive.

Everybody gathered at the Adamses' rooms that night found failure in the Mayday election hard to face. Indulging in a postmortem was natural. They'd carefully followed Samuel Adams's Boston practices in maneuvering, encouraging, and directing. In the months leading up to the election, the apothecary Marshall, a powerful member of the City Committee, met with Adams every few days. Marshall felt he and Adams had a special bond. He brought Adams universalist tracts to read. Adams's Calvinism actually despised both Quakerism and universalism. It despised Anglicanism, too—Adams's Puritan ancestors had defined themselves by rejecting it—but on the Congress's first day, Adams had reached out to apostate colleagues and endorsed an Anglican minister's giving the blessing.

His own faith was certain. It made him practical. He knew how to draw people in.

Thus advised and coordinated by Adams, the locals had acted in concert to try to win the election. The City Committee petitioned the Pennsylvania assembly to expand representation. Western counties had fewer assembly seats than eastern ones, and the Adams coalition believed that if seats were more fairly apportioned, independents would gain a majority in the Mayday election. Of course the assembly rejected that petition, so the committee made a real threat. It moved to preempt the election by calling a provincial convention. In the crisis with England, such conventions had taken charge of government in most other colonies. In other colonies, Whig gentlemen remained in charge of conventions and committees, but in Pennsylvania, if such a convention occurred, James Cannon's privates were ready to respond. Pennsylvania might be taken over by its working class even without American independence.

The assembly countered. It agreed to broaden representation by seventeen seats for the Mayday election. This, it argued, should satisfy demands for greater fairness. In return, the committee agreed to call off the convention. Members of the secret coalition, from Thomas McKean to Thomas Young to John Adams, thought they had reason to celebrate.

But to the coalition's dismay, expanded representation didn't help. The Mayday election went for reconciliation anyway. In one smart move, the Pennsylvania assembly had preserved its existing government and won the election for those who wanted to stay within the empire.

The men gathered in the Adamses' rooms tried to explain their defeat in theories that became circular. Had the turnout really been as heavy as it had seemed? Anyway, there were still property qualifications for voting, and although people tended to lie about their qualifications and vote illegally, maybe there had been some extra effort at enforcement on the part of the elites? Or had legal German voters been turned away?

In any event, electoral politics had failed them.

⁓

Samuel Adams was genial and polished, but he always evinced quiet intensity. Meetings usually involved food, drink, smoke, and loud, long talk. Adams largely abstained from eating and drinking, and he spoke softly and briefly. He thought.

While he had the useful knack of getting along with almost anybody, he was not in sympathy, putting it mildly, with his local allies' goals for a democratic government, the Levellers' old dream. He didn't share Christopher Marshall's universalism, he certainly didn't share Thomas Young's scoffing rationalism, and unlike James Cannon, he'd never encouraged working-class crowds to seek their own political power. Quite the contrary. True, in Boston Adams had deployed Young and appreciated Young's results. But, Adams had kept Boston's working class from gaining control of the resistance to the crown. He would by no means have tolerated in Massachusetts what he was helping the radicals bring about in Pennsylvania. He'd put this coalition together for the purpose of using the class war that had developed in Pennsylvania to win the local election and swing the keystone vote in the Congress for American independence.

Since his local allies had now failed to win him the election, Adams might have been expected to write off the relationship and back away from the alliance. He might have sought new means of moving delegates in the Congress and members of the Pennsylvania assembly toward independence.

But that wasn't his decision tonight. He went the other way.

It was late when the Philadelphians left the Adamses' rooms. The rain had stopped. As the radicals walked home, the moon shone high and bright. A new plan was in effect.

It took to extremes what the radicals had already been doing. Young, Cannon, and Marshall, along with their friends Paine, Matlack, and Rush, would no longer merely push socially radical ideas. They would make an actual working-class revolution in Pennsylvania. They would overthrow the keystone province. Their radical government would swing the Continental Congress to independence.

Sheer last-ditch ruthlessness made the thing simple. There would be twists and turns, setbacks and unintended consequences. Yet only nine weeks after the May 1 election, which determined on reconciliation with England, Samuel Adams's unlikely coalition would turn Pennsylvania, the Congress, and the British government upside down.

3

The Revolution Is Now Begun

May 3–May 8

Samuel Adams knew he couldn't control events, but events did work in his favor sometimes, and this was one of them. On May 6, the Continental Congress returned to the State House after the Sunday break, and his secret coalition began carrying out its drastic new plan. That day, two events occurred in Philadelphia to encourage Adams's hopes.

One was a galvanic piece of news. For months there had been two competing theories in town as to what the king and Parliament had in mind for the rebellious colonists. An act of Parliament, it was known, had authorized the formation of a royal peace commission. One theory was that the king would soon be sending commissioners to negotiate with the Congress for peace, on good terms. The commissioners might already be on their way.

Why would the Congress declare independence, the reconciliationists asked, and turn a just war of defense into an unnecessary war of choice against the world's most fearsome army? Why not at least wait to see what the commissioners had to say?

The commission was a phantom, Samuel Adams and the independents had been replying. The very act of Parliament authorizing a peace commission, the American Prohibitory Act, also authorized pirates to seize American ships as prizes for the king himself. The king had thereby removed the colonists from his protection. The fight had been with Parliament, but now it was with the king, too. The whole British government was declaring the colonies independent, said the independents.

Secretly Adams and the independents feared the peace commission more than anything else—more than an invasion. Any offer by the British to negotiate would shatter the colonial alliance. Everybody would be looking for an out. With each delegation to the Congress rushing to make a separate peace for its own "country," as people called their colonies, the Congress would be impotent. If the middle colonies, most eager for reconciliation, left as a bloc and made a deal, New England and the South would be cut off from one another and quickly brought down. Any one colony, big or small, making such a deal would place all the others in jeopardy.

In response to the Prohibitory Act the independents moved to call the king "the author of all our miseries." Liberals in England had been pushing for a negotiated settlement, but independents hoped personal attacks on the king would make liberals despair of American reason and a commission seem pointless. So the reconciliationists had that language removed. More defiantly still, independents proposed opening American ports to foreign trade. To reconciliationists, that would break the basic mercantile rule of empire, declare independence tacitly, and preempt any peaceful conclusion. That's why the independents wanted it, and they achieved a victory in March 1776 when the Congress did vote to recommend to the colonies that they open their ports to foreign trade.

What the independents really wanted was an official resolution of the Congress openly calling all the colonies independent. They wanted that resolution passed unanimously, and accompanied by a plan of union to be enforced by rules of confederation, binding all colonies to moving forward together. Then foreign countries might ally openly with them.

So the independents had been broadcasting their own theory about what the king and Parliament really had in mind for the colonies. The king was about to send, Samuel Adams predicted, not commissioners to negotiate, and not just the crack British troops gathering on the ships at Halifax, but something far worse. Mercenary troops would be hired from various German principalities, especially Hesse. They would probably number sixteen thousand, Adams calculated.

"Foreign mercenaries": it seemed to many almost unthinkable. People from Massachusetts and people from Pennsylvania were strangers. Actual foreigners—Germans, but also Scottish highlanders—could make Americans feel ill with horror, and the thought of the intrusion could make people from Massachusetts and people from Pennsylvania suddenly see one another as comrades. Could their king in Parliament have so little feeling for them, had he turned his back on them so utterly, did he disdain them so much, that he could even consider subjecting them to that violation?

On May 6, people in Philadelphia got the answer. News arrived that the king had hired German mercenaries. Adams had read the royal mind clearly. Treaties called for twelve thousand "Hessian" fighters—they came from Hesse and elsewhere—to go to America to suppress the colonists.

The second thing to happen in Philadelphia that week was more dramatic. Norfolk had been shelled, and Boston had been occupied for years, but Philadelphia had not seen war. Suddenly that changed.

Down the Delaware River, at the mouth of the bay, the water supply of HMS *Roebuck* was running low. *Roebuck* was a fast, new British man-of-war, mid-size, an 886-ton chasing-and-fighting vessel of power and agility. Its full complement was 130 sailors and 120 Royal Marines, and it carried both eighteen- and nine-pound batteries. Under command of Captain Andrew Hamond, *Roebuck* had sailed from Portsmouth, England, to Halifax, then to Virginia, and ultimately to the Delaware. Its mission was to blockade Philadelphia.

Roebuck had been busy chasing and capturing small schooners whose captains were running products into and out of the Delaware from Philadelphia, Bermuda, and Boston. The bay was a long, slow estuary, opening wide to the Atlantic and narrowing upstream below Philadelphia. Every day at the mouth saw adroit sailing between Cape May on the Jersey side and Cape Henlopen on the Delaware side. Some runners got past by staying in shallow waters where *Roebuck* couldn't go. But the mission rarely required serious fighting. Trade schooners were weakly armed, and a cannonball across the bow could inspire quick surrender. Captain Hamond either burned the captured schooners or, if they were worthy, reflagged them and sent them chasing other shallow-draft ships.

Roebuck had come to the bay with two armed tenders. Soon another man-of-war, *Liverpool*, arrived with its own tenders in support of the blockade. With the addition of the seized schooners, *Roebuck* was now flagship of a small fleet.

On May 5, *Roebuck* entered the Delaware Bay and began sailing against the current toward Philadelphia. Captain Hamond had lightened his casks to reduce the big ships' drafts, and now he badly needed drinking water. He also wanted to check American positions and defenses up the river. There was no effort, and no way, to conceal the expedition. *Liverpool* accompanied *Roebuck*. Three tenders sailed ahead of the two big men-of-war and took depth soundings.

A coast-watcher at Lewes, Delaware, saw the convoy and sent word upriver. News of *Roebuck*'s movements came to Philadelphia by the afternoon of the 6th. That was the same day the news of Hessian mercenaries arrived. The city's alarm guns began firing. The militias turned out. Rumor had it, wrongly, that the men-of-war had burned New Castle, Delaware; had already reached Chester, Pennsylvania; and were nearing the city itself. The militias readied themselves for an attack.

Philadelphia had no men-of-war, but it had muscle power. Thirteen galleys, rowed by ranks of strong Philadelphia men, started downriver to confront the British. They were assisted by the few brigs of the Continental navy, such as it was, which were stationed in Philadelphia's harbor. Captain Hamond had meanwhile kept his fleet tacking slowly up the river. A cutter launched from one of his ships chased and burned an American sloop navigating near the shoreline, but there was no other incident. That night the British fleet anchored below Chester. Morning brought clouds and drizzle. Still carefully advancing, the fleet took bread and flour from another schooner it chased down. Captain Hamond had hoped to forage at New Castle, but from the deck he could see that town being abandoned as citizens hauled away food and boarded up stores. There was no point in landing there. *Roebuck* anchored and awaited the American galleys.

Shortly after noon on the 8th, a thick fog cleared and the galleys appeared upriver, about a mile away. They lay in shallow water where the men-of-war couldn't go. Hamond was forced to sail upriver to fire on them.

For two hours the British and Americans exchanged cannon fire on the Delaware. The boom of the big guns was heard in Philadelphia. The city militias turned out. War had come to the middle colonies.

The galleys made low targets, and by late afternoon only one American had been killed, and only one galley hit. Captain Hamond had lost one of his brigs to an American schooner while *Roebuck* was distracted by cannonfire. Still, the galleys were running low on ammunition. They had to row back upriver into the shoals.

Just then, *Roebuck* ran aground. Stuck on the mud, the ship began heeling. *Liverpool* and the tenders sailed quickly over to protect the helpless flagship. Her crew worked hard to seal the gunports to keep water out. Hamond was ready to burn his vessel to keep it from becoming an American prize. Yet the Americans were still upriver. After midnight, British crews unloaded *Roebuck* to lighten her. Three rowboats went back and forth before her to watch for attack. At four in the morning, on the rising tide, *Roebuck* sailed free in a thick fog.

At eight, when the fog lifted, the Americans were again visible, two miles upriver. Captain Hamond's fleet sailed up to meet them. The Americans withdrew toward Philadelphia, oarsmen stroking hard. They were luring the British toward narrow waters, where local batteries commanded the river from the banks. The tide was going out again, and *Roebuck* soon had only six inches of draft in the best channel. There was no maneuvering. Grounding was growing likelier by the second. Defense obstructions were visible in the water. The British came about and retreated downriver. In wider and deeper waters, they anchored. At two the next morning, the Americans began rowing hard downriver, on the attack. The British sailed quickly downstream, hoping to draw the galleys into wider water, where canvas sails could outmaneuver oars. But the chase upriver had brought the ships near the city, and the river widening was far away now. The Americans leaned on their oars and pursued. At a distance of less than a mile, American cannons began firing steadily on *Roebuck*. Musket fire from shore supported the attack.

It was daytime now, and the noise was loud in town. People began traveling down the riverbanks to watch. The American galleys were using up their ammunition in forceful, economical fashion. They hit *Roebuck* over and over, fore and aft. Cannonballs shattered the hull. Gun carriages splintered. Rigging, sails, and masts broke and began toppling. Men were killed; more were badly injured. Four hours later, HMS *Roebuck* was crippled.

That night the firing stopped. The American galleys had no more ammunition. The British fleet retreated downriver, and the Americans didn't give chase. Hamond's men refilled water casks without incident near Lewes. They began repairing their ships. They determined to avoid fighting in the Delaware again without better support.

The galleys and Continental schooners were damaged, but only one man had been lost, with a very few wounded, and they'd forced the British navy to retreat. The working men of Philadelphia and their officers, along with a small contingent of the Continental navy, had held off a British approach on the city. Men-of-war were not invincible. Jubilant news traveled quickly to Philadelphia.

"There is reason," Samuel Adams wrote an ally, a week before the battle, "that would induce one even to wish for the speedy arrival of the British troops . . . one battle would do more toward a declaration of independency than a long chain of conclusive arguments."

With explosions on the river supporting the independents' worst characterizations of British intentions, at the State House John Adams spent most of the week of May 6 trying to take the first step in the coalition's new plan to overturn Pennsylvania government.

Samuel Adams sat unreadably silent, even remote, in his chair at the Massachusetts desk, but John was voluble. He couldn't conceal effort or passion and he didn't make this opening move in the plan look easy. He only had to introduce a resolution, but the reconciliationists in the Congress had ploys for putting off even hearing it, never mind debating and voting on it. John had become accustomed to fuming that his enemies excelled at distraction and interruption.

He was a loner in Philadelphia. He'd long ago given up being popular. He was dogged in the execution of Samuel's plans. He waited out his enemies, he tried again.

The room was a graceful and intimate space for such a tough contest. Compared to the English House of Commons, say, with its rows of benches and galleries, where members had to shout histrionically to be heard, the borrowed Pennsylvania assembly room was nearly domestic. Right off the street, on the grand floor, it was a high-ceilinged meeting room without galleries or upper tiers. Light poured in through high, clear windows in the north and south walls. Members sat grouped by the thirteen state delegations, at desks set close together, facing the chair, where the body's president, John Hancock of Massachusetts, sat slightly elevated on the east wall. Voices carried at normal volume. During sessions, the big doors were closed and guarded.

The mood inside was bad. The delegations had first met in 1774, and many of the men had been together too long, in too-close quarters, under too much pressure. Other delegates were new. No rules governed how many men any colony could send or how long they could stay. Some colonial governments had only three men eligible to serve, others had at least eleven, and with the delegates' coming and going on both public and private matters, numbers in the room, and at any given desk, could fluctuate seemingly at random.

People from different colonies disliked one another anyway. Getting to know the habits, smells, tropes, and pomposities of fellow delegates, under unpredictable circumstances, in an unsettling city, kept the delegates skittish and prickly.

And they were exhausted. They'd served on legislative bodies at home, but the Congress wasn't a legislative body. It didn't make laws for colonies or citizens. It was an administration, with unrelenting work. For all their differences, the delegates had to debate and decide everything together, in an endless succession of detail, from the army's equipment, food, clothing, and pay to hundreds of petitions, some on matters of importance, many frivolous. Committees were legion, responsibility overwhelming. The men didn't know one another, sometimes didn't understand one another's accents, and lacked any precedent for the job they'd taken on together. They relied on elaborate forms of politeness just to get through each day without breaking the alliance and losing America everything.

The touchiest thing, of course, was the overall purpose of the war that had broken out at Concord and Lexington the previous year. By now the idea of American independence was alive in the room. Members held a variety of opinions about it, and felt a variety of emotions. Many were in flux, some were confused. Shifting alliances, old power struggles back home, and groping personal judgments meant that no delegation could be certain that all its members favored either reconciliation or independence. Even Massachusetts, where war had broken out, and where people thought Samuel Adams ruled, had a divided delegation. John Hancock, once Adams's top deputy, had turned against the Adamses and independence. Hancock wore lavender suits embroidered with gold and silver trim and traveled in a bright yellow carriage pulled by six bays. His personal style was everything Samuel Adams disdained, but he'd been a major funder of Adams's work in Boston. In this, the second Congress, he'd expected to be president. Adams, hoping to dispel fears of a Massachusetts hegemony, wanted a Virginia president. The Virginian Peyton Randolph got the position, but when he left to engage in politics at home, Hancock took over temporarily. When Randolph returned, Hancock refused to give up the chair. Adams was furious.

Hancock also wanted to be named commander of the Continental Army. Here again Samuel Adams's tactic was to name a Virginian. John Adams took pleasure in rising in the Congress, speaking fulsomely and at length of the man who so richly deserved the job of commander, then watching Hancock's face fall when he nominated George Washington. Since then, Hancock had been working with the reconciliationists against the Adamses, and John had replaced Hancock as Samuel's chief lieutenant.

The Virginia delegation was also divided. Benjamin Harrison, from Virginia's James River plantations, favored reconciliation, and Richard Henry Lee from the Potomac, was closely allied with the Adamses for independence. But regardless of any susceptibility or rigidity within any delegation, no member was free to vote as he chose. Each delegation was bound by explicit instructions from the home government. In no event, many of those governments had said, might their delegates vote for any measure that even tended toward American independence, or insulted the king, or suggested change of government or a formal union of the colonies. If anything like that came up, the delegates must submit it to the home government for assessment and refuse to be bound by acts of the Congress.

Pennsylvania was explicit in charging its delegates to obstruct independence. And even Massachusetts wouldn't yet support any move toward it.

Samuel Adams therefore worked on the divisions within the delegations. In the coffeehouses, in taverns, in rooming houses, and in the State House yard ("out of doors," the term was), the Adamses, along with allies in the Congress like Lee and the local man Thomas McKean, lobbied potential sympathizers. They pushed those delegates to ask their home governments directly for new instructions that would allow them to vote for independence. Meanwhile, Lee and the Adamses were writing home to push Virginia and Massachusetts to do even more than that. They wanted their own governments to take the lead. They wanted instructions to propose independence to the Congress.

Out-of-doors efforts helped. There was movement, though it was mainly tentative. In March the South Carolina government told its delegates to go along with a majority in any necessary defense. Yet it also declared itself only a temporary government, awaiting reconciliation with Great Britain. Georgia instructed its delegates that, in the event of a proposal for independence, the delegates would know best what to do. North Carolina told its delegates they could go along with a majority, even if it meant independence. Rhode Island gave its delegates powers to annoy England to any degree. But none, so far, was stepping out actively in favor of independence, not even Virginia and Massachusetts.

And no instruction to follow a majority passively—not even leadership by Virginia or Massachusetts—could defeat Pennsylvania and the middle-colony bloc, which also included Delaware, New York, Maryland, and New Jersey. In April, Pennsylvania's assembly explicitly reaffirmed instructions to its delegates to oppose any tendency in the Congress toward independence. The Mayday election reaffirmed that measure by referendum.

Hence the Samuel Adams coalition's new plan to overturn the host colony.

Hence also John Adams's oppositional relationship with the other members of the Congress. The middle-colony reconciliationists were only waiting for royal peace commissioners. On big issues, they sought delay, and delaying a parliamentary body is not difficult. The Adamses, by contrast, needed a unanimous adoption of independence, and they needed it soon, before any peace commission arrived. All the reconciliationists in the Congress had to do was fritter away what to John Adams was the most precious thing of all, time.

On Monday, May 6, John Adams proposed a resolution, cosponsored by Richard Henry Lee, which amounted to a sneak attack on Pennsylvania. The Congress was resolved in what parliamentarians call the committee of the whole. The president of the Congress, Hancock, had temporarily given up the chair, and Benjamin Harrison of Virginia had taken his place, serving as chairman of a committee that included the whole body. This "committee" would then make a report to the Congress—that is, the Congress would report to itself—on what it recommended the Congress do. The mechanism went back to the time of the Stuarts in England, when speakers of the House of Commons were spies for the king, and the whole body needed to meet without the speaker, in fake committee. Hiding was no longer the point, but on tricky and painful issues, the committee of the whole allowed members to debate freely with less commitment. Delegates tested the wind and selected their fights. The Congress resolved itself into a committee of the whole whenever a member, often

John Adams, insisted that it consider what members called the "state of the united colonies."

John Adams and the reconciliationists had become adept at using the committee of the whole at cross purposes. This week was no exception. Monday, the committee squandered its energies on small matters, so had to promise to reconstitute itself on Tuesday. Tuesday, it didn't have enough time to reconstitute itself: forming a committee of the whole often waited until business coming in that day was assigned to new committees, and old business, handled by regular and ad hoc committees, and ready to be reported on, could be debated. The issues could be as challenging as poor relations between officers and men in Washington's army, as small yet meaningful as a requisition for soldiers' shoes, and as trivial as reimbursing somebody ninety-nine and seven-tenths dollars for express communications. Minutiae, John Adams believed, was what reconciliationists loved most.

So on Tuesday the committee of the whole couldn't even form. On Wednesday the committee did reconvene, but at the end of that day discussion was still ongoing. Lacking a resolution for the Congress to report to itself, it reported to itself that it would reconvene on Thursday to arrive at a resolution to report.

By late Thursday, members were indeed able to report to themselves that there had been a resolution, whose substance, they reported, they were ready to report. But as time was running out for the day, report, debate, and vote were postponed till next day. In a move that might as well have been intended to drive John Adams crazy, the Congress now turned its attention to the passport application of a Mr. Bellew, a Tory, for his wife, who wanted to come to Philadelphia and then go to Marblehead, Massachusetts. The committee that had been assigned to deliberate that issue (an actual committee, in this case) recommended that the Congress approve the passport. Congress took a vote. Mrs. Bellew got a passport. The delegates left for the day. All Adams could do was harangue against wasting time. The reconciliationists always heard out his harangues, because haranguing wasted more time.

Nevertheless, on Friday the reconciliationists had run out of excuses and postponements. Maximum delay was their only goal. They'd achieved it. The resolution's existence was officially acknowledged at last.

The body had convened again as the Congress. President Hancock was back in his chair, ready to hear the report of the committee of the whole. The chairman of the committee, Harrison, formally reported to the president what the president already knew. At the urging of John Adams and Richard Henry Lee, the committee of the whole had determined that the Congress ought to do something extreme: encourage the member colonies to throw out their chartered governments and put in whatever new governments they wanted. The resolution proposal that the Congress recommend

> to the respective assemblies and conventions of the united colonies, where no government sufficient to the exigencies of their affairs have been hitherto established, to adopt such government as shall, in the opinion of the representatives of the people, best conduce to the happiness and safety of their constituents in particular, and America in general.

As bold as the proposal was, not all of the delegates would have discerned the real purpose. Certain colonies, in confusion over where to place authority during the conflict with England, had earlier requested guidance from the Congress on forming new governments. The Congress had answered them in terms very much like this.

True, the Congress had never before made sweeping pronouncements regarding provinces that conspicuously hadn't asked for advice, but still, the resolution's language was drily procedural. Few would have deduced that the immediate target was the host colony itself, Pennsylvania.

At the Pennsylvania desk sat a man who understood what was happening, John Dickinson, the target's bull's-eye. To him, every word in the resolution would come as a stinging pellet. The Adamses, taking what they hoped was their final shot at John Dickinson, were asking for a fight.

4

The Farmer Immovable

1757–76

The Pennsylvania State House, where the Congress met, was John Dickinson's house. Upstairs he led the majority in the keystone Pennsylvania assembly. He led Pennsylvania's delegation to the Congress downstairs. He used the staircase at will. If John Dickinson didn't want a declaration of independence, declaring independence was all but impossible.

John Adams had an explanation for Dickinson's obduracy in opposing independence. The man was timid and indecisive, Adams said. He told people that Dickinson's reconciliationist attitudes—the entire Pennsylvania assembly's, actually—were Quaker, a religion that Puritan-descended New Englanders loathed. Adams also believed that Dickinson was loyal to the Penn family, the proprietors of Pennsylvania. Another theme, picked up from local gossip: Dickinson's wife and mother-in-law made political decisions for poor henpecked Dickinson, Adams said.

Apodictic certainty and riffing command of insult could make John Adams sound as if he knew what he was talking about. But Dickinson was serving in the militia, unlike Adams. He was no pacifist. He'd espoused the most aggressive measures against England long before Adams did, and he led the war effort for Pennsylvania. He was frail, but toughness had brought him here. He'd never shown any doubt about confronting the most powerful forces on earth. He had no doubt now about confronting Samuel and John Adams.

⁓

Had John Adams really wanted to know what he was up against, he would have had to consider the daring moves Dickinson had been making all his career, his insurgency in Pennsylvania's troubled politics, the stubbornness that contradicted a fragile appearance. Dickinson wasn't raised to be an urban politico. Growing up on immense properties in Delaware and Maryland, which made his father one of the biggest planters on the eastern shore, John Dickinson knew only the river-fed plantation life. As a boy he was already thin and sickly. His father was robust, a Quaker with deep ancestry in the meeting, and in the meeting's decisive effect on the shore's culture. Yet the father stopped attending the meeting abruptly when it censured his daughter for marrying an Anglican. He was really a freethinking planter and merchant. He raised John in the classic operations of colonial development, the ferocious pursuit of landholdings, the fighting of title battles in court, and the advancement of business through service in local government. The Dickinsons acquired the best land all over the eastern shore for growing tobacco, wheat, and corn. They administered tenants, indentured laborers, and slaves, all harvesting and baling grain and tobacco, sending the grain from wharves to Philadelphia, loading the tobacco for London and the British West Indies. The Dickinsons prospered in a network of Quaker business-men operating under British laws that balanced imperial trade from China to the Ohio Valley.

They lived in a new, pedimented mansion on the Delaware coast, only a few hundred yards from flapping sails and loaded hulls on the St. Jones River. By his teens, John was doing his father's business on long rides to collect rents from the tenants. He would spend his life in the pursuit and management of property and the art and science of trade.

When he moved to Philadelphia at eighteen, and began clerking in the office of the king's prosecutor for Pennsylvania, he encountered the higher meanings of property and trade, and their ancient connec-tions to English liberties. Clerks were law students who learned by doing, dependent for their studies on their bosses' day-to-day sched-ules. In Philadelphia, Dickinson learned how seriously Pennsylvania law took itself as a form of English law. Relationships with London were gathering intensity as empire and business advanced through mercantile rules.

So it was with great excitement that he embarked upon the Ches-apeake and sailed the Atlantic, to study in London at the Temple and the Inns of Court and at court sessions at Westminster, accompanied on his trip by Cato, the body servant his parents had assigned him when both slave and master were children. During the passage, he suffered what he called his "fits," mysterious physical and emotional collapses that he would struggle with all his life. His time in London was punctuated by retreats to the country to recover his health. But he saw Garrick on stage, felt astonished by the bustle on the streets, and visited the "cockpit" at Whitehall, where colonies' agents presented American petitions to the Lord Commissioners for Trade and the Plantations. He studied the great common-law scholars Blackstone and Coke, as well as the Whig libertarians Sidney and Bolingbroke and the Roman historian Tacitus, whom Whig libertarians embraced as one of their own. He fenced. He played shuttlecock.

Dickinson's interest in law and liberty, and what their interdependence might mean for Pennsylvania, grew. He kept postponing his return, writing home for money in part because of his illnesses, but also because he couldn't stop immersing himself in his studies. He wanted to become a barrister.

But his ideas about England were growing complicated. In what was supposed to be liberty's ancient fountain, he saw unabashed corruption. The election of 1754 shook him because it was rife with bribery and perjury. He was thrilled to stand at Westminster where Coke had argued cases, and in the House of Commons he thought of John Hampden, the Buckinghamshire landowner who worked in Parliamentary committee to resist the king and helped inspire the English Civil War. Yet he felt a decline, even a decadence. Parliament's noble history of opposition seemed diminished by hack members who enjoyed easy places in the king's service. Freedom was lapsing.

He was becoming a shrewd observer. British officials, he began to think, were eager to start restricting American freedom, too. In 1757 he was home in Philadelphia, having been called to the degree of the Utter Barr and made barrister. He was twenty-five now, and still passionate about the big ideas.

Dickinson lived on South Street and opened a law practice that he made busy and successful. Philadelphia, almost a small town when he'd first arrived from Delaware, had boomed in his absence, spreading west and south, with Market Street the center of trade. The city competed with London for sophistication, yet without, in Dickinson's view, the decadence he'd observed in the capital. In America, Dickinson and other American Whigs believed, the noblest ideas of English liberty, law, and representative government thrived. He wanted more than anything to protect those things. He would always be physically weak and vulnerable to stress, but the son was growing into a ferocity something like his father's, on a more dangerous plane.

⁓

Dickinson's opening move in politics would inform his struggles with the Adamses in 1776. In 1764 he opposed the most powerful man in Pennsylvania, Benjamin Franklin. That wasn't a cautious or even prudent thing to do. Born in 1706, Franklin had escaped a hard-knock, printer's-devil apprenticeship in Boston and risen from hunger on the Philadelphia docks. Self-starting enterprise made him rich enough to retire from the printing business in his forties and engage full-time in the pursuits and responsibilities of a gentleman. In his unique case, that meant philosophy, laboratory experimenting, practical inventing, chart making, monetary theory, and city planning, along with various forms of writing, from propaganda to scientific papers to aphoristic pronouncements to comedy news.

He sent a kite up in a storm in 1752, when he was already known for transforming the study of electricity. Earlier he'd proved that a single kind of electricity exists, with positive and negative charges, but the kite was drama. From the gusts it sent current down a hemp string to a primitive capacitor. Men had tried that experiment by raising iron rods and they'd been killed like village idiots. When Franklin held his string, a silk ribbon protected his hand. Filaments of charged hemp stood on end. The delicacy and strength of his materials—silk and cedar, hemp and wire—made Promethean adventure out of Yankee practicality and childlike fun. Soon he fitted his roof with a lightning rod. For his delight, thunderstorms rang bells throughout his house while arcs lit dark corners.

If that was all Franklin ever did, his renown would have been assured. But like other gentlemen, and those recently made gentlemen and eager to be known as such, he devoted himself to the art of government. Here, results were mixed.

When John Dickinson took him on, Franklin had risen to what seemed permanent authority in Pennsylvania. He'd done that by confronting two Pennsylvania interests whose clashes had paralyzed government for too long, with awful results: the founding Penn family and the Penns' enemies, the strict Quakers who dominated the assembly. Pennsylvania had no royal governor. Under a grant from the King to William Penn, Pennsylvania's founder, the Penn family administered the colony as its "proprietor." The colonial governor was the Penns' hired agent, sometimes an actual family member. He had veto power over all the assembly's laws. He was bound by secret instructions from the Penns. He lacked freedom even to bargain with the assembly. The Penns were no longer Quakers. They weren't even Pennsylvanians. They were Anglicans living in England, and living large, since they held the best lands in the province, with perpetual rights of landlordship and development. They collected high rents and paid no tax on land or rent.

The Quakers who dominated the assembly were forever pushing back against the governor and the Penns on behalf of representative government and limited executive power. But they crippled their own efforts. They refused to make strong laws protecting the province from military attack. Quakers were pacifists. While they did sometimes pass militia and supply-requisition laws, covering their religious compromises with vague language, the purpose of those laws was mainly to harass and annoy the Penns. The assembly requisitioned money for defense by taxing the Penns' lucrative proprietary lands, so the governor had no choice but to veto all defense laws.

As the Penns and the Quakers went on blaming each other for weak defense, the hardest fact of ordinary people's lives was war and rumor of war. The War of the Spanish Succession was known to Americans as Queen Anne's War. What Americans called King George's War was known in Europe as the War of the Austrian Succession. Americans called the Seven Years' War the French and Indian War—but in fact warfare in the colonies always involved the French, and the Indians allied with the French, against English-speaking colonists and British army regulars and the Indians allied with them. At the worst times, settler families were cut to pieces in their homes and Pennsylvania's frontier fell back almost to Philadelphia. Then even Mennonites, normally pacifists, were ready to fight. But the Pennsylvania assembly balked at defense unless the Penns would be taxed, and the Penns wouldn't be taxed.

Ending that paralysis became Benjamin Franklin's goal. He personally organized and paid for private Philadelphia militias. He lent his prestige to raising supplies directly from farmers across the province. He wrote against the Quaker lawmakers' attachment to pacifism: they could govern or be pacifists, he argued, but not both. He accused some Pennsylvanians of cowardice, famously observing that people who would trade their liberty for personal safety deserve neither liberty nor safety. Amid the horrors and losses of the French and Indian War, Franklin and a new party in the assembly demanded a legitimate militia bill and an enforceable bounty on Delaware Indian scalps.

Under pressure from Franklin and his party, certain Quakers held to pacifist principle and resigned from the assembly. Others found their principles flexible enough to let them keep their seats while allowing military funding. Franklin didn't care which they chose. In the 1756 election, Franklin and his allies took a majority in the assembly. The Quaker monopoly in Pennsylvania was over.

Franklin's party was the new anti-Penn party. It was dedicated to the supremacy of the representative body, to harassing governors, to loosening proprietary controls, and to submitting the Penns to taxation. But it also built forts. So potent was the anti-Penn, pro-defense combination that Pennsylvania had one-party rule for almost ten years, with Benjamin Franklin in charge.

That's when he started going too far. In the year John Dickinson arrived home from studying in London, Franklin was sailing the other way. With his party in control at home, he spent almost five years bearding Thomas Penn in his town house in London and lobbying British government. He wanted the king's ministers breathing down Penn's neck. He wanted royal prerogative to force the proprietor to let the governor negotiate, to submit to taxes, and to give up the power, especially outrageous to liberty-loving Whigs, to fire judges at will. In meeting after meeting with high-level officials of Whitehall, Franklin argued that the power of the Pennsylvania executive must be limited, just as the king's executive power was limited in England. He argued that the Pennsylvania assembly was really a kind of House of Commons.

Home in Philadelphia in 1763, he called more and more openly for pushing the proprietor out of Pennsylvania. He wanted to tear up the founding charter. He would create a new government, based on a new charter, with no proprietor.

But he'd misread the attitude of the ministry. British officials were unmoved at best, and at worst deeply disturbed, by Franklin's elevating a colonial assembly to the level of the House of Commons.

In Philadelphia, Franklin remained confident. He said he only wanted a new "tumult" to justify a final blow against the Penns. When the tumult came, it led to his last great act in colonial politics. The French had lost the war and left North America. Now the natives began a new war against the British and Americans in the west. Known as "Pontiac's Rebellion," that Indian war caused an actual rebellion, a white one, against Pennsylvania's government. A frontier posse calling itself the Paxton Boys believed the assembly was appeasing natives. They attacked a peaceful Indian village, killed inhabitants, burned a cabin. The governor—now an actual Penn, John—placed peaceful natives in protective custody in Lancaster. The Paxtons raided the Lancaster site and slaughtered the natives. Then, in early 1764, hundreds of armed Paxton Boys marched on Philadelphia itself. Their stated intention was to kill any Indian who had taken refuge there.

The city fell into panic. As westerners approached, easterners grew terrified by the rowdy, lower-class anarchy that the Paxtons seemed to bring with them. For this, even Quakers armed with muskets and daggers.

John Penn, at a loss what to do, came to Franklin's house and handed over control. Here was the tumult. Franklin mustered local militias and a gang of laborers and artisans loyal to his party. British soldiers were in town mopping up after the war, and they joined in the effort. With the city ready to resist attack, Franklin led a delegation out to Germantown to meet with the Paxtons.

Somehow he persuaded them to write up their grievances. The Paxton Boys marched home. This time Franklin had literally saved the province.

With Philadelphians still shaking from the threat, he began his most aggressive campaign to end what he now had good reason to call the incompetence of proprietary government. The assembly brought up all the old complaints about Indian attacks—but now they added the lawlessness of western rowdies like the Paxtons. They said the province needed a new level of military protection.

In March 1764, the assembly adopted twenty-six resolves. Some of what they said was familiar. The assembly blasted the Penns for all that had gone wrong in the province and restated the grievances Franklin had taken to London. But one new accusation signaled Franklin's real purpose. The proprietor had interposed himself, the assembly complained, between the king of England and that great king's most loyal subjects, the citizens of Pennsylvania.

Here was Franklin's plan, out in the open. George III must exercise his prerogative and remove the proprietor. The provincial charter must be rewritten. The king must rule. Benjamin Franklin wanted royal government in Pennsylvania.

＊

That, John Dickinson decided, he could not allow.

If Franklin believed the proprietor was a tyrant, Dickinson thought, he must have no idea what the king and his ministry might do. By now Dickinson had experience in office, but nothing like a mandate to oppose anything proposed by Franklin. He'd established his law practice and served in the assembly of his home province, Delaware, and his eloquence had made him speaker there at only twenty-eight. In 1762, he was elected to the far more important assembly of Pennsylvania. After his father died, richer than ever, Dickinson not only practiced law but also oversaw planting, trade, and management of the eastern shore properties.

In politics, he'd served only as a minor member of Franklin's ruling party. He'd supported all of Franklin's moves against the Penns.

Nobody concurred more strongly than Dickinson in limiting their power. When he was a promising Pennsylvania youth in London, he'd been given an audience with Thomas Penn, and had even been invited to dinner. He grudgingly reported to his parents that he was civilly received and that Penn had been helpful. Yet even then, in the spirit of Coke and Hampden, he expressed fears of proprietary tyranny.

Hence his fury with Franklin's plan to replace the proprietor with, of all people, the king. Kings had changed American charters before. Loss of liberty inevitably followed. Pennsylvania's charter dated from 1701, closely based on the founding one of 1689. For generations that charter had kept the crown far away. It was becoming obvious to John Dickinson that 1763 might be the worst possible time to encourage British intervention in American affairs. The new government of the young king, George III, looked ready to reach out and, in the view of certain American Whigs, slap down English freedoms where they still really flourished, in the new world.

So what was Franklin thinking? Was the great genius mad? Naïve? Was he feigning dedication to representative government while pursuing a career as a courtier (he certainly seemed to enjoy himself in London)? Did he seek preferment for himself and his family and friends in a new provincial regime of his own devising? In London, Franklin had been told point-blank that in royally governed colonies, instructions to governors were no more negotiable than the Penns' and had the full force of crown law.

Dickinson didn't know about that conversation. It would have made his infuriated amazement even greater. When it came to government and law, was the great genius a dolt?

His scorn for Franklin would grow over the years. Later people would say he wouldn't have a lightning rod on his house. For now,

John Dickinson, a little-known junior legislator, decided that royal power must not be allowed in Pennsylvania. He decided that if Benjamin Franklin was tearing up charters that enforce natural rights and gambling with the autonomy of the representative body in foolish obsession with removing a lesser evil, then Franklin too must be resisted.

~

Part of what kept Franklin's party in power was merciless bullying. Franklin's second in command was Joseph Galloway, a lawyer of Dickinson's generation and a crony of Franklin's son, William. Franklin played philosophical eminence, sometimes far away in London. Galloway was the local enforcer. Together they'd fended off calls for fair representation. Their assembly refused to establish new counties in the west, despite population growth there. Galloway kept the party hierarchical, distributing war contracts and other patronage to Franklin, himself, and their friends, using elective offices to reward loyalty. When two dissenters published hostile criticisms of the assembly, under Galloway's aegis the assembly prosecuted them for libel. The Whig ideal of a free press, supposedly dear to printers like Franklin, didn't apply. Both critics were imprisoned.

Nobody openly criticized the Franklin-Galloway party anymore. Its tickets ran unopposed.

So Franklin and Galloway didn't see John Dickinson coming. In the spring of 1763, with the fall election nearing, Franklin brought the assembly a petition to the king, asking His Majesty to bring royal government to Pennsylvania. Franklin and Galloway had prepared the way with a mass meeting outside the State House. Galloway, a noted orator, entertained the crowd with the usual attacks on the proprietor. Franklin published an essay called "Cool Thoughts," heatedly mocking all fears of royalty. Pennsylvanians' right of representation was in no danger from George III, Franklin said, and only hysterics could think otherwise.

They did get signatures on their petition—but only fifteen hundred, relatively few. John Dickinson saw an opposition developing. It cut across religious and ethnic lines. Presbyterians and Germans, natural enemies, joined in opposition to royal government on the grounds that Anglicanism might one day be imposed on the province. But Anglicans joined the opposition, too—officeholders appointed by the proprietor. Some strict Quakers joined, not to support their old enemy the proprietor but to oppose any change in charter rights. Western settlers came in because they feared British troops' promoting eastern interests by force.

The opposition, while broad, was motley. In May, the Franklin-Galloway assembly did resolve to petition the king for royal government, and it assigned Franklin and Galloway to write the petition, which they'd already done. Their own reelection would serve, Franklin and Galloway felt, as ratification. Things were humming along for the hegemonic party when late that month, debate on the petition began in the assembly room at the State House. In the same room where he would one day do battle with Samuel and John Adams, Dickinson made his first move in politics.

It was irregular for a minor member of the assembly to stand and reject a petition sponsored by Joseph Galloway and Benjamin Franklin. Dickinson firmly asserted all the arguments against crown changes to charters. He scorned the petition, saying it could be "regarded in no other light than as a surrender of the charter, with a short indifferent hint annexed, of a desire that our privileges may be spared if it shall be thought proper." He made tactical arguments, too, with humor: "If . . . we inform his majesty that 'though we request him to change the government, yet we insist on the preservation of our privileges,' certainly it will be thought an unprecedented style of petitioning the crown, that humbly asks a favor and boldly prescribes the terms on which it must be granted."

And in this formative moment, he echoed both Cicero and the old Parliamentarians. "What life will be saved by this application?" he asked at the climax. "Imaginary danger! Vain remedy! Have we not sufficiently felt the effects of royal resentment? Is not the authority of the crown fully enough exerted over us? Does it become us to paint in the strongest colors the follies or the crimes of our countrymen? To require unnecessary protection against men who intend us no injury, in such loose and general expressions as may produce even the establishment of"—some published versions italicized and others changed case to let him shout—"AN ARMED FORCE AMONG US?"

Joseph Galloway stood at once to rebut. If a British standing army was needed in Pennsylvania to control men like the Paxton Boys, so be it, he said. The British government would always respect chartered limits. Dickinson and Galloway, two proud young orators, now started quick-publishing their speeches. The summer of 1764 saw the escalation of what became known as the Philadelphia pamphlet war. Each man prized rhetorical skill above all else, and so did readers. Each accused the other of having no integrity, of lying about what had been entered in the assembly, and every pamphlet drew a response attacking the previous one. The pamphlets drew comment in other pamphlets by new authors. Broadsides proliferated. Doggerel poems and crude cartoons mocked both men. Some claimed to have been outside the State House when the two had a fistfight there. Part of that comedy was that both chevaliers were supposedly Quakers.

Scurrility made both men look silly, but that was good for Dickinson, because it helped him become known, and bad for Galloway, who had seemed unassailable and now found himself on the defensive. Benjamin Franklin's party was under attack.

By the time Franklin and Galloway had ostensibly won their wish—the assembly did vote to send the petition to the king—the upcoming fall election result was no longer inevitable, for the first time in years. As election day neared, Dickinson made royal government the only issue. Franklin wrote articles mocking Dickinson's suspicion of the crown, and Galloway came up with a new tagline: "royal liberty." He hoped to allay Whig fears that monarchical power threatened freedom. The line would come back to haunt him.

In the election, Dickinson and his allies formed tickets for the city of Philadelphia, Philadelphia County, and outlying counties. On election day, Franklin and Galloway worked their networks, too. Their gangs banged doors and got out the vote by carrot and stick. Polling took a day and a half.

Franklin and Galloway were badly defeated. Dickinson's new ticket scored in Philadelphia city and county. There was still a majority in the assembly for Franklin's "old ticket," as it was now called, but since the assembly had long been stacked by Franklin and Galloway to make Philadelphia all-powerful, the downfall of the two city bosses and the arrival in the assembly of Dickinson's city party represented a startling turnaround. The bosses were used to nothing but success. They charged fraud. They schemed to run the assembly by outside cabal. But they'd let Dickinson take the initiative and had lost control of the province.

And yet their petition for royal government had passed. With the petition's author in defeat the situation was uncomfortable. In November 1764, over Dickinson's objections, Franklin's party in the assembly succeeded in making Franklin the Pennsylvania agent to the British government. They sent him back to London, his task to shepherd his petition through the Privy Council.

Franklin loved London. He was an intellectual and scientific celebrity there. He'd spent much of his previous visit conducting experiments and dining and chatting at the Royal Society and the Club of Honest Whigs. He was content to disappear from Philadelphia, even while continuing to assert power as the colony's agent. If he did get his petition through, and thereby changed Pennsylvania's government, he would return in triumph. By then he might even have a place in the British government.

Yet even before Franklin sailed for London, for what he thought might be a brief stay—even before the election, while the pamphlet war was on—John Dickinson's future as an American leader was foreshadowed. In a session of the assembly, Benjamin Franklin himself read aloud a circular letter, addressed by the assembly of Massachusetts to the assemblies of other colonies. It was 1764. New Englanders were seeking unified colonial support for an American protest against the Sugar Act.

⁓

When Franklin was mocking fears of royal overreaching and Galloway was floating the idea of "royal liberty," Parliament had begun passing trade laws that inspired anxiety and then outrage in so many Americans. John Dickinson turned out to be right, and being right made his name. The Pennsylvania assembly was timid about joining Massachusetts in petitioning Parliament, and Dickinson found its timidity intolerable. Amid the protests over the Sugar Act, and then rioting over the Stamp Act in Philadelphia, Charleston, New York, Boston, and beyond, he pushed for binding nonimportation agreements among Pennsylvania merchants. But the assembly was weak and the merchants' greed made them forever backslide. Dickinson sought new ways of directing and enforcing boycotts on British trade.

In 1765, he called for a colonial congress to frame an articulate, concerted American dissent from the Stamp Act. He corresponded with Samuel Adams, who was working in Boston toward a congress, too. Dickinson pushed the Pennsylvania assembly to send a delegation (it agreed, but by only one vote). He traveled to the congress in New York. The body adopted bold and confrontational language, which Dickinson had crafted.

In 1768 he became known around the English-speaking world. He published a series of fervent articles, *Letters from a Farmer in Pennsylvania to the Inhabitants of the British Colonies,* an ideological reference point and a call to fierce, concerted action. Samuel Adams, organizing in Boston, echoed and approved the Farmer's sentiments in his own scathing articles. People from Massachusetts to Georgia went around signing "The Liberty Song," a ditty attributed to the Farmer. Patrick Henry, a rising Virginia lawyer and orator, quoted him, and throughout the colonies men of like mind about ancient rights and liberties lifted hot cups in smoky rooms and said, "The Farmer!"

The pseudonym suggested anything but the city politician, practiced lawyer, and rich planter that John Dickinson was. The Farmer was a character out of high-Whig fantasy. A semiretired American landowner of ample but not ostentatious means, ensconced among his Tacitus, Sidney, and Harrington, the Farmer took up his pen as an Enlightenment amateur to speak plainly against the cant that enables tyranny. But what the Farmer had to tell all Americans, in tones that roused them to action, was just what Dickinson had been telling Pennsylvanians since his first repudiation of Franklin, Galloway, and royal government; what he'd been worrying over since his time at the cockpit at Whitehall and in the courts of Westminster; what he'd been excited about when underlining his student copy of Tacitus. The ultimate question, the Farmer said, wasn't whether it was wise or poor policy for Parliament to impose taxes in America, or whether Americans were over- or undertaxed, or whether the king might rightly expect Americans to contribute to the staggering cost of driving the French out of North America, or whether Americans had long been smuggling—to the French enemy, indeed, in the time of war—and otherwise ducking trade laws. The real question was an awful one. Did Parliament have the *right* to impose what even the British government admitted was a new kind of tax?

For with these taxes, the home government wasn't merely seeking to balance and regulate trade across the empire. That, the Farmer knew, was a necessary and legitimate use of Parliamentary power, which the British had been exercising for generations. The new laws sought instead to raise revenue for the treasury directly from American trade. That kind of tax was unacceptable, unless imposed by consent given through representation. To the Farmer, essential principles of English liberty, brought to constitutional climax in the 1689 settlement and preserved from corruption in the American legislatures, made the taxes tyranny.

Some might argue that since the amount and impact of the taxes were negligible, the issue was, too. The Farmer reviewed ancient and modern history to show how each seemingly trivial incursion on liberty has led, incrementally, to a police state, arbitrary oppression, and terrorism by hired soldiers. He differed too from the American patriots who called the stamp tax wrong because it was "internal"—that is, a tax on products and services within a country—as opposed to a tariff on imports, which those patriots held constitutionally innocuous. One problem with that line of reasoning was that when Parliament began taxing imports as well, patriots decided that they did object to tariffs after all, and then swung all the way around to the even more irrational claim that Parliament had no right to tax them for any purpose at all, even to regulate imperial trade. Those inconsistencies, based on what could easily be read as mere American self-interest, played into Parliament's desire to dismiss American arguments about rights wholesale.

The Farmer withstood all veering. There was no relevant "internal/external" distinction, he was sure, and of course Parliament had legal power to regulate its mercantile system. The Farmer fixed his objections relentlessly on the illegality and immorality of taking property in the absence of consent. That was tyranny. It justified—it required!—protest and resistance, without ambiguity.

So when the Continental Congress first met in Philadelphia, in 1774, Samuel and John Adams expressed their delight at meeting John Dickinson at last. The Farmer's identity had become known, and Dickinson was the most important resistance leader in the colonies. Benjamin Franklin, meanwhile, was in deep trouble in London. He'd spent a decade getting nowhere with his petition for royal government. He was unpopular with British authorities, who had come to suspect him of treason, and was suspected by patriots back home of Tory loyalism.

Dickinson's nemesis Galloway had nevertheless managed to return as speaker of the Pennsylvania assembly, and Galloway prevented Dickinson at first from serving as a delegate to the Congress. But the Farmer was so famous that John Dickinson was the only man on the scene known by reputation to all delegates. Meanwhile he'd helped create the City Committee in Philadelphia to enforce anti-British boycotts in opposition to Galloway's loyalist assembly. He presided over a meeting of eight thousand people in the State House yard. The meeting was extralegal, yet firmly in Whig tradition, open only to those with the right to vote.

That was the committee to which the artisan allies of James Cannon and Thomas Young demanded entry. In 1774, admitting some artisan membership worked out well for Dickinson. To demonstrate popular support for nonimportation, the City Committee even met at Carpenters' Hall, the artisan headquarters. Set back from the street by a brick courtyard, modest in comparison to the great State House a few blocks to the west, Carpenters' Hall had finer, more nuanced detail, with fancily inscribed mortar between randomly dark-glazed bricks, giving the façade a ruddy, two-tone glow. Carpenters' Hall was the pride of the artisan class. It reveled in utility and beauty.

Working with Samuel and John Adams, Dickinson made sure the delegates to the first Congress got a good look at Carpenters' Hall. Galloway had offered the Congress the State House, where he was speaker, as a meeting place, but the Congress rejected Galloway's offer and chose Carpenters' Hall instead. That was a victory for the Adamses and Dickinson against loyalists. Another occured when the first Congress spurned a plan Galloway presented for stronger American unification with England.

In Pennsylvania's October election that year, with the Congress still in town, John Dickinson became Philadelphia county's nearly unanimous choice for the assembly. As soon as the new assembly met, it made Dickinson officially a delegate to the Congress as well. When Dickinson joined the Adamses at Carpenters' Hall to excoriate Tories, Galloway was finished as a leader in Pennsylvania. Dickinson had written a list of grievances against the king and Parliament, and John Adams read and approved it. After the first Congress left town, Dickinson led the Pennsylvania assembly in approving the Congress's journal. That committed the province officially—through its old, chartered representative body, not just extralegal committees—to collaboration with the other colonies in the resistance. Loyalism was out. By the time the second Congress met in March 1775, Joseph Galloway had begged off being a delegate. Soon he would join the British army and he would die in England.

To the second Congress, Dickinson proffered an invitation to convene, not at Carpenters' Hall this time, but at the State House. He no longer relied on the City Committee or the artisan headquarters. The Farmer led Pennsylvania's great assembly and American resistance to England.

5

The State House and the Street

May 6–May 10

In the first week of May 1776, Dickinson faced the Adams-Lee resolution in the Continental Congress. He was forty-four and still sickly. He'd grown even skinnier, and notably pale and gray. Still, this tall man with a prominent nose stood up straight and walked gracefully. At war with England, he'd organized Pennsylvania's deeply rooted institutions around the positions he'd been acting on all his life.

But nobody knew better than Dickinson how vulnerable he was now, and what the Adamses were really up to. When Dickinson and the Adamses had taken the Congress away from Joseph Galloway and the loyalists, they'd praised one another's firmness in the cause. Their mutual sympathy was unfounded. The Adamses had been concealing a desire for American independence, and Dickinson hadn't concealed his objections. His commitment to the war was intense. "Our towns are but brick and stone and mortar and wood," he said. "They are only the hairs of our heads. If sheared ever so close, they will grow again. We compare them not with our rights and liberties. We worship as our fathers worshipped, not idols which our hands have made." But commitment to war only reinforced his position on law, liberty, and imperial relations.

He wanted the Congress to adopt reconciliation as an official goal, on terms of restoring American rights to their pre-1764 state. He tried to prevent "independence" from being uttered in the State House. He worked with the Virginia delegate Thomas Jefferson to craft "A Declaration of the Causes and Necessity of Taking Up Arms," the Congress's most uncompromising statement of grievances, which coupled toughness with sincere hope for reconciliation. Dickinson wrote a petition arguing for the legitimacy of using defensive force against British troops and asking the king to intervene on behalf of reconciliation. Just this January, a Pennsylvania congressman and protégé of Dickinson, James Wilson, had proposed a resolution denying that the colonists sought independence.

John Adams called Dickinson's petition to the king "a measure of imbecility." He wrote to James Warren, a Boston ally, calling Dickinson "a piddling genius whose fame has been trumpeted so loudly" and saying Dickinson gave "a silly cast to our whole proceedings." The British intercepted Adams's letter and had it published in Tory papers, hoping to embarrass and divide the Congress. It worked. One morning soon afterward, Adams and Dickinson were going to the State House. Adams made the customary bow. Dickinson didn't return it. They hadn't acknowledged one another's presence since.

Meanwhile, with Samuel Adams's help the Philadelphia City

Committee, which Dickinson had once led, turned against him. Dickinson had been using his place on the City Committee to harass Galloway, take back the assembly, and get into the Congress. With those ends achieved, he lost control of the committee. The radicals Thomas Young, James Cannon, Christopher Marshall, and their crew organized the artisans and mechanics who took it over. Infiltration by obscure, lower-class men disturbed Dickinson, as did their Levelling ideas about social equality, their connections to out-of-town independents, and their effort to supplant the assembly's chartered authority.

By early 1776, the City Committee, aligned with the Committee of Privates, was at odds with Dickinson's assembly over who was running Pennsylvania's resistance to England in conjunction with the Congress, and to what end. With the Privates agitating to gain the vote for the unpropertied, and the City Committee threatening to call a provincial convention to reconsider the charter, Pennsylvania was in a new tumult.

Dickinson and his assembly hung on. The radicals' ultimate hopes for Pennsylvania required American independence, and the assembly retained power to instruct its delegates in the Congress to prevent any move for independence. Dickinson made the canny deal with the committee to expand representation for the Mayday election. He thereby avoided a provincial convention that would have replaced his chartered government. He campaigned personally in the election, going from house to house to bring out the vote for reconciliation. With victory on May 1, he gained what he had reason to hope were time and room to move.

Hence the force of the Adams-Lee resolution, as it was read on Friday, May 10, by the chairman of the committee of the whole. It sounded so simple:

Resolved, That it be recommended to the respective assemblies and conventions of the united colonies, where no government sufficient to the exigencies of their affairs have been
hitherto established, to adopt such government as shall, in
the opinion of the representatives of the people, best conduce
to the happiness and safety of their constituents in particular,
and America in general.

Masked as a suggestion to all the colonies, the resolution was really recommending that the Congress support Philadelphia's radical
City Committee in calling a provincial convention after all, throwing out the Mayday election result, and creating a new Pennsylvania
government solely on the City Committee's authority. That would do
two things at once. It would end the old, chartered government Dickinson had fought for all his career, and it would remove Pennsylvania
as the insurmountable obstacle to independence.

The Adams-Lee resolution thus exemplified every one of John
Dickinson's reasons for objecting to American independence. Ancient precedent existed for wars to defend representative assemblies,
property rights, and constitutional law, but no precedent existed for
colonies' breaking off, on their own self-declared authority, and im-
provising new governments. The resolution itself showed why. The
Adams coalition wanted to reverse an election by force, empower a
self-appointed local committee to overturn an entire province, tear
up a charter guaranteeing rights, and lure the Congress into exceed-
ing its mandate by bullying one of its members. That was American
independence, in Dickinson's eyes. At least as dangerously as Parliament, the Adamses were threatening the sacred connection between
law and liberty in Pennsylvania.

There was one more vulnerability of which Dickinson was aware as he faced down the resolution that week of May 6. Benjamin Franklin was back. Right off the boat from London in 1775, Franklin had been prevailed upon to become a Pennsylvania delegate to the Congress, and immediately he'd taken a seat in the borrowed assembly room he'd once dominated. He was seventy now, after ten years in London, surrounded in the room by some who hadn't even been born when he retired. He was august, famous, and he lent charm and gravity to the upstart body.

But Franklin was battered. He was angry. Only a few years earlier, he'd been delighted to think he was making a place for himself in high circles of imperial politics. When his petition for royal government had grown irrelevant amid the mounting American resistance, he'd assigned himself a new role: liaison between Americans and the home government, a savior of empire. He'd believed he might even get a ministerial position out of it.

He'd decided he might best serve that purpose by sharing some letters that had come into his possession. They were from Thomas Hutchinson, the royal governor of Massachusetts. In them Hutchinson appeared to damn himself, in American eyes, by urging the ministry to bring military force against the Massachusetts resistance. Franklin's thought was that if he could, as he put it, scapegoat Hutchinson (once his friend), making everything appear to be the fault of one man, the Americans would settle down and the British would be off the hook. Negotiations could then begin, with Franklin, the honest broker, at their center.

It didn't go that way. Hutchinson's letters, when published, intensified American hatred of royal government and sent Boston and all of Massachusetts into crisis. In London, Franklin was called to the cockpit at Whitehall, and before jeering crowds in the galleries, he stood in silence as the solicitor general subjected him to an uninterrupted hour of shouted abuse. Then more humiliation. Desperate now to claim a role as reconciler, Franklin worked with William Pitt, Lord Chatham, on a proposal for reconciliation that Pitt brought into the House of Lords. Franklin's involvement in the proposal was the Lords' excuse for insulting and rejecting it out of hand. Franklin was in the gallery when the proposal was shouted down as a traitorous American's work.

Clearly he wasn't about to be offered a position in the ministry. He left London shocked by disappointment, in danger of arrest.

Now he was passionate for American independence. In the Congress, he'd kept his own counsel at first. He'd even seemed to doze during debates—some members thought he was only pretending to doze while sizing up the situation. Some even feared he was a British spy. Since then he'd made proposals for an American union, not very well timed, and had taken up committee work. He didn't speak much.

But he'd become a firm ally of the Adamses and, in the room where they'd had their first contest, a renewed enemy of John Dickinson. Once he'd wanted the king to rule Pennsylvania, and then he'd hoped to broker reconciliation, and now he was certain that only a complete break with England would do. Anyone who thought otherwise was a fool, a traitor, or both.

Franklin wasn't in the chamber the week of May 6. He was trying to get back to Philadelphia, beset by illness, from a diplomatic mission from the Congress to Quebec. Yet in the struggle to oust John Dickinson and overturn the government of Pennsylvania, Benjamin Franklin would play his strange part.

⁓

Now Dickinson made a surprise move in the chamber.

The obvious thing for him to do was point out that the Adams-

Lee resolution was really yet another half-veiled attempt at independence and crusade eloquently against it. That would comply with the letter of the strict instructions, issued by himself and his assembly upstairs, to himself and his delegation down here, to oppose all such resolutions. He could legitimately argue against letting his state be taken over by what the Adams-Lee resolution called "the representatives of the people." He could object to bullying by the Congress, which had no legal right to meddle in its members' governments. And he could warn other colonies about placing power in the hands of people like Samuel Adams, who with this resolution showed contempt for rule of law where it interfered with his goals.

Yet Dickinson astonished anyone in the chamber who also got the resolution's purport—certainly he had to startle John and Samuel Adams—by not opposing it. He saw something. The Adamses had set themselves a trap when wording the resolution in committee, and Dickinson sprang it.

The resolution said that the colonies should form new governments where none "sufficient to the exigencies of their affairs have been hitherto established." In that context, Dickinson didn't just decline to oppose the measure, he endorsed it wholeheartedly. He praised it as a good way to *achieve* reconciliation with England, for as everybody knew, Pennsylvania did have a government, and of all governments, Pennsylvania's might be the most capable of meeting exigencies. Indeed, Pennsylvania had one of the only functioning governments left in North America based on a founding charter, and that charter was not a royal one. Other legislatures had been disbanded by royal governors and taken over by patriot committees and conventions. Pennsylvania's charter had never allowed the governor to disband the legislature. It had always guaranteed the representative rights of the people that Congress now espoused. The Mayday election gave proof that representation was flourishing here. Pennsylvania was actually modeling the sort of government the others might want to emulate.

So the resolution couldn't possibly apply to Pennsylvania, Dickinson said. Its government would stay intact, thanks to this very resolution.

His play was at once ingenious and desperate. Had Dickinson begun attacking the Adamses for meddling in local politics, he would have revealed his province to be in the turmoil that it was, in fact, in. He pretended instead that the Adamses' schemes with the radicals were having no effect, that the province was stable. With the resolution, John Adams had charged at him, and Dickinson sidestepped. He even held out a friendly hand to pull Adams flying past him.

There was no floor fight. To members unsure of their own positions on independence and how their instructions might apply in this case, the Adams-Lee resolution appeared as that rare and reassuring thing, a measure on which Adams and Dickinson actually agreed. It passed with virtual unanimity. Dickinson had rendered it useless to the Adamses' purpose. One more time the pale, skinny man stood in his chamber and used close analysis, lawyerly skill, and parliamentary eloquence to save Pennsylvania's charter from dismemberment.

Then Dickinson did something else surprising. After his victory that day, he left town for his family plantation on the Delaware shore. That would turn out to be a mistake.

⌒

Another shot in the assault on Dickinson had already been fired. Thomas Paine, an English-born writer, published an article under one of his pseudonyms, "the Forester." John Adams's task in the secret coalition was to press John Dickinson from the Congress. Thomas

Paine's was to press him from the street. Coming out on May 8, in conjunction with the Adams-Lee resolution's progress in the Congress, the article helped render Dickinson's May 10 victory less complete than it first looked. Like many of Paine's articles, this one was more than a piece of writing.

Paine was one of the radical group whose core had met in Samuel Adams's rooms on May 3. In the past year, he'd been discovering new capacities both in himself and in the political situation of Philadelphia. He'd worked hard with Thomas Young, James Cannon, and Christopher Marshall in the failed effort of the Mayday election. The night before the May 3 meeting, he'd met with Marshall, Young, and Cannon to review the election failure and consider next steps. His relationships with the local radicals were new, and they'd been leading Paine to new places. He shared Marshall's dissenting Quaker background and departure from orthodox religion into universalism and mysticism. He shared Young's defiant love of reason and need to wander. He shared Cannon's belief in the transforming spirit of ordinary people. He believed, with all of them, in a future where such people will have power. With them, Paine saw American independence from England as a way to bring that future about in Pennsylvania. And as Pennsylvania went, so might go the country.

Yet there were important differences between him and his fellow social radicals. He was English. He'd arrived on the continent only in late 1774. Marshall was from Ireland, Cannon from Scotland, but Marshall lived almost all his life in Philadelphia, establishing a business, raising children, and leaving and founding churches. Cannon had come in the 1760s when anti-British ferment was gearing up, and became a leader in working-class Philadelphia society and revolutionary politics. They were Americans.

Paine came late, left early, and brought something different.

Never a colonial, he grew up in the heart of empire. He struggled in London and other towns when they were becoming industrial. For all of the poverty and oppression that Cannon and Young abominated in Pennsylvania, Paine knew slums more miserably crowded than anything Americans had ever seen. At sixteen he served as a sailor in a privateering man-of-war. That was one of the worst experiences the empire could offer its multitudes of poor young men with few options and a crushing feeling of boredom.

So Paine was old-world, a refugee from degradation and an exponent of long philosophical traditions. He was improvisatory, too, imagining new worlds. Even when barely published, he was already a kind of international intellectual like Voltaire. He was a new kind, a working-class kind, downwardly mobile, the critic with no Latin. Unlike Young, Marshall, and Cannon, Paine would travel on. He would live in London again, in Paris, and on Bleecker Street in New York. He knew the artisan poet, engraver, and visionary William Blake, the radical intellectual William Godwin, the pioneering feminist Mary Wollstonecraft. He linked English traditions of dissent with an emerging English Bohemianism. He became a new kind of celebrity, someone everybody had to have an opinion on, "Mad Tom" to his detractors. His enmities could be terrible. He was a friend of General Washington, then a foe of President Washington. He served with Robespierre in the French revolutionary government, then was imprisoned by the Terror. One of his books gave a name to an era, *The Age of Reason*. Following his astonishing American successes of 1776, history embraced Thomas Paine.

Yet Paine's future couldn't have been predicted as late as December 1775. He arrived in the city an unknown failure at thirty-nine. He'd been fired twice from a low-level job as a tax collector. He'd tried his father's trade, corset staymaking, and had run a tobacco shop, both to no avail. He'd separated from his second wife (the first had died) under mysterious circumstances that brought him a settlement of thirty-five pounds, some of which he spent traveling first-class to Philadelphia. When his ship came into port he was so sick with typhus he had to be carried ashore in a blanket. He knew nobody in Philadelphia, nobody in all of America. This was a last gasp.

What he did have was a set of letters of introduction written by Benjamin Franklin and addressed to well-connected men in America. Paine had met Franklin in London at a meeting of the "Club of Honest Whigs." Outclassed by the membership, Paine nevertheless chatted with Franklin about their shared love of science. Franklin's recommendation of Paine, while wholehearted, was modest. The bearer might be profitably employed as a clerk, assistant tutor, or assistant surveyor, it said.

On the basis of that introduction and no successful experience, Paine moved fast. He met Robert Aitken, who owned a Philadelphia bookstore, where Paine drank coffee and talked ideas. Aitken made him the editor of *Pennsylvania Magazine*, a startup Aitken was publishing. Paine had done some writing before, mainly poems and songs. His fellow tax collectors had appointed him to frame an appeal to Parliament on their behalf, take it to London, and lobby for it. But now he was writing all the time, and after a few months of putting out articles for the magazine, he was confirmed in a career.

In a time of big ideas, it turned out Thomas Paine had bigger ideas than anyone else. He attacked African slavery in emotional, evocative terms. He described the sufferings of American Indians— and of Indians in India. His protest against empire was unusual for being made on behalf not of himself, or even of his class, but of others. The whole world should change, he began to say, for all kinds of people. America's revolution against England would make America a haven for liberty, reason, and goodness, which would then spread around the world. He seemed to find himself fearless, with no limits on what he imagined and no inhibition about giving imagination a crackling voice.

The crucial moment in this unexpected career came sometime in 1775, when the boldness and facility of Paine's writing at once captivated and terrified an idealistic doctor almost a decade younger, Benjamin Rush. The two met at Aitken's bookshop, where they drank coffee and discussed dozens of new ideas. The thrill of their shared vision, Paine's fearlessness, and Rush's trepidation made their friendship creative in a way neither of them could have predicted. In tense closeness to Rush, Paine abruptly became one of the most famous people in the English-speaking world.

Dr. Rush was a Philadelphian, and one of the radical crew. He worked with Young, Cannon, and Marshall to organize the radical committees. He served on the board of the American Manufactory. He campaigned for the independents in the Mayday election. Yet Rush's hopes were divided. He was the son of an artisan—but a prosperous artisan, a gunsmith, who had sent him to the medical college in Edinburgh. Not flamboyant like Dr. Young, Rush nevertheless irritated the Philadelphia medical community. He brought back to town such controversial practices as childhood inoculation. He questioned older doctors and showed them up. So he was ostracized, and with no referrals and few patients, he began treating Philadelphia's poor, often for nothing. He became a fervent Presbyterian evangelical, working for social justice as part of the millennial Christian transfiguration, the last redemption of humankind.

Yet he also liked knowing famous people. He'd tried at times to cultivate both John Dickinson and Joseph Galloway. He didn't like being ostracized by the establishment. Defiant of authority, filled with desire for spiritual and social change, he was less a rowdy populist than an advanced social thinker, and he wanted to rise up. He worried about the low status and legal oppression of women. He hated slavery, and had written against it even before Paine. His sympathies made him at once radical and genteel.

With Paine, the most down-at-heels of the radicals—and no Christian evangelical—Rush had long talks at the bookstore on women's rights, abolishing slavery, and the ultimate potential of American independence. A part of Rush wanted to write a polemic that would change people's minds in favor of independence. Another part of him quailed: authorship might lower his status and income even further. His friend Paine had the manifestly greater talent for writing, and no status or income to risk. Paine should write it, Rush thought.

Thus occurred a long and remarkable pamphlet. It drew inspiration from Rush's desire to shout out, which his professional and social ambition blocked. It was written by Paine, whose own desires and ambitions were no longer blocked in any way. While Paine wrote, Rush stood by, egging the author on and hand-wringing. Don't mention independence directly, he counseled. But Paine didn't take the advice.

The pamphlet's title expressed the contradiction in the friendship. Paine wanted to call it "Plain Truth." That was confrontational, absolutist, preaching—a challenge and a demand. Rush advised calling it "Common Sense," and that became the title. "Common Sense": how midlevel gentry defend their least-examined everyday opinions. Rush's title packaged Paine's hair-raising radicalism in banality.

There was nothing commonsensical about Paine's vision. The pamphlet certainly did mention independence, and mentioning it was startling enough when *Common Sense* was published at the beginning of 1776. The Adamses had only just begun to use the term *independence* publicly. And Paine redefined it. For one thing, he castigated the king. Americans were routinely ascribing the king's failings to a wicked ministry. Even the independents in Congress wanted only to call the king "the author of all our miseries." That was a whine of children disappointed in their too-big, too-distant father. Paine assailed George III as "the royal brute," "the sullen-tempered Pharaoh," "the wretch" with "blood upon his soul." That sounded like a man calling out another man and hoping for a fight. Pulling the king down from his throne and using only a string of words to do it, Paine displayed outlandish confidence.

His attack went further. Whigs blamed George III for departing from the appropriate role of a king, as constitutionally defined. They thought this king was at fault because he was indulging in tyranny; he was not being a good king. But to Paine kings *are* tyrants. There can rarely be such a thing as a good one, he said. The American colonies must separate from England, but kings, and kingship itself, must go down everywhere.

Paine went still further. Whigs, wherever they fell on the issue of independence, believed their king was checked—specially and gloriously checked—by the English constitution's balancing of powers, which accommodated the interests of the one, the crown; the few, the Lords; and the many, the Commons, elected by non-noble property owners. England was a monarchy, in other words, but not an absolute one. It enjoyed what Whigs called balance. The king didn't have sole lawmaking power and wasn't absolved from obeying the law. The representative aspect of English government made it a kind of republic in the tradition of the Athenians, the early Romans, and the Tuscan city-states.

Paine denied that whole story. The vaunted English constitution is nothing but a fantasy dedicated to tyranny, he said. The English don't have a constitution. Checks are falsehoods; so-called balance is oppression. Paine was thus questioning the prevailing rationale for American war against England. So-called English constitutional rights or even American independence weren't worth fighting for. A new kind of government, an authentically republican one, a democratic one—that was worth a fight.

Paine was expressing his Philadelphia comrades' working-class radicalism in a powerful new language. In *Common Sense* and in follow-up letters to newspapers, he designed an American republic. It would of course have no king. It would have no sole, strong executive at all. Paine rejected covalence, the separation of equal powers of government. He wanted a dependent executive branch, a committee, elected by the people or appointed by a vote of the representative legislature, the republic's mainspring.

And the legislature must not, Paine argued, be divided in two houses, like the corrupt British version. In most of the colonial legislatures, one large house represented the people, and a smaller "upper" house kept representation from going too far. That check, that balance must be removed, Paine said. He called for a single house in the legislature, and he wanted the house to be far more representative of all the people than had ever been tried before. Like his fellow Pennsylvania radicals of 1776, Paine wanted representation proportional to population, elected through "manhood suffrage," a franchise open to white male adults regardless of property.

In *Common Sense* he kept his discussion of voting qualifications somewhat vague. He called explicitly only for what he termed broad suffrage. The pamphlet was meant in part to bring readers of all classes over to independence. Yet Paine was working every day toward removal of the property requirement in a new Pennsylvania, and he would soon have an opportunity to make his feelings better known. Even more radically, he held that any white male of majority age should be allowed to hold elected office, regardless of property. Laborers, tenant farmers, and lower artisans would thus gain lawmaking power.

With Marshall, Cannon, Young, and Rush, Paine broke sharply with hundreds of years of Whig tradition. He connected American independence with the hopes of the Levellers at Putney. Paine's vision would come to inspire not only working-class white men but also women and members of other races. He and the French revolutionaries would one day call those rights "the rights of man and of the citizen." Writing in endorsement, yet with concern about their scope, Mary Wollstonecraft published *A Vindication of the Rights of Men*. Then Paine published *Rights of Man*, and Wollstonecraft published *A Vindication of the Rights of Woman*, condemning marriage as legalized prostitution and calling for women's suffrage.

But all of that was still to come in January 1776, when *Common Sense* was published in Philadelphia. It was signed only "an Englishman."

Now in the week of May 6, Paine brought the lesson home. In *Common Sense* he'd dispensed with the legitimacy of kings. In the May 8 Forester article, he called for the immediate overthrow of the government of Pennsylvania. Even while the Adams-Lee resolution made its veiled attack on Dickinson's government in the chamber at the State House, Paine's article openly denied the legitimacy of Dickinson's government and the validity of the Mayday election.

The assembly had to go, Paine said, and the recent expansion of representation for the Mayday election only made the body's fraudulence worse. That expansion was something Paine and his friends had

fought for. Dickinson had avoided a provincial convention by allowing it, and the radicals had lost the election. Now Paine said that the
bigger a body that "derives its authority from our enemies, the more
unsafe and dangerous it becomes for us." He called for a provincial
convention. He urged the people of Pennsylvania to throw out their
government, in alliance with the independents in the Congress. To
support that exhortation, he accused the Pennsylvania assembly of
deriving its authority, ultimately, from the king of England. Given
the king's enmity, the assembly thus had no legitimate authority at
all, he said, and it could no longer operate legally.

The elected Pennsylvania Assembly wasn't merely wrong about
independence or in need of advice from the Congress—it was illegal.
That was a new and powerful idea. Right after Dickinson eluded him
on May 10, John Adams began working up his own version of it to
take back to the delegates in the Congress. The local radicals meanwhile readied themselves to overthrow Pennsylvania. Paine's Forester
article wouldn't be remembered as *Common Sense* or *Rights of Man*
would be. Yet in identifying Pennsylvania's elected government with
the king's cruelty, it gave new life to the Adams-Lee resolution that
Dickinson thought he'd finessed on May 10. A week after its publica-
tion, the article brought American independence one step closer to
reality.

6

Der Alarm

May 13–15

Nobody would ever know what made John Dickinson leave for Delaware on May 10. He was exhausted. Maybe he hadn't read or taken Paine's Forester article seriously, and maybe his old "fits" had overwhelmed him. Whatever his reasons, leaving town wasn't a good idea.

On Monday, May 13, John Adams returned to the room at the State House to make a second attempt on Pennsylvania. He had a new weapon.

Most resolutions of legislatures, as well as those of the Congress, came with preambles. They framed resolutions' purposes for the public. But a preamble could serve other purposes, too. Some "whereas . . ." language, tacked on the front, could reshape an official statement's meaning.

That's what the Adamses decided to do. John had written a pre-amble to the May 10 resolution. Its new and crucial idea was shared, tactically, with Thomas Paine's Forester article. The secret coalition's plan, parts synchronized and meshing, began to accelerate.

The May 10 resolution had only advised the states that if they didn't feel they had effective governments, they should form them. But on May 13, John Adams's preamble to the resolution was read in the Congress. A heavy-breathing tirade, it said all this:

> Whereas his Britannic Majesty, in conjunction with the Lords and Commons of Great Britain, has, by a late act of Parliament, excluded the inhabitants of these united colonies from the protection of his crown; and whereas no answer, whatever, to the humble petitions of the colonies for redress of grievances and reconciliation with Great Britain has been or is likely to be given; but the whole force of that kingdom, aided by foreign mercenaries, is to be exerted for the destruction of the good people of these colonies; and whereas it appears absolutely irreconcilable to reason and good conscience for the people of these colonies now to take the oaths and affirmations necessary for the support of any government under the crown of Great Britain, and it is necessary that the exercise of every kind of authority under the said crown should be totally suppressed, and all the powers of government exerted, under the authority of the people of the colonies, for the preservation of internal peace, virtue, and good order, as well as for the defense of their lives, liberties, and properties, against the hostile invasions and cruel depredations of their enemies; therefore, resolved, & etc. . . .

And here would follow the actual resolution, advising the states—but now for the specific reasons listed above—to dissolve their governments and form new ones.

John Adams was a member of a committee the Congress had appointed, when the Adams-Lee resolution passed on Friday, to write a preamble, but he would always claim he'd written it alone, and nobody could seriously doubt it. It made whole new point after whole new point, piling on *whereas*es until the preamble was three times longer than the resolution it purported to frame. Where the resolution was precise and technical, the preamble was full of recrimination and justification, revealing a determination, inelegant but strong, to leave Dickinson and the reconciliationists not an atom of room. Dickinson's argument of Friday had gracefully excluded Pennsylvania from the scope of the resolution. The preamble sweatily wrestled Pennsylvania back in.

Never discussed during the debate over the resolution itself was something the preamble now treated as critical. It called illegitimate any government that required taking loyalty oaths to the king.

Pennsylvania's government wasn't royal. But it did take oaths to the king. For as long as anybody could remember, assembly sessions had begun with that observance. Amid the inveighings in Adams's preamble, a novel provision—neatly matched to Paine's article—made mere oath-taking to the king a cause for branding a government royal, hence illegal, and replacing it. If the Congress adopted this preamble, it would tacitly be lending the gathered colonies' support to Paine's call for a revolution in Pennsylvania.

Debate was postponed until the next day, but the preamble was already starting anxious arguments "out of doors." On Tuesday the 14th other matters took precedence in the Congress while private arguments escalated, and on the sunny morning of Wednesday, May 15, when the Congress began climactic debate on the preamble, consternation prevailed in the room.

~

Congress's business was secret, according to the dire regulations of the body itself. The doors were closed and guarded. Debates weren't even recorded by the secretary.

But Congress's business wasn't secret from the local radicals. Along with the Adamses themselves, with whom the radicals were meeting and planning in detail, they had McKean, the Pennsylvania Whig representing Delaware in the Congress, to fill them in on what was said in sessions at the State House.

And they had Timothy Matlack. He was a clerk of the Congress, assisting the secretary, and a member of the radical coalition with Paine, Rush, Cannon, and Young. Matlack had a following as a roisterer in Philadelphia's smelly taverns and smoky theaters, where members of every class mingled. He was the son of a Quaker artisan, but he'd taken on debt by gambling, horse-racing, bull-baiting, and fistfighting. He not only entered his cocks in fights but also entrepreneurially sponsored cockfights. He spent time in debtors' prison. In 1765 he was disowned by the Quaker meeting for being disreputable and welching on debts.

But they loved him on the street and in the taverns, and he was elected a colonel in the Fifth Rifle Battalion of the Philadelphia associators. He moved easily among classes. He'd even spent time with Joseph Galloway. He read papers at the American Philosophical Society. And at most sessions of the Congress, Timothy Matlack was in a position to know, hour by hour, what the body was doing and to pass information to his radical friends.

As the delegates began their debate on the morning of the 15th, the local radicals outside were fully aware of what was going on at the State House. They'd been preparing with the Adamses to overturn Dickinson's government upon passage of the preamble. On May 10, after the original Adams-Lee resolution had been passed by the Congress, James Cannon and Christopher Marshall met with their congressional ally McKean, and then with the Adamses themselves. On May 13, when John Adams's preamble was first read in the Congress, Marshall and Cannon went to seek guidance from Samuel Adams about putting together a big local meeting that night. The Adamses weren't home. The radicals sought them at a coffeehouse but to no avail. A group met that evening at Marshall's anyway. It made a plan to bring leaders of working-class Philadelphia to an even bigger meeting the next night, at a schoolroom they'd been using for organizing. The radicals hoped to create a sense of the local people as a whole putting the City Committee under pressure. Paine, Rush, Cannon, and Marshall took up the task of visiting people and calling them to the schoolhouse meeting.

On May 14, the eve of debate on the preamble in the Congress, Philadelphians from many neighborhoods and religions met at the schoolroom. The radicals wrote up a list of protests against the assembly of Pennsylvania. Their plan was to call an even bigger meeting and to present the protests to the City Committee, which the radicals of course already directed. On the 15th all they needed for their revolution in Pennsylvania was tacit assent from the other states.

⁓

First to speak in the Congress that morning was James Duane of New York. He was a supporter of reconciliation in the middle-colony bloc led by Dickinson. Duane moved that New York's instructions to its delegates in the Congress be read aloud.

They were read. It was clear that New York had instructed its delegates to work against independence and toward reconciliation. Duane reminded the chair that when first invited by Massachusetts to join a congress of colonies, New York had raised a concern that votes in such a meeting might be used to bind the states to innovative policies of the Congress itself. It was not the Congress's place to consider how justice was administered in any state, Duane said, let alone to pass a resolution like this one. The Congress had no more right to do that, he added, than Parliament did.

He meant to raise a murmur in the room. Americans were resisting Parliament for encroaching illegally on the sovereignty of representative governments. Now the Adamses were using the Congress to do what Parliament was doing, in Duane's view. There was a basis for his suspicion. In the letter published by the British, where he'd called Dickinson piddling and silly, John Adams had written that "we ought to have had in our hands a month ago the whole legislative, executive and judicial of the whole continent, and have completely modeled a constitution, to have raised a naval power and opened all our ports wide, to have arrested every friend to government on the continent and held them as hostages for the poor victims in Boston." Changing states' governments from the Congress could seem to be accomplishing those overbearing purposes.

For the members' benefit, Duane dissected the preamble itself. He noted that Adams had snuck in, without explanation and for the record, not only that no favorable response had yet come from the king but also that no such response was likely to come, and had coupled that foregone conclusion, made as if factual, to the hiring of Hessian mercenaries. Duane reminded the members that every British act providing for foreign troops also provided for peace commissioners.

"Why all this haste?" he asked, cannily enough. He could smell something brewing. "Why this urging? Why this driving?"

He closed by registering a formal protest against the preamble as a "mechanism" and announced that he would take no part in this breach of faith with his home country. He suggested, for a bitter flourish, that the preamble wouldn't have been proposed unless the Adamses had already counted the votes in caucus and made sure of victory. Duane sat down.

At Delaware's desk, Thomas McKean rose. Samuel Adams had, of course, counted votes the best he could, and McKean's vote for the preamble was assured. Yet now McKean made no case for independence. This was a classic caucus diversion, perfected in Boston by Samuel Adams. McKean played the moderate. He said the measure would actually be the best thing for producing harmony between the colonies and Great Britain, and that far from being a shadow act of independence, it was only the toughest kind of defensive measure. Foreign mercenaries were coming to destroy Americans. Without taking this step, he said, Americans would lose their liberties, properties, and lives. He didn't say how adopting a preamble would prevent such losses. But for any member nervous that the preamble might go too far, McKean separated it from independence, and for members frightened by news of foreign troops, he connected it to the paramount goal, security.

Samuel Adams rose to speak.

This was a rare event. Members would listen closely and with tension, wondering how to take whatever he said. Adams underplayed. His speeches were rarely memorable. His tremor was noticeable, and he spoke quietly, as if commenting with interest from an objective distance on the logic of a current situation. He expressed his gladness that the New York instructions had been read. They only meant that James Duane was excluded from voting for the preamble and not, Adams noted carefully, that there was anything wrong with the preamble itself. The king had thrown the colonies out of his protection, he said, and had answered petitions with fleets and armies and unscrupulous foreign hirelings—"myrmidons," he called them.

Why then would Americans support any government operating under the king's authority? He was amazed only that the people had put up with such governments as long as they had.

That was a signal, working two ways. "The people," in this case, meant the City Committee in town and the Committee of Privates across Pennsylvania. Adams was assuring them that if they responded to the call in Paine's Forester article and overthrew Pennsylvania's legislature, the Congress would support them via the preamble and resolution.

But Adams was also preparing the delegates in the Congress for what was about to occur in Philadelphia, indeed right there in the State House, in the yard, and up and down the staircase. When the people of the province rebelled, it would be because their patience had run out with their government's taking oaths to an evil king. Nobody could say an uprising had anything to do with him.

James Wilson of Pennsylvania rose. He was a protégé of Dickinson, having begun his studies in Dickinson's office and become an astute lawyer and reconciliationist. With Dickinson out of town, it was left to Wilson to try to protect Pennsylvania's government. He pointed to the difference between Pennsylvania and those colonies that had actively sought advice from the Congress on how to form governments. They had been royal governments, he reminded the members, needing help during a war against a royal army. But

Pennsylvania had never been governed by the king. It had a working representative body. It didn't need this kind of supposed help. It had done much for and asked little from the Congress, and the preamble was a nasty repayment.

Wilson also pointed out that on the authority of the voters, Pennsylvania's delegates were under instructions, from a duly elected assembly, not to vote for anything like the current preamble. Instructions could change, but only legally. What would be the harm, Wilson asked, in waiting five days for the newly elected assembly—where representation, he reminded the Congress, had recently been increased—to take its seats upstairs? That body could then consider whether to modify its instructions to the delegates, or it might pass a law ending oath-taking to the king. The May 10 resolution, Wilson assured the members, could be published now, just not with this preamble, which, if it were really only a preamble, wouldn't make any difference to the resolution's force anyway.

Waiting was just what the Adamses couldn't allow. The meeting of Philadelphians had occurred just the night before, in preparation for passage of the preamble today. The radical crew was poised to bring up protests against the Pennsylvania assembly for adoption by an even bigger meeting tonight.

To the radicals, the issue came down to what "the people" meant. When Wilson referred to the people as the author, through their representatives, of instructions to vote against independence, he meant people with the right to vote and hold office. But the unenfranchised white men of the province, and their military wing, the Committee of Privates, had a different definition of "the people." They were ready to end the old charter, take over Pennsylvania, and seize the franchise.

Wilson knew it. "In this province," he now admitted to the delegates, "if that preamble passes, there will be an immediate dissolution of every kind of authority. The people will be instantly in a state of nature.... Before we are prepared to build the new house, why should we pull down the old one," he pled, "and expose ourselves to all the inclemencies of the season?"

Richard Henry Lee of Virginia rose. Having co-sponsored the May 10 resolution with Adams, he noted simply that objections raised today attacked not the preamble but the original resolution itself, which had been passed and was beyond debate. Lee was right. The reconciliationists had lost control of Dickinson's strategy. Duane's attack was on the resolution; he argued that the Congress had no right to pass it. Wilson, expressing anxiety for Pennsylvania, was really complaining about creating a new government. The preamble had done its job. The reconciliationists were failing to frame an argument for rejecting the preamble alone. Yet combined with the resolution, the preamble spelled doom for Pennsylvania's elected government.

There was no way to know what might have happened had Dickinson been present to argue. It was undeniable that Pennsylvania's legislature and judiciary did take oaths to the king. But Dickinson might have noted, with asperity, how attacking Pennsylvania on this novel issue was at best fantastically unfair and at worst vicious and arbitrary. Pennsylvania never had a royal governor, because John Dickinson himself, opposing Benjamin Franklin in the early 1760s, had prevented it. That his achievements on behalf of representative government and process of law should be turned against Pennsylvania represented the bitterest irony.

Benjamin Franklin was recuperating at home from the rigors of his trip to Quebec. He might have liked to savor this twist to an old story in his political life.

~~⌒~~

It was time for what would be a critical vote. But the Maryland members stood, cleared their desks, and packed up their papers. Like New York's, their instructions were explicit. They announced that they couldn't now deem the May 10 resolution binding on their state. They would submit an account of today's proceedings, which they called alarming, to their home government, and they wouldn't be back unless they had instructions on how to act in this case. Maryland's delegates walked out of the State House.

This was a crisis. Without all thirteen acting as one, the separate colonies were in jeopardy. If peace commissioners, or the British army, or both, arrived now, America would lack a united front. That was the last-ditch risk Samuel Adams had decided to take in order to set Pennsylvania up for overthrow.

The vote proceeded. In the Congress, each delegate got one vote, and each delegation's vote was determined by the majority of votes within the delegation. If votes within a delegation split evenly, the delegation had no vote.

Pennsylvania's reconciliationists couldn't vote for the measure, but voting against it would have left them vulnerable to accusations of royalism by both the Adamses and the street. Pennsylvania abstained.

Georgia's delegation wasn't present. A majority of members in six delegations voted for adopting the preamble. A majority in four voted against. It was close, but the preamble passed.

~~⌒~~

As the spring evening fell on the city, word was out. If some of the congressmen didn't know what they'd brought down on Pennsylvania's government, many people in the province, on all sides of the issue, did see what was happening. At the London Coffee House on Front Street, people were saying the Congress had just effectively declared independence. That night, as scheduled, Philadelphians packed into a space normally used by the American Philosophical Society, which, lacking its own building, often met at Christ Church School on Second Street. The radicals brought in the protests against the legitimacy of the assembly, written the night before at the schoolroom.

Tactical debate went on for three hours that night, without a conclusion. Another session was scheduled for three the next afternoon.

But by the time the meeting reconvened, the city was in turmoil over the preamble. Dickinson was still in Delaware. His newly elected assembly was scheduled to meet on Monday and start a new session in its temporary quarters upstairs at the State House. Yet that assembly was being denounced as illegitimate by a growing number of citizens.

Marshall met with Cannon. The Committee of Privates offered the best means of organizing support outside Philadelphia, so the two men decided on a forthright move. At the reconvened meeting at Philosophical Hall, the radicals proposed that a crowd gather outside the State House on May 20. The crowd would protest the elected assembly and adopt resolutions, which the local chapter of the Committee of Privates would endorse and disseminate to militias across Pennsylvania. The city's action would gain support from the armed rank and file of the whole province.

But to give that mass meeting as much formality and legitimacy as possible, the radicals wanted the City Committee to appear to be succumbing to overwhelming pressure in the form of a petition from the citizenry. Monday the 20th, when the assembly was scheduled to sit, was only two business days away. Time to circulate petitions and have them signed was short.

Luckily for the radicals, they had an extra day. Months earlier, the Congress had declared Friday, May 17, a special kind of weekday holiday throughout the colonies, dedicated to prayer and thanksgiving. These "Congress Sundays" were meant to serve inter-colonial unity. The May 17 Congress Sunday served the Philadelphia radicals. People were off work after church on Friday. They hung around the coffeehouses and on the corners, talking about turbulence in the city and the Congress. The radicals spent that day getting signatures on their petition. They also called on city and nearby inhabitants to attend a mass meeting at nine in the morning on Monday, May 20, at the State House. They didn't qualify attendance by property.

For even greater urgency, Paine wrote another call to action. This one was titled "The Alarm." The radicals had it set in type in two versions, English and German (*Der Alarm*). *The Alarm* called again for a change in government. The elected assembly, it said, ruined by an ineluctable history of royal connection, couldn't legally change itself to comply with Congress's resolution. It had to be replaced. The people must form a convention, *The Alarm* said, and write a constitution, with no interference from the assembly.

When the City Committee officially convened on the night of Saturday, May 18, it was presented with the petition signed by many citizens. The committee voted to hold the mass meeting of protest at the State House on the morning of May 20. On Sunday, the radicals began distributing *The Alarm* in both languages. They wanted the rally at the State House to be a big one. Marshall, Young, Cannon,

Paine, Rush, and Matlack had been working for a long time on bringing about not improvement of government but a change in its nature, a government committed not only to liberty but also to equality. They saw an independent America transformed and redeemed. Their moment seemed imminent.

7

Blind Eyes

May 20

Of all the people John Adams hated—in 1776 the list was already long—he may have hated Thomas Paine the most. Adams called John Dickinson piddling and silly. He called Paine, his ally in the secret coalition, "a star of disaster," and he meant a meteor leaving a crater. Paine's writings were "worthless and unprincipled," "profligate and impious." The one good thing in *Common Sense* was its call for independence, Adams said, and that was stolen, he said, from him. Paine's indelicate language—calling the king "the royal brute," for example—revealed the author's roughneck and possibly even criminal origins. The pamphlet, as Adams summed it up, was "a poor, ignorant, malicious, short-sighted, crapulous mass."

That indelicacy went pretty far, even for John Adams. Paine's thinking disgusted him violently. The new government proposed by *Common Sense* was "so democratical," Adams said, "without any restraint or even an attempt at any equilibrium or counterpoise, that it must produce confusion and every evil work." Such ideas could only arise, he was sure, from ignorance or hypocrisy. *Common Sense* became an international bestseller, and its authorship was known early. Paine's fame showed Adams only that ignorance and hypocrisy might coexist in one low, demonic fake.

For Adams believed fervently in just what Paine condemned— the checks and balances in the English constitution. He believed that the useful part of English government was indeed republican, with the king its first magistrate. He also thought elected representatives tended to pander irresponsibly to constituents, so he wanted an independent solo executive with power to check the legislature. When it came to the breaking of ancient ties between property ownership and the right to vote, Adams was disdainful. People are self-interested and weak, he said. If the unpropertied get the vote, they'll still be dependent. Tenant farmers dependent on landlords will vote with the landlords, urban laborers dependent on bosses with the bosses. Powerful individuals and machines will control elections and constitutions, pushing laws around to suit immediate desires. They'll be like kings, but far worse than the British one, because their power will be absolute and arbitrary, backed by the mindless will of a mob.

Even a legislature elected only by property owners is at risk of excessive democracy, Adams believed. He called Paine's single house a "crude, ignorant notion." A big representative house must be balanced by a smaller house, less immediately representative, providing ballast. Paine wanted judges elected locally and democratically, answerable to working people, the debtor class, not to wealthy creditors. But the appeal to economic justice didn't move Adams. He wanted the judiciary independent of politics. Judges must be appointed by the executive, he insisted, with the advice and consent of the upper house of the legislature, and should serve for life, free from both popular opinion and executive branch convenience. If a judge misbehaved, he should be impeached by process of law.

Lacing power tightly against power would achieve a government "of laws," Adams echoed the old liberty writers, "not of men." Like his enemy Dickinson, Adams was an astute and experienced practitioner of common and criminal law and the science of government. Like Dickinson, he staked hope for the American future on preserving the ancient connections among law, liberty, and property.

Yet Adams was working with Paine and the Philadelphia radicals to destroy Dickinson's representative, lawfully elected government. Thanks to his doggedness in the Congress, in the third week of May the coalition was moving to replace Pennsylvania's charter with everything Adams loathed. He'd been engaging in contradictions like this for as long as he'd been involved with Samuel Adams. They caused him anxieties that demolished him physically and mentally, making him literally sick. Trying to end that turmoil, he'd sniffed around the resistance in Boston, coming and going and coming back. He'd moved into Boston itself, then out, then back in. He'd made strong determinations and turned away from them. The circling had exhausted him.

As a youth, he'd discovered in himself an immense yearning. He wanted to be admired, deferred to, and remembered after death: a great man. But to pursue fame, he also believed, was to indulge selfish desire, a weakness. In his diary, the young man fought a battle with himself. "The love of fame," he told himself, "naturally betrays a man into several weaknesses and fopperies that tend very much to diminish his reputation, and so defeats itself. Vanity, I am sensible, is my cardinal vice and cardinal folly." Fame would be manhood fulfilled, but wanting fame unmanned. "Oh!" he wrote, "that I could wear out of my mind every mean and base affectation." If only he could "conquer my natural pride and self conceit, expect no more deference from my fellows than I deserve, acquire that meekness and humility which are the sure marks and characters of a great and generous soul."

In that struggle, he was drawn by a line from Tacitus, the Whig-republican hero: "Contempt of fame is contempt of virtue." Those with no desire for fame will never commit big, good acts, Tacitus said. Denying the desire is what tyrants have always done. The worst crime would be hypocrisy.

The best thing, John Adams decided then, is to admit desire for fame, yoking it always to the pursuit of high principle. That was virtue in public life, at once Puritan and classical. He would be a great citizen of a place that mixed the old Bay Colony with the Roman republic. He would be a Cicero or an Increase Mather, living in edifying service to others, evincing the greatness that brought fame worth having. That goal also inspired devotion to success in business, and John Adams made his devotion an outright busy-ness. He lived in a way that would come to be called "Yankee." He was always doing dozens of things, big and small. He would not be idle.

Yet he faced frustration. As a lawyer in Braintree, the rural community where he'd grown up, he rode the court circuit almost without stopping, from Braintree to Boston to Worcester to Barnstable to Martha's Vineyard, rarely home, always overwhelmed, never getting rich. He wanted to rise in local politics, as respectable men did, yet he hated to reveal ambition. He wanted to be courted. And he annoyed Braintree's legal and political establishment with open disdain for "pettifogging," amateur fly-by-night lawyering by which men he saw as mediocre got ahead.

He believed he had greatness in him. He wanted a big event. He was fitful and irritable. He blamed himself for his frustration, and he blamed everybody else, too.

In the mid-1760s, when Adams already felt both overworked and left behind, Samuel Adams began bringing him into a new relationship with Boston. Up in town Samuel and his allies were reacting to the Sugar Act and the Stamp Act by harassing the royal element in Massachusetts government and protesting Parliamentary trade and tax laws. They were sending their own people to represent Boston in the Massachusetts assembly, turning that body against the royal governor and the upper house, crashing one part of government into the others. The men who would become Sons of Liberty were organizing civic and professional life in Boston so thoroughly that getting ahead there was coming to mean being allied with them.

Samuel Adams was reaching out to younger men. He wanted to bring new talent to the service of Boston, the Bay province, and charter liberties in opposition to royal government. Dr. Joseph Warren was one of them. So was John Hancock, scion of a shipping fortune and fleet, well able to fund Samuel Adams's efforts. Josiah Quincy, Jr., was another; like John Adams, though more refined, he was a lawyer with Braintree roots.

That group had strong attractions. But there were risks involved. For John Adams, they were both practical and emotional.

John and Samuel Adams didn't know each other well then. Second cousins share only great-grandparents, and the Adamses weren't close as youngsters. There was the thirteen-year age difference; also their family branches had diverged. John was country. His father was a Braintree farmer. When John went to Harvard, his father sold acreage to pay the tuition. Harvard class ranking had recently come to be determined by family social status, and John ranked fourteen of twenty-five.

Samuel's Harvard rank was five of twenty-two. Having moved from Braintree two generations earlier, the Boston Adamses were merchants and investors. Boston had poor soil and short rivers. Trade at sea was the source of profit, and the Hancocks were adept at eluding imperial regulations to enhance profit. The Boston Adamses were investors in the Hancock business, and Samuel grew up in a house on Purchase Street fronting the harbor. The roof featured a railed observatory platform accessed by outside stairs, and a big, windy view, the merchant view. Immediate profit came from a malthouse contiguous to the home, where grain was prepared and sold for brewing. Wharves bounded the property, and Samuel's father owned one of them, along with houses and land parcels ready for development.

Unlike John, Samuel knew what he wanted. When his father died at fifty-nine, young Samuel was already editing and writing an anti-imperial newspaper he'd founded himself with a few friends, a weekly remonstrance against corrupt power, in favor of traditions of liberty going back to the English Civil War. Samuel wrote most of the pieces, signing them with a variety of aliases. He wrote fake letters to the editor, praising his essays. He was conjuring a movement.

He wasn't rebelling against his father or establishment Boston. Quite the contrary. The Boston Adamses and their merchant friends lived in opposition to royal government and imperial regulation. Boston was a town more than a city, almost an island, with Boston Neck, which connected the town to inland Massachusetts, so narrow it had room for the road and not much else. Puritan ancestry and oceangoing commerce meant toughness, isolation, and unity. There were living memories of the Mathers and other ministers as powerful spokesmen for a special covenant between New Englanders and God. Old, natural connections between Puritan religious ideals, freedom of conscience, and Whig liberties thrived. "Help, Lord," Samuel's paper pled when Adams Sr. died, "for such wise and godly men cease, and such faithful members fail from among the sons of New England."

The condemnation was of Samuel's generation. The plea was for new, young leadership, in an old New England spirit, a son in the image of the father.

Samuel lived in his late father's house on Purchase Street and inherited his father's public life, which he began taking to extremes. He inherited problems, too. Adams Sr. had been a director of a "land bank," which issued paper currency, secured by land. Real money was gold and silver coin, which was scarce in Boston. Boston Whigs blamed economic ills on English "hard money" laws prohibiting paper currencies, and, they thought, keeping their town submissive. The Adams land bank, an alternative to gold and silver, was associated, in the minds of its founders, with liberty. But Parliament declared the land bank illegal. Worse, its directors were made personally liable for all the paper they'd issued. That gave the colony's royal government a chance to come down hard on the Adamses. The family lost nearly a third of its wealth, became subject to lawsuits, and had property attached. For twenty years, first the father and then the son would strive to keep home, malthouse, and other holdings from seizure and sale by authorities.

Samuel also inherited his father's relationship to the Boston town meeting. In the hands of men like Samuel Adams, Sr., the town meeting had become a machine for opposing British innovations, preserving Congregationalist autonomy and Whig liberties, and consolidating virtue by elevating right-thinking men. Its unity came from an entity known as "the caucus." A few men met in tavern upper rooms to predetermine agendas for the town meeting. Around the punch bowls, amid pungent smoke, they decided whom the meeting would elect to represent Boston in the Massachusetts assembly, and whom to appoint to town jobs. By rigging the town meeting, the caucus controlled politics in Boston and, as far as possible, throughout the colony.

Samuel began using the caucus to take his father's lifelong struggles against the royal element in government all the way. His chief ally in the project was James Otis, the province's most brilliant lawyer, and Adams and Otis were bringing in young Warren, Hancock, and others. Influenced by the caucus, the town meeting began electing Samuel Adams to jobs with income: clerk of the market, scavenger, tax collector. His influence grew. When he fell behind in his tax collection accounts, royal elements of provincial and local government wanted to indict him for malfeasance in office. The town meeting showed itself unwilling to support indicting Samuel Adams, and the charge was dropped.

Samuel married the daughter of his father's friend the Reverend Checkley, minister of New South Church. He sang psalms at the church in the fuguing, unaccompanied way with his friend William Billings, a self-taught composer. Billings was making an American sound in canons, anthems, and hymns. Tense harmony, voice against voice, made wooden floors tremble with what Billings called agreeable suspense. It was the Puritan way of old Boston, held in suspense and freely covenanted.

$\backsim$

In Braintree, with not enough to do, John Adams received a letter from the Boston town meeting. It was 1765, and Boston courts had been closed by decree. Nobody would use the hated stamps, required by the Stamp Act for court documents, so legal business stood still. The letter invited John to join with James Otis and Jeremiah Gridley, the most celebrated lawyers of the town, to argue before the royal governor and council against the Stamp Act, and for opening the courts without stamps.

It couldn't have been more exciting. Adams didn't know who in Boston might have thought of him—a distant, little-known lawyer—for the third partner. He wasn't yet familiar enough with Boston politics to know that without Samuel Adams's involvement, the invitation could not have been made. He went to Boston and conferred with the other lawyers, and then, by candlelight, met in the assembly room at the Massachusetts State House with the town meeting committee handling the case. Samuel Adams was in the chair.

While they were meeting, word came from the governor and council, across the hall, that the lawyers were to make their case, tonight, with nobody else present. John was startled. He had no books or notes. When they stood before the governor, Gridley volunteered to speak last. Otis said he'd speak second. All turned to the little-known man from Braintree. Adams began a classic Whig argument against taxation without representation. He backed it up with a practical argument about the act's unenforceability. When he finished, Otis and Gridley addressed the tangled constitutional issues in closing courts.

Adams stayed overnight in Boston. He gathered that as counsel for the town, he was expected the next day at the town meeting, where the committee would report on the governor's response. The meeting convened in the big, echoing chamber in Fanueil Hall, and the committee reported that the governor and council had rejected the lawyers' arguments. Adams was asked by the town to give his opinion on how it should respond, and to consult further with Otis and Gridley.

He was in—a junior member, but a member nonetheless of both the elite Boston bar and the resistance to England. He took deep pleasure in being depended upon and solicited for advice. Constitutional traditions of continuous royal justice made this court-closing question a big one, and Adams made it even bigger. "It is the first time, I believe," he reflected in his diary, "that such a question was ever put since William the Conqueror, nay, since the days of King Lear." His excitement advanced until he spooked himself: "If we are out of the king's protection, are we not discharged from our allegiance? ... In short, where will such an horrid doctrine terminate? It would run us into treason!"

Soon he was riding eagerly back and forth from Braintree to Boston to help Otis, Gridley, and the town meeting form the response to the court closing. He went to club meetings with the town's social and lawyerly elite, where they swapped stories and joked and cheered one another on. At the clubs' behest, he wrote newspaper articles against the Stamp Act.

One evening Samuel Adams told John he was glad that John had been nominated to bring the case against the governor. Samuel told John he wanted his cousin to enter more fully into Boston life. Joining, Samuel said, would build up John's business and reputation and—the real hook—might even get John elected by Braintree to the Massachusetts assembly.

Back in Braintree, John wrote instructions from the town to its representatives in the assembly, basing them on resolves written by Samuel Adams, telling Boston's representatives to oppose the Stamp Act. The American resistance was successful. In early 1766 Parliament repealed the Stamp Act. Americans celebrated, and some became emboldened to further resistance; certain leaders in England, meanwhile, began seeking ways of reasserting Parliamentary authority. In Massachusetts, the courts re-opened. Now as John Adams rode the circuit, crowds cheered him as a patriot defender of liberty.

But he lost the Braintree assembly election. He was made selectman, a local and lesser position. The pettifoggers controlled everything, he seethed, and the very worst of them was now chosen over him for the assembly. His Boston adventure had come to nothing. Samuel Adams was meanwhile entering the Massachusetts assembly from Boston, having already influenced much of what that house did anyway. When Samuel became clerk of the assembly, the legislature's resolves began to resemble, some thought, a colonial Magna Carta, a case against the royal governor. Samuel was bringing rich, flamboyant John Hancock along, making him not only a source of funds but also his chief deputy, roles that naturally enhanced one another. Hancock was elected to the Massachusetts assembly at the age of twenty-nine.

Down in Braintree, John fretted. Everybody else had advanced by opposing the Stamp Act. He might have won the local election, he thought, if only he'd stayed out of the Boston protests. He hated the gangs, the smelly air and dirty streets, and what he saw as the crowd's mindlessness. Yet he vacillated: Maybe he'd hurt himself by being too timid in supporting the protest?

He'd been self-sacrificing, he thought. In service to others, he'd given of himself and lost favor.

⌐‿⌐

So John Adams made a problematic helpmeet for Samuel Adams. As things advanced to rebellion in Boston, John became at times a hysterical one. The goal, Samuel said, was to build a Christian Sparta.

He was single-minded. Every bad act of England only made his path clearer. "What a blessing to us," he later remarked of the Stamp Act. But John went from fervent support of Whig and Puritan traditions of liberty to terror at where his support might lead him and lead Massachusetts. He took positions, reversed them, chided himself for miscalculation. He kept being urged by the Sons of Liberty, the lawyers, and Samuel himself to move into Boston, and in 1768 he did shift his practice and family there. But while he worked in secret for the Sons, handling writing and law assignments, he wouldn't take a public stand. Joseph Warren kept asking him to speak against ministerial crimes at Boston town and mass meetings. Adams refused.

When people accused him of being weak in cause, he went to a Sons of Liberty excursion. The Sons were well-off merchants, and the event a rich men's picnic, with dining and drinking and entertainment. Guests arrived in gorgeous coaches. That was a far cry from the artisan and laborer actions that John so hated, the effigy-burning and house attacks, the Pope's Day parades politicized, which these same Sons were at once helping organize and trying to restrain. But John didn't enjoy the Sons' ostentation, either. The picnic seemed frivolous. He didn't join the Sons.

Samuel Adams was nothing but patient. The cousins spent time together in Boston. One day after a ride in a chaise, they had dinner. Samuel assured John that nothing Samuel was doing had the object of piling up wealth or ensuring his posterity's security.

To John, that summed up their difference. He'd had to work all his life; Samuel hadn't. "If that had been true of me," he told Samuel, "you would never have seen my face." They were reaching an understanding.

And in the end, it was his apparent distance from the core of the resistance, and his evident stand as a moderate that made John

Adams useful to Samuel Adams's purposes and brought him into public view at last. By 1768, resistance in Boston had advanced to the point where regiments of British soldiers occupied the town. The people harassed the soldiers, sometimes to great effect. On a cold March night in 1770, four hundred citizens gathered outside the Custom House, where eight soldiers under the command of Captain Thomas Preston stood in a semicircle, holding the people off with bayonets. People chanted and jeered: "Shoot! Shoot!" A thrown club hit a soldier. A shot was fired into the crowd. There was a pause. Then came a full round of shots. As people fell, Captain Preston screamed at his men to stop shooting. He marched them quickly away, leaving the Custom House unguarded and ending the standoff. Enraged but stunned, the crowd milled about as the wounded were carried off. Five men would die.

Royal governor Thomas Hutchinson arrived at the scene. The people poured out their grief and shock. They showed Hutchinson the blood on the snow. Hutchinson climbed to a balcony and addressed them. He promised that Preston and the soldiers would be tried for murder. The crowd dispersed.

Samuel Adams quickly named the event "the Boston Massacre." The upcoming trial gave the Sons of Liberty a powerful opportunity to build support, both in Massachusetts and among other colonies, for what they saw as a virtuous resistance to brutal occupation. Because the king's justice would be brought to bear on the king's soldiers, the royal part of government would be under stress. Governor Hutchinson would set the schedule and the venue and assign judges. The Sons could, however, improve prosecution of the soldiers. The king's attorney should have led the prosecution team, but he ducked the assignment, busying himself with matters out of town, and the court made the solicitor general a special prosecutor. He was a loyalist, unlikely to prosecute royal troops vigorously. So the Sons had the Boston selectmen and town meeting vote to pay prosecution expenses. That gave them a right to place one of their own on the team.

Having chosen half the prosecution team, Samuel Adams made some careful calculations regarding the defense as well. If the soldiers were weakly defended, their conviction would seem weak, too, robbing Boston of a moral victory. On the other hand, the last thing the Sons could afford was to have the defense attacking Boston in general, expounding on the violence of the people, putting the town's resistance movement—the Sons themselves—on trial to justify the shootings. The Sons needed just the right lawyer defending Captain Preston and the soldiers.

John Adams took the job. Precisely because John wasn't a creature of the Sons of Liberty, he wouldn't have to pretend to be a moderate. He really was a moderate. He wouldn't have to pretend to believe that everyone, even a British soldier, deserves a defense regardless of public opinion. He really believed that. He wouldn't have to pretend to disdain mobs. He disdained mobs. He wouldn't have to pretend to be one of the province's best lawyers. He was one, and because Samuel Adams believed victory for the prosecution was certain, John could be every bit as brilliant as he'd always wanted to be.

Nor did John have to pretend to be unpopular in Boston for defending British soldiers. People didn't know the Sons of Liberty approved his taking the case. People believed he was defying the Sons and fragmenting civic unity. Some called John Adams a traitor to the cause.

That public disdain was painful and infuriating, but the case touched John's drive for fame and concern for his own virtue at their tenderest joint. This wasn't just the most sensational thing in Massachusetts or in the American colonies. It was imperial business, watched from Whitehall and the palace. A ring of big tapers was being lit. John Adams, too long obscure, was getting his chance to step into its center.

How closely he scrutinized the calculation that made him, in effect, Samuel Adams's secret agent in the Boston Massacre trials would never be clear. John was too perspicacious not to have gotten the whole thing. Perspicacity would not serve him here. He stuck throughout his life to the cover story: this was his profile in courage. As he told it, he'd risked safety, lost business opportunity, and been made a mockery, all in the service of the principle of equal rights before the law. Reveling in the vastness of his own integrity, he even complained about being paid almost nothing for the defense.

In fact he was well paid by Samuel Adams and the Boston town meeting for his part in their strategy. There was a blatant quid pro quo, and it was worth far more to John Adams than any fee. Even before the trials were over, he was elected to the Massachusetts assembly, a representative from Boston. That reward was arranged, as all such elections were, by Samuel Adams, the caucus, and the Sons, through the town meeting.

So it all worked out—for John Adams, that is, but not for Samuel Adams and the Sons. They'd miscalculated. Believing conviction was certain, Samuel Adams pressed for speedy trials. Governor Hutchinson, believing conviction was at least likely, kept postponing. When two of the judges conveniently got sick, the trials were put over to June, but Samuel Adams and his allies, along with a crowd, walked into the courtroom to demand trials be held in the current term. Under that pressure, the judges agreed to try the cases in April. Hutchinson found ways to run out the term, and the trials didn't in fact start until fall, but that was still fairly speedy, and speed actually worked against the prosecution. The state's case was based on contradictory eyewitness testimony. It would have needed either bolstering or imaginative development or both. And John Adams did some adroit lawyering. He got Preston's case separated from the soldiers', since Preston wasn't accused of murder. He based the captain's defense on having not ordered the shooting and the soldiers' on following orders. In the Preston case, he used juror challenges to great effect, filling the box with loyalists and people with army business. The soldiers' trial restricted his latitude in challenging, but he somehow managed not to put any Boston residents on that jury.

Yet the weakness of the state's case, and his own delicate position, forced him to proceed carefully, too. He refrained from beating up on state witnesses, Bostonians loyal to the resistance. He refused to use evidence that would suggest Boston crowds were constantly threatening just this kind of incident. In his memorable summation for the soldiers' trial, he argued against taking personal revenge on the soldiers, and he famously demeaned the crowd outside the Custom House as a motley, lower-class rabble: "saucy boys, Negroes and mulattos, Irish teagues, and outlandish jack tars." But he did articulate the Sons' primary message to the crown and ministry. Sending soldiers to Boston was the real crime, Adams said. Blame the deaths on England, not the troops.

Preston was acquitted, as were most of the soldiers, with two convicted of manslaughter. As he took his big step toward fame, John Adams got to have things both ways.

John Adams entered the Massachusetts assembly room at the old State House, backed by the Boston caucus, elected by the Boston town meeting, leaving country pettifogging far behind. He joined Samuel Adams, Hancock, Otis, William Cushing, and other famous

Boston men as a lawmaker and defender of high Whig values. He handled the biggest caseload in the province, with up to three clerks working for him and a clientele that ranged from the Hancocks to a former royal governor. He was a man of the town and of the province. The fame he'd always longed for was his.

He had a breakdown.

The contradiction in entering the house by virtue of his work on the Boston Massacre cases was overwhelming. Contradictions only proliferated after he got in. To enforce boycotts against British products, the Sons were supporting rallies and meetings that sent self-appointed committees of inspection, tough gang members, to threaten and abuse noncomplying merchants. Two importers were visited by Thomas Young with a huge crowd of men and boys. The importers were seized, terrorized, humiliated, and dragged through town in a cart. One importer agreed, in lieu of being tarred and feathered, to run a gauntlet of men spitting in his face. A crowd did tar and feather a customs inspector. Boston's unity was being enforced by the kind of terror and torture that John Adams saw as the height of lawlessness.

"They call me a brainless Tory," said an observer of one Boston riot. "But tell me, my young friend, which is better—to be ruled by one tyrant three thousand miles away, or by three thousand tyrants not one mile away?" That's how John Adams felt, too.

Meanwhile, his main job in the house on behalf of the resistance was to attack Governor Hutchinson. That might have seemed easy, even enjoyable, given that Adams and Thomas Hutchinson had always hated each other. When he'd been a judge, Hutchinson humiliated Adams in court. As governor, Hutchinson represented what Adams most despised. He was an American, with New England ancestry at least as old as the Adamses', yet he was an imperial courtier. Unalloyed ambition characterized Hutchinson, Adams believed. The man had risen through preferment, connections, and patronage. Adams had no sympathy for the governor.

But he did object to the assembly's attacks. They were vicious and personal, based on a caricature of Hutchinson as a secret plotter against New England, a traitor to his country. Adams knew this was character assassination. He had to speak against the governor for hours every day in the assembly, carrying out a program he didn't believe in and wearing himself down. And all of this was designed to serve a goal that, he could not fail to see, was starting to involve not protest against the horrors of British overreaching but a push toward something hard to imagine: American independence. Samuel Adams was becoming clear about that. John Adams loved the British constitution. The idea of independence was strange and fearsome.

So the machinations that had placed him where he'd always wanted to be were undermining his virtue, the reason for being there. He was carrying out plans, every day and with all of his might, that he couldn't honestly support. Meanwhile, the demands of his profession mounted. His sense of himself as virtuous became harder to maintain as he became physically and mentally exhausted.

In February 1771 he endured a night of horror. He was, he said, never in more misery in his whole life. The next day he brooded. The day after that he stopped writing in his diary. He'd always striven with himself there. He wouldn't make entries again until April, when at the end of the assembly session, he packed up and moved back to Braintree.

Boston had made him one of its own. The foul air of that town, he believed, was destroying him. In Braintree, which had rejected him, good, clean air was blowing, he was sure.

Being home didn't help. He gnawed on resentment. He tried to get Samuel Adams elected to a minor Braintree post. When Samuel was defeated, people at the courthouse openly mocked John, big Boston mover and shaker, for having no influence at home, or possibly even a negative influence. "Thus are the friends of the people," he wrote, "after such dangerous efforts, and such successful ones too, left in the lurch even by the people themselves. . . . I have very cheerfully sacrificed my interest, and my health and ease and pleasure, in the service of the people."

Late that May, he gave up. He went for a rest cure at the Stafford mineral springs in northern Connecticut. He swam in the water and drank it. He lived a simple life, boarding with a farm family who fed him plain food and said prayers before bed each night. He rambled and read. He chatted with people he found pleasing but dull. He heard little about the great events in Boston. Idle, he described his brains as barren.

Yet some delight in the world seemed to return. He was writing at length in his diary again, describing nature and weather, speculating about farming and English history. On his way home from the springs, he had a new thought.

"I believe there is no man in so curious a situation as I am," he mused. "I am, for what I can see, quite left alone in the world."

In the fall of 1772 he was back in Boston, but he was determined to quit politics for good. No more clubs, he instructed himself. No town meeting. He felt well, in good spirits, happier than he'd ever been. This time, he was done with Samuel Adams's operation, he decided.

In the spring of 1776, John Adams hadn't merely come back to Samuel's operation; he was its top operator, its most vociferous fighter in the Congress for independence. And he wasn't looking back.

At first, after the nightmare of his breakdown, he refused invitations to politics. Samuel personally asked him to give what had become the annual speech, before crowds, on the anniversary of the Boston Massacre. He declined, pleading weak health and the irony of his role in having defended the soldiers. He dined and chatted with the various Sons without joining their efforts. He helped Samuel with some writing against Hutchinson, but he toned down Samuel's language. One night in December 1773, a Boston crowd, garishly costumed and made up, enforced a boycott against the Tea Act. They boarded ships in the harbor, which were laden with tea, broke open chests, and threw the extremely valuable cargo into the water. Adams took no part in what became known as the "Tea Party." He gloried in the event's effectiveness but worried about where it might lead.

Then he stopped writing in his diary again. During that period, news arrived in Boston that Parliament had passed a law closing the city's port. The news sent patriots around the country into a new state of anxiety. John began writing in his diary again. This law seemed to give the question of resistance, and possibly even of independence, new clarity. England herself was telling John Adams that there might be no way back for him. Events were becoming profound. He chose.

He served on a town committee, then became moderator of the town meeting. In the fall of 1774 came the First Continental Congress. He went with Samuel to Philadelphia. There he revived the feeling of inclusion he'd felt when first called to Boston from Braintree. He enjoyed meeting the most important men from all over the country. He took pride in his importance to Samuel Adams's plans, and pleasure in their secrecy. "We have been obliged to keep ourselves out of sight, and to feel pulses, and sound the depths," he wrote with excitement about the Adamses' lobbying and scheming. As the first Congress went on, he grew bored, frustrated, and angry again, yet when John Hancock rebelled against Samuel Adams's leadership and made common cause with the reconcilationists, John replaced Hancock as Samuel's chief deputy.

Soon he would be more than that. Events began to seem great, possibly the greatest ever. Now he lived with frustration and anger. Some symptoms were mysterious. For the second Congress, he arrived depressed and "suffering infinitely," as he put it, with what he called "blind eyes." He wasn't literally blind, but he wasn't being metaphorical, either. He'd known Dr. Thomas Young back in Boston, when Young was helping organize for Samuel Adams. Despite his disregard for Young's populism—he called Young an "inveterate fisher in troubled waters"—John was no conservative when it came to medicine. After chiding Adams for not taking care of himself, Young brought newfangled electrical contraptions to bear on Adams's vision.

Still, as the secret collaboration with the local radicals progressed, Adams became what he called "always unwell." He was "lonely," he said, with "not one creature here that I seem to have any kind of relation to." Everything for him now came down to declaring independence.

On May 10, 1776, the Congress adopted the Adams-Lee resolution. Adams wrote home to James Warren: "This day the Congress has passed the most important resolution that ever was taken in America." Greatness was imminent. After his preamble passed on May 15, he wrote to his wife, quoting Moses: "who am I, that I should go in and out before this great people?" He went on: "I consider the great events which are passed, and those greater which are rapidly advancing, and that I may have been instrumental of touching some springs, and turning some small wheels, which have had and will have such effects, I feel an awe upon my mind which is not easily described."

On Monday, May 20, the mass meeting planned by the radicals and endorsed by the City Committee took place. Four thousand people gathered within the brick-walled yard behind the Pennsylvania State House. They were wet. It was pouring rain. A stage had been hastily erected, and on it were members of the secret coalition, Thomas McKean, the haughty Whig, and Timothy Matlack, the radical roisterer, along with Daniel Roberdeau, who served with Marshall and Cannon on the board of the American Manufactory. Roberdeau had a booming voice.

The yard had been the scene of mass meetings before, and some had been bigger. Rain was a factor. Yet John Adams was right to call the moment an "epoch." Roberdeau began by reading aloud the Adams-Lee resolution of May 10, beginning, of course, with the preamble that had brought the meeting together. When addresses were read aloud, the reader had to shout and pause to allow phrases to drift to the back, so everybody could hear. Into the storm Roberdeau bellowed each phrase of the preamble, accusing the king of malfeasance, and then bellowed the resolution advising Americans to adopt governments that would best conduce to their happiness and to American safety. Hats flew in the rain. The crowd gave three lusty cheers. By acclamation they accepted the advice of the Congress to overturn the government elected on May 1.

Now the real business began. Roberdeau shouted to the crowd a series of resolves, written by the committee. The idea was that the crowd would vote by voice to accept or reject them.

But there was a pause after the resolutions had been announced.

John Cadwalader, also on the stage, was moving to edit them slightly. He was an old man, in favor of independence and well liked by the crowd. But he was making the mistake of treating the rally as a genuine town meeting. In what would be ordinary procedure for such a meeting, he moved to discuss a mild revision to the resolutions' language, not to change the substance but to clarify it.

So the crowd changed its mind about Cadwalader. Wanting to discuss the resolutions branded him not just a bore but a traitor. Insults began flying. Cadwalader was shouted and jeered at. Abuse overwhelmed him. He was silenced.

Now came the vote. The first resolution condemned the Pennsylvania assembly. That body had shown a dangerous tendency, the committee said, to withdraw the province from union with other colonies, a union that the committee considered the province's glory and protection. To this characterization of the assembly, the wet crowd responded in the affirmative with what seemed forceful unanimity.

But regarding the second resolution, somebody tried to vote no. This resolution said that the assembly had assumed arbitrary power, lacking the authority of the people. The man expressing dissent was a grocer. Another man in the crowd was considering voting against some of the resolutions, too, but he changed his mind when he saw the lone grocer "abused and insulted" by the others.

After that, the responses were unanimous. The final two questions took the first to conclusions devised by the men who had met on May 3 in Samuel Adams's rooms. Was the current government of Pennsylvania competent to the exigencies of affairs (as Congress had put it)? The crowd said no.

So should a new government, favoring independence, be created by a constitution, on advice of the city committee, the authority of the people, and the support of the Congress? The crowd said yes.

John Adams watched the proceedings in the yard. Here was the result of his work in the Congress in collaboration with Paine and the radicals. He saw thousands of people, enfranchised and unenfranchised alike, stand in the rain and toss up their hats to condemn their newly elected legislature as dangerous and nullify it by a shout. He saw them shout down dissent and shout down discussion.

That night he wrote home again to James Warren. Calling the mass meeting in the yard an "entertaining maneuver," he reviewed the proceedings step by step, with satisfaction. He called the event not a mass meeting but a town meeting, not mentioning the absence of a qualification for voting. He didn't mention the humiliation of Cadwalader, or the intimidation of the grocer. It was the first town meeting he'd seen in Philadelphia, he said, and it had been conducted with "great order, decency, and propriety."

8

⁓

Black Silk

May 20–May 27

Something else happened on May 20. John Dickinson came back to
town.

What he found in Philadelphia might have been hard to predict ten days earlier, when he'd left for Delaware after winning his
round against John Adams. But in another sense, conditions were exactly what Dickinson might have predicted, and had warned against,
should independents and the radical City Committee ever get the
support of the Congress. The law-giving charter he'd fought for all his
career was slated, through backroom maneuvering, to be removed by
crowd fiat. To Dickinson, this was just what an independent America
would look like. Law was barely in force.

That same rainy day, some assemblymen did arrive at the State

House. The more extreme implications of the crowd's resolutions declared the assembly dangerous and arbitrary, even illegal if it sat. But men elected on Mayday nevertheless mounted the staircase to the committee room, their temporary chamber.

Only twenty-seven were present, not enough for a quorum. Still, Dickinson had more room to move than the Adamses might have hoped. Physically exhausted, politically weaker than he'd ever been, he determined to do everything he could to uphold the principles that had brought him to war with England in the first place. He began a desperate rearguard action for the survival of legal government.

Meanwhile Samuel Adams, John Adams, Thomas McKean, Richard Henry Lee, and the other independents in the Congress had work to do, and they started doing it. Even if Pennsylvania tumbled, a declaration of independence wouldn't come all by itself. Weakening Dickinson was critical because it opened a breach in what had seemed an impenetrable middle-colony bloc. Now the independents had to move into the breach with force. That meant gaining support for independence—or at least acquiescence in it—from other colonies' governments.

The independents had kept working out of doors on sympathetic and susceptible delegates, and certain delegates had asked their home governments for new instructions. Certain governments had loosened up. Some delegations were now permitted to go passively along with a majority, even, as North Carolina said, to the point of independence.

But no colony other than North Carolina had used the word *independence*, and the middle colonies remained firmly against a break with England. And when the Adamses forced the vote on their preamble, the Maryland delegates had walked out. They'd since returned—but only after Maryland flatly rejected any compliance with either the resolution or the preamble, giving the delegates the tightest possible restrictions, prohibiting them even from discussing a measure related to independence without first checking with the home government.

Still, it was now or never. With some members of the Congress no longer required to oppose independence categorically, and Dickinson's grip being pried loose from Pennsylvania, one government had to take the lead and actively propose a break. The Adamses and Richard Henry Lee had kept pushing allies back home to act. Now the South began to take the lead.

Caught in conversation outside the State House, Samuel Adams and Richard Henry Lee would have caricatured the unlikeliness of any Massachusetts-Virginia partnership. Adams, genteel compared to his Braintree cousin, with pleasing, low-key manners in conversation, was nevertheless short and awkward, all brain and will, afflicted with the tremor. He spoke quietly when he spoke at all, and rarely gave memorable speeches. Whether his shabbiness was a display of nondisplay, or whether he really never thought about clothes, nobody would ever know. But before he'd first come to the Congress, the Sons of Liberty had pitched in to buy him a new outfit.

Richard Henry Lee dressed. He spoke publicly to great effect. He loomed over Samuel Adams. He was a sportsman. While he was shooting geese his gun barrel had exploded and blown off the fingers of his left hand. Addressing the House of Burgesses in Williamsburg and the Congress in Philadelphia, he gesticulated with that hand, which he kept wrapped in black silk to make a single glove. He hid yet displayed his wound, and the effect was hypnotic.

Even without black silk, Lee's gaunt, long-boned majesty could be intimidating. He had a high forehead, a shock of hair, and an aquiline nose. In Philadelphia, all of the Virginia delegates seemed gigantic in every dimension, physically tall and straight but also the owners of tobacco empires and tamers and riders of prancing mounts. They bet on cockfighting. They danced. Richard Henry Lee had once attacked the African slave trade in Virginia's House of Burgesses. Yet the Virginians came to Philadelphia attended by human chattel in dazzling livery. Retinues of black men waited at the doors of the Congress to serve the masters.

That wasn't the Adamses' style. It was John Hancock's, and the Adamses had come to despise Hancock for it. Despising Lee was harder. At one of the first Philadelphia dinners, John Adams observed with fascination that Lee had already been drinking Burgundy all afternoon, with John Dickinson, and that when it came time for the late-night toasts, Lee was, Adams said amazedly, "very high." Manifest drunkenness would cost a respectable Bostonian his dignity. But being visibly drunk all day with fellow drunk gentlemen was among the Virginia elegances.

Lee was not, in short, a Yankee. When the Adamses, Puritan dissenters, farmed hard ground in Braintree, the Lees, Stuart loyalists, went galloping about plantations and estates on the Potomac, buying land, raising tobacco, and driving slaves. An old family of Virginia's northern neck, the Lees' origins were obscure, but they saw themselves as descended from men who were knights before the ancestors of the current English peerage had even emerged. Their home on the Potomac, called Stratford, was ugly and uncomfortable, like the drafty piles of the old English gentry. They were part of a hereditary aristocracy, with the Lightfoots, Randolphs, Harrisons, Carters, Peytons, and others. Like other aristocracies, the Virginians intermarried and recycled names to advertise ancestry. Peyton Randolph was a Peyton and a Randolph, Landon Carter a Carter and a Landon. Lines made new lines, staked out new holdings, piled up new fortunes or borrowed themselves into penury.

And they harbored rivalries. Richard Henry Lee and his brothers and cousins were going a new way in politics. The Virginia upper house, and the lower house known as the Burgesses, were far from ideally republican institutions. Aristocratic James River planters dominated both. Potomac men of the same type, the Lees lacked natural republicanism, too, but they were at odds with the James River men. They looked westward, toward and even over the Blue Ridge. They bought vast lands there, investing in what they hoped would be agricultural bounty, speculating in becoming landlords, and so, they hoped, leaders of white settlers. In the House of Burgesses they made common cause with representatives from the west. Their English blood lent credence to the hopes of Scots-Irish up-and-comers.

In that process, the Lee brothers began espousing republican principles. With Richard Henry the most eloquent of them, they'd decided to oppose the monarch. Virginia must become a republic, the Lees now believed. That could not come about by reconciliation with England, only by American independence.

Richard Henry Lee found a partner in Patrick Henry, a lawyer from the middle plantation gentry near Richmond. Both men were renowned speakers, Henry known as the Cicero of the Burgesses, Lee the Demosthenes. Henry had mastered a form of rhetoric that structured emotion musically. As he worked it up, listeners' blood started to run cold, their hair prickle. Lee's rhetoric, by contrast, was intellectual. He carried listeners along on lines of thought. With black silk weaving, his whole bearing in gentle motion, he made himself hard to look away from. Fellow burgesses muttered that he must practice in front of a mirror, but really it was his voice, John Adams thought. He cajoled and coaxed. You wanted to listen.

Virginia's Cicero and Demosthenes were tightly allied for independence. They'd served together in the first Congress in Philadelphia in 1774, but for the second Congress, Lee worked in Philadelphia and Henry at home. Virginia was a royal colony, and in the new situation its administration was a provincial convention at Williamsburg. That convention was divided, and Patrick Henry worked to push it toward independence. The delegation in the Congress was divided, too, and Lee worked to the same end there.

Moving in concert against reconciliationists in Williamsburg and in Philadelphia, Patrick Henry and Richard Henry Lee began collaborating with Samuel Adams. Other delegates to the Congress called the alliance "the Lee-Adams junto."

The relationship with the Adamses was intricate. Richard Henry Lee differed in some important ways from his brothers and cousins. For all of his sportsman's derring-do, he was the scholar in the family. The strictness of his analysis, along with the gauntness of his face, made him seem almost Presbyterian. And he'd begun to consult with John Adams about the nuts and bolts of republican government.

The Lees would naturally see the quest for American independence in the light of an aristocratic adventure, a dashing errand for the kingless state. John Adams was no aristocrat, and his views on government were decidedly non-Virginian. The New England town meetings, Adams insisted—in the face of his experience of how they really worked—offered the most virtuous, least corruptible model for an American republic.

Richard Henry Lee, like all Lees, had his heart in Virginia, and he wanted to ensure the best kind of government. He was coming to admire the north and John Adams. New England had a more modern society, he thought, less dependent on slave labor, more in keeping with both republican principle and economic practicality. Lee concluded what for some Virginians was heresy: in its attitudes about independence and about government, Virginia should act more like Massachusetts.

John Adams wished Massachusetts were acting more like Massachusetts. If this was a race between Virginia and Massachusetts to take the lead for American independence, Adams's home was falling behind. The Adamses' man on the scene back in Boston was James Warren, brother to their old ally in the Sons of Liberty, Dr. Joseph Warren. The doctor had been killed during the Battle of Bunker Hill. James Warren replaced his martyred brother as president of the provisional wartime convention that administered the province. Like his brother, he was hot for independence.

So when James Warren received a request from his delegation in the Congress in Philadelphia for new instructions, not to loosen them but to turn them into an outright call for American independence, he might have been expected to start pushing the plan right through the Massachusetts provincial convention. The first request came as early as April 1776. If Warren had responded to it as hoped, events in Philadelphia might have looked quite different.

But Warren couldn't give the Adamses what they wanted. In Boston he was coping, and often felt he was failing to cope, with a situation that made changing instructions in favor of independence a low priority, even possibly a dangerous one. For as in Pennsylvania, radical democracy was loose in Massachusetts.

Boston wasn't the main problem. The Pope's Day topsy-turvy, the dress-up and disguise, the blackface and Indian costume, the hangings in effigy, even the tearing down of the royal governor's house in 1765—those had a basis in tradition. Deliberately creepy and weird, festive assaults had regulated village life from what seemed time immemorial. The Sons of Liberty had struggled to keep rioting within their idea of reasonable bounds, and through a top-down network of town committees of correspondence, Samuel Adams had managed to run the whole province's resistance from Boston.

But with Parliament's Government Act, the shooting at Lexington and Concord, the breakdown of provincial government, and the departure of British troops, people in the western towns and counties, especially in the rugged Berkshire mountains, began taking ideas about liberty to new conclusions. Westerners had never felt ideally served by the caucus-elected Bostonian elite. Now war inspired the lower class to reconsider its goals. Like the Committee of Privates in Pennsylvania, rank-and-file militiamen in the Berkshires connected military to political purposes. At a convention in Stockbridge, farmers voted to keep their courts closed, on the basis of the judges' appointment by the royal governor's council. Some of the judges were Tory, the farmers complained. But they also complained that some of the judges were simply rich.

Six other towns condemned the court closing as anarchic. But people in Pittsfield went along with Stockbridge, and then went further. Pittsfielders said that towns and counties should have the right to nominate their judges. They said that their town was operating well on its own, under the new circumstances, and that Pittsfield didn't need any higher provincial government at all.

This free-for-all was just what reconciliationist patriots had been warning would emerge, inevitably, from a quest for American independence. So it was hard for leaders in Boston, especially independents, to deal with towns' assertion of new rights and sovereignties. Berkshire farmers weren't wearing disguises. Armed, drilled militiamen in a time of war, they didn't rely on theatrics. To close courts, they didn't riot. They went through procedures and took votes and passed resolutions. They behaved as if government had simply lapsed to them.

When organizing the Massachusetts town meetings for Samuel Adams, Thomas Young had explicitly pointed out to Adams the desire of indebted farmers for control of government. Young was a westerner, too, and he knew and encouraged these people. Amenia, New York, and Salisbury, Connecticut, were in the Berkshire foothills. Up in the Green Mountains, under Young's friend the outlaw Ethan Allen, settlers would soon declare Vermont independent of New York, Great Britain, and everybody else, and they would write their own constitution. Like Vermonters, Berkshire militiamen were crying out at once for American independence from England, for western independence from the powerful east, and for debtors' independence from predatory creditors. But Samuel Adams wanted unity in the cause of Massachusetts liberty, not social change. He had no sympathy for Berkshire dissent and paid little heed to Young's exhortations.

Now, from Philadelphia, John Adams goaded Warren. "Why don't your honors of the general court," he said, ". . . give instructions to your own delegates [in the Congress] to promote independency? Don't blame your delegates. . . . The southern colonies say you are afraid." But whereas in 1775 Warren had railed against the royal part of Massachusetts government, now he said that mostly he feared the "Levelling spirit." He admitted miserably that the spirit had been encouraged by the resistance. He felt paralyzed by the populists' demands. He warned Adams that if the Congress didn't declare independence soon, western Massachusetts men might march down to Philadelphia and do it for them. He wanted the Congress to serve as a higher power.

"We need veneration for persons in authority," Adams naturally agreed, "or else we are undone." But to get independence declared in the Congress, the Adamses needed instructions from Warren. "The vehemence of the southern colonies puts you to shame," he told Warren, and he exaggerated South Carolina's commitment to independence to push the point.

The stalemate was painful. John was starting to view American independence as a great epoch in world history. He thought possibly his was the greatest epoch ever. To take his rightful place in it, he was suffering illness, exhaustion, loneliness, and drudgery. He was certain that an independent Massachusetts must avoid radical democracy, and he'd begun to see himself as a great framer of orderly republican government. His disgust with populism and with the international bestselling success of Paine's *Common Sense* had inspired him to write a pamphlet of his own, *Thoughts on Government*, which laid out his plan for balance: bicameral house, independent solo executive, property requirement for the franchise, judiciary appointed by the executive. In contrast to *Common Sense*, his *Thoughts on Government* was not, putting it mildly, an international bestseller. It gained no public recognition at all.

But now, in the race between Virginia and Massachusetts to announce first for independence, *Thoughts on Government* began playing an unexpected role. Adams's pamphlet had first been written in the form of letters, with lists of suggestions for various other states, including North Carolina, New Jersey, and Virginia. Richard Henry Lee saw the one addressed to George Wythe of Virginia and encouraged Adams to publish it. Lee sent the published pamphlet to Patrick

Henry and others in Virginia. Members of the governing convention in North Carolina were reading it, too.

Thoughts on Government was earning a reputation as a blueprint, a reputation that would grow and spread northward. It was in the South, not in New England, that John Adams was first hailed as the great American thinker on republican government.

Samuel Adams, for his part, had no wish to publish thoughts. John's pamphlet was far from tactical in Philadelphia. It contradicted *Common Sense* outright. Samuel knew what was wrong with *Common Sense,* but Paine's work served the purpose. Samuel's plan was to make a secret alliance with the social radicals, not remind the radicals that after independence, elites would retain control. (Fortunately for the Adams coalition in Philadelphia, *Thoughts on Government* had no local impact, although John Adams would later say, with pleasure, that it had badly upset Paine himself.) Samuel Adams wasn't a student of government. He was an activist for the Christian Sparta in New England. He worked with luxuriating Virginians, anarchic radicals, scoffing Deists, ambitious, vacillating John Adams, or anybody else to get it. When writing home on Massachusetts government to James Warren's brother Joseph, Samuel had kept his voice low and firm. Restore traditional order, intact, except for the royal component, he had advised. Unity was all. Independence came first.

He would rely on Virginia and deal with insubordinate Berkshire farmers later.

＿〜

And the timing was perfect. Just when John Dickinson's government was becoming seriously damaged in Philadelphia, matters started moving quickly in Virginia. Not that Virginia didn't have its own problems with the less enfranchised. Militiamen everywhere were starting to believe they'd be included in the benefits of independence. But so authoritarian, hierarchical, and aristocratic was Virginia society that many there considered Massachusetts, with its town meetings and instructed officials, a terrifyingly democratic place. To a Virginia planter, Boston could look as anarchic as Paine's vision of the future looked to John Adams.

Richard Henry Lee and Patrick Henry took a different view. They promoted John Adams's *Thoughts on Government* as a basis for forming a new government in Virginia. Henry even hailed Adams as "a democrat"—the very word Adams himself used to blast Paine, Matlack, Cannon, and Young, his allies in the coalition he preferred not to acknowledge. By "democrat," Henry didn't mean to suggest that unpropertied men should get the vote in Virginia. But Adams's ideas were so republican, and to such a forthright extreme, excluding monarchy and endorsing strong representation, that to describe them Henry had to use the riskiest word that he could think of.

When Virginia's provincial government scheduled a meeting for spring of 1776, Richard Henry Lee wrote to Patrick Henry. He asked that the convention send new instructions to the delegation in the Congress. Virginia, Lee exhorted Henry, now must lead the way.

Henry agreed. And Virginia Whigs turned out to be surprisingly receptive. Bombardments of Norfolk, along with Governor Dunmore's appeal to the slaves to rise up against their masters, made Virginia's planter gentlemen readier than many people in other colonies for a complete break. One hundred and twenty-eight delegates gathered at Williamsburg and stayed for weeks. Like the Congress in Philadelphia, they had a war administration to run, and much time was spent on detail.

But on May 6, the convention opened its deliberations on forming a government and on American independence. That same day in Philadelphia, Richard Henry Lee and John Adams were bringing their resolution against the government of Pennsylvania into the Congress. Even while the Adamses and Lee were aiming the resolution at Dickinson and Pennsylvania, three sets of resolutions in favor of independence were being introduced in the Virginia convention.

The third set, written by Henry, reflected the Adamses' and Lee's tactics. Henry brought to the resolutions none of the emotional rhetoric he was famous for. Hoping to lower the temperature, he didn't even introduce them himself but had them read by a duller speaker. There was reason for caution. His resolutions were not just endorsing independence; they referred to the colonies as "united." That treated the colonies as having made an agreement that would bind them, giving no way out but civil war, forming an entity that could enter into foreign alliances. The colonies hadn't, in fact, formed any such union. Regardless, treating union as accomplished fact accorded with Samuel Adams's desire to prevent a royal peace commission from breaking up the American alliance.

And Henry supplied Lee and the Adamses with what they needed most. His resolution proposed giving new instructions to Virginia's delegates in the Congress. The delegates, Henry wrote, should "exert their ability in procuring an immediate and full declaration of independence."

Information usually took about ten days to travel between Williamsburg and Philadelphia. On May 15—the day John Adams's preamble made it through the Congress, and the Philadelphia radicals met at the schoolroom to begin removal of Dickinson's assembly—the Virginia convention adopted Patrick Henry's resolutions instructing the Virginia delegation to propose independence to the Congress. On May 20, the day of the mass meeting at the Pennsylvania State House, Henry wrote to John Adams, "before you get this, we will have done it." Lee's friends and family had already sent the good news to Lee. By May 27, with Dickinson badly weakened as an opponent, Lee and the Adamses had word that Virginia, not Massachusetts, would take the lead.

The resolutions had been watered down, Henry complained. They were good enough, John Adams said in congratulating him by letter. Each member of the "junto" had reason for satisfaction and excitement. The Virginia convention began setting up a government that looked a lot like the one John Adams proposed in *Thoughts on Government*. In the struggle for a Christian Sparta in Massachusetts, Samuel Adams had endorsed the Virginian Peyton Randolph as president of the Congress and the Virginian George Washington as commander in chief. Now Virginia again won the prize of making history. On May 27, Richard Henry Lee laid Virginia's instructions to its delegation to exert itself for American independence before the Congress.

9

⁓

"They are not represented in this house"

May 27–June 14

Meanwhile, right after the mass meeting in the State House yard, John Dickinson started making the toughest moves of his life. He still hoped to prevent American independence and the dissolution of his chartered government. And his assembly was operating, in defiance of the most extreme hopes of the people in the yard.

Yet circumstances had changed so totally since May 1 that the minority of independents in the assembly had new strength. They were allied not only with the City Committee and the Committee of Privates but also now with the apparent intentions of the Continental

Congress itself. Dickinson had to deal with organized opponents not only in his lent room downstairs but also in his displaced legislature upstairs. And it was clear that the provincial convention, scheduled for June 18, meant to throw out his assembly for good.

But he had ideas. The State House yard crowd interpreted the resolution and preamble as the Adamses had intended: dismantle Pennsylvania's government. Dickinson knew that many delegates in the Congress never envisioned the end of his government. They'd seen the preamble as a suggestion for a change within government: stop taking oaths to the king. Indeed, other middle colonies—Delaware, New Jersey, and New York—were in the process of complying with the Congress's advice without overturning their governments. Those governments hadn't been set up to be overthrown from below. Pennsylvania's had, by Samuel Adams's secret coalition. The Adamses' resolution did technically apply to all colonies. But its real purpose was to remove the obstacle to independence, using the pressure of Congress to expose Pennsylvania to the radicals' uprising, which the Adamses had helped prepare.

So Dickinson thought that if he could take the issue right back to the delegates downstairs—he was still one of them, a leader—they might withdraw the Congress's support for the local revolution. Not one of the delegates was a democrat. If enough of them were forced to confront having aided a radically democratic movement to end a chartered government, they might correct the resolution's wording and let Pennsylvania's elected assembly live.

The assembly sent a petition downstairs, asking the congressmen to please clarify and amplify the meaning of their preamble and resolution. Had they really meant that Pennsylvania, of all governments, was incompetent? If oath-taking ceased, wouldn't Pennsylvania be in compliance with the recommendations of the Congress?

That request had potential to reverse all that the Adamses had achieved. The secret coalition therefore moved smoothly to block Dickinson's maneuver. The independents in the Pennsylvania assembly upstairs tipped off members of the City Committee outside. Dr. Benjamin Rush, Paine's partner in *Common Sense*, acted for the committee. He sent an urgent message to Richard Henry Lee downstairs in the Congress. The seemingly innocent request coming down the stairs was in fact, Rush wrote Lee, a low attempt to undermine the crowd's May 20 resolutions and the Congress's resolution and preamble. He begged Lee to keep southern delegates in solidarity with the crowd in the yard and to be sure the Congress refused to amplify or clarify the resolution.

Meanwhile Rush, Paine, Christopher Marshall, and Timothy Matlack met at Marshall's to write a City Committee petition to the Congress, objecting to giving the assembly any clarification at all. Marshall had conferred with Samuel Adams to get advice on wording the petition.

Dickinson's request for clarification tried to blow fog away, to show the delegates in the Congress what they'd really done. The City Committee's counter-petition—submitted to the Congress on May 25—took a chance. It told the Congress openly what the Congress's own resolution had never admitted. The assembly of Pennsylvania, in particular, should be shut down, the petition said. It described the assembly as no longer having public support. In Pennsylvania, the committee now spoke for the people.

⌒

Dickinson kept trying new ideas. To remove the stated reason for closing down the assembly, he made sure the session opened with no loyalty oath to the king. That would comply with the advice of the

Congress. Independents in the assembly, trying to force a balk, moved that Germans therefore also be allowed to vote in Pennsylvania without taking oaths of allegiance. Dickinson countered by agreeing to explore the question, and a committee was duly assigned. That was his only available tactic: agree. He wanted to lead the assembly into full conformity with what the Congress had advised, like Delaware, New Jersey, and New York, making it logically impossible to end his government.

The independents didn't want Dickinson's government to be in compliance. The minority in the assembly started blocking Dickinson's every move.

But Dickinson had a seeming advantage. A movement was forming in Pennsylvania against losing the province's charter and turning out its elected government. Pro-assembly men, both in and outside the assembly, wrote an appeal to the people of Pennsylvania, in opposition to the City Committee and the State House yard resolutions. They called it "the Remonstrance." It was read to the assembly on May 23. The Remonstrance made no show of agreement. It described the Congress as interfering in the government of a member colony and overruling elected representation. It reviewed the manifest competence of Pennsylvania as a government. It noted that two New England colonies, Connecticut and Rhode Island, rested on charters similar to Pennsylvania's. Yet no move had been made by the Congress to turn those colonies over to conventions.

The Remonstrance didn't mention American independence or reconciliation with England. Its plea was to respect legitimacy in government. It asked people to sign a petition to preserve their legal charter. Pro-assembly men started carrying copies of the Remonstrance throughout the city, and then into the rest of Pennsylvania.

John Dickinson drawn from life—flatteringly, perhaps,
yet with the prominent nose—in an engraving from 1781
(when spelling was often improvised).

Lightning strikes while the famous doctor studies an electrical device in this mezzotint of Benjamin Franklin, made in London about 1763 for sale to an eager public.

An admiring and somewhat fanciful lithograph of a thoughtful Thomas Paine, made in 1851, when his work was being rediscovered by abolitionists and other reformers.

This 1873 rendering of the 1776 Pennsylvania State House—made well before the restoration of Independence Hall, and not accurate in every respect—gives a feeling of the building's location on the city's outskirts and the workaday mood outside.

Less august than the State House, yet representing a height of beautiful craftsmanship, Carpenter's Hall, the artisans' headquarters, is seen here in an architect's drawing.

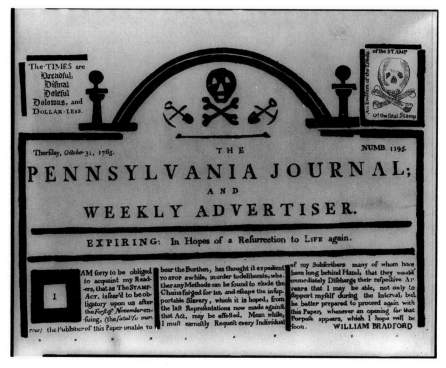

The TIMES are Dreadful, Dismal, Doleful Dolorous, and DOLLAR-LESS.

An Emblem of the Effects of the STAMP. O! the fatal Stamp.

Thursday, October 31, 1765.

THE

NUMB. 1195.

PENNSYLVANIA JOURNAL;

AND

WEEKLY ADVERTISER.

EXPIRING: In Hopes of a Resurrection to LIFE again.

I

I AM sorry to be obliged to acquaint my Readers, that as The STAMP-Act, is fear'd to be obligatory upon us after the First of November ensuing, (the fatal To morrow) the Publisher of this Paper unable to bear the Burthen, has thought it expedient TO STOP a while, in order to deliberate, whether any Methods can be found to elude the Chains forged for us, and escape the insupportable Slavery, which it is hoped, from the last Representations now made against that Act, may be effected. Mean while, I must earnestly Request every Individual of my Subscribers many of whom have been long behind Hand, that they would immediately Discharge their respective Arrears that I may be able, not only to support myself during the Interval, but be better prepared to proceed again with this Paper, whenever an opening for that Purpose appears, which I hope will be soon. WILLIAM BRADFORD

The front page of a Philadelphia newspaper showing an angrily humorous response to the Stamp Act.

Sam.ᵗ Adams

This portrait of Samuel Adams, unusual for revealing physical frailty along with personal determination, is also mysterious (what document is under his foot?).

In this drawing, John Adams looks youthful and optimistic—unusual for his portraits—and characteristically well-fed and well-dressed.

JOHN ADAMS.

The Massacre perpetrated in King Street Boston on March 5th 1770, in which Mess.rs Sam.l Gray, Sam.l Maverick, James Caldwell, Crispus Attucks Patrick Carr were Killed, six others Wounded, two of them Mortally.

Samuel Adams's one-sided construction of events outside the Boston Custom House in March 1770 that would be known as the Boston Massacre: on orders of the officer raising his sword, a British rank opens fire on innocent civilians.

The Virginian Richard Henry Lee, imposing and elegant, with his famous high forehead, shock of hair, and Roman demeanor.

As both majority leader of the Pennsylvania assembly, which had moved upstairs, and head of the Pennsylvania delegation in the Continental Congress, which met downstairs, John Dickinson went up and down the elegant State House staircase in his tireless effort to oppose independence.

COMMON SENSE;

ADDRESSED TO THE

INHABITANTS

OF

A M E R I C A,

On the following interesting

S U B J E C T S.

I. Of the Origin and Design of Government in general,
with concise Remarks on the English Constitution.

II. Of Monarchy and Hereditary Succession.

III. Thoughts on the present State of American Affairs.

IV. Of the present Ability of America, with some mis-
cellaneous Reflections.

Man knows no Master save creating HEAVEN,
Or those whom choice and common good ordain.
THOMSON.

PHILADELPHIA;
Printed, and Sold, by R. BELL, in Third-Street.
MDCCLXXVI.

Thomas Paine's famous pamphlet *Common Sense,* which became an international bestseller, called not only for independence but also—to the indignation of John Adams—for a democratic American republic.

They rode far, emissaries on behalf of the elected body. They were gathering signatures.

~~~

This was the moment that James Cannon and Thomas Young had been working toward for so long. They were prepared. Before the pro-assembly Remonstrance had even been written, the radicals had sent all the towns in the province the State House yard resolutions condemning the assembly. McKean carried copies to Reading. Cannon and Matlack went throughout Philadelphia County. Young went to Lancaster. Others went all the way to York, and from there, riders could carry the news and the protests into the far backcountry. The protests came with circular letters, and the radicals published articles in the papers to frame and develop the protests' meaning for ordinary people in Philadelphia and across the province.

Through the Committee of Privates, Cannon meanwhile had the resolutions sent to every battalion of military associators in the countryside. Militias everywhere held their own mass meetings. The resolutions were read aloud and put to rousing voice votes, just as in the State House yard. The message was exciting: with the support of the Congress itself, the old charter of Pennsylvania, which barred so many of these militiamen from voting, would be replaced through a representative process that included them. The fruit of declaring America independent would be equality in Pennsylvania. The militias condemned reconciliationists in the assembly as rich traitors. Working people across the province adopted the State House yard resolutions with hope.

So when riders showed up in country towns carrying a Remonstrance against the resolutions of the State House yard, and in favor of the old charter, they were met with unified, organized hostility. Militiamen and town committees had police powers. The committees called the emissaries from the assembly criminals. The militias arrested them. The towns burned the Remonstrance in public. There was no margin for dissent. People who had signed the Remonstrance begged to have their names removed; they sent letters to the papers to recant publicly.

On May 27, with the Remonstrance still going around the countryside, Virginia's instructions for independence arrived in the Congress. Their impact on Pennsylvania's gasping assembly upstairs was just what Samuel Adams had hoped.

In the Congress's chamber, the Virginia instructions were read aloud to the delegates. Their last words, "a declaration of independence," so recently unspeakable, hung there. Then the resolutions were laid on the table. Their presence made it clear, every day, that Richard Henry Lee was about to bring matters in the Congress to a head.

John Dickinson couldn't step outside an American union. He'd been an uncompromising resister from the beginning, committed to American rights, colonial alliance, and war with England. He was the Farmer. But in his own State House, he was losing his place. To prove it to him, on the day the Virginia instructions came into the room downstairs, his enemies upstairs stayed home. The minority in the assembly had the power to boycott, thus denying the body a quorum. Without his enemies, Dickinson couldn't operate at all.

Two days later, with a quorum regained in the assembly, supporters of elected government had a moment of hope. The Remonstrance that had gone around Philadelphia city and county came into the assembly room. Six thousand people had signed it—half again as many as had attended the meeting in the State House yard. Despite intimidation, many people in Pennsylvania were objecting to letting the City Committee speak for them.

But it was getting hard to imagine how to act on that news. Downstairs, the Congress was spending days in meetings with George Washington. He'd moved his troops to New York, where the British fleet was expected to arrive, and he'd come to Philadelphia to plan defense and strategy. Along with the usual press of business, from regulating the price of salt to paying a certain waggoner two pounds and change, the Congress now mobilized militias, determined how many troops to raise from each state, wrote a proclamation calling on Americans to sacrifice in the coming fight, named new ships, and recommended to the provincial conventions and legislatures means of supplying arms, camp kettles, and tents.

War powers led the Congress to treat the colonies as a union, with the militia the union's driver. In Pennsylvania, the militia was organized east to west around a plan for social equality, and it had shown what it thought of a Remonstrance to preserve Dickinson's assembly.

Meanwhile, Richard Henry Lee acted on his instructions from Virginia. In consultation with the Adamses, he wrote a resolution proposing independence, confederation, and pursuit of foreign alliances. He planned to introduce it to the Congress in the session on Saturday, June 7. Any effort Dickinson might have made to parry that event now met total obstruction. Independents in the Pennsylvania assembly stayed home three workdays in a row. With Lee's resolution coming, Dickinson was immobilized.

Immobilized but not finished. Anyone else might have been, but only two days before Lee was to bring the resolution for independence into the Congress, there was a quorum in the assembly, and Dickinson took advantage of it to do exactly what he'd refused to do all these months. He proposed loosening the Pennsylvania assembly's instructions to its delegates in the Congress. Bending on this issue might just mute the crowd's criticism of the assembly. New York and Maryland were still instructed for reconciliation anyway, and New Jersey, Delaware, and South Carolina would go along with them. Many members of the Pennsylvania delegation were reconciliationists, and mere loosening wouldn't prevent them from voting their consciences. The change might do no harm and buy some time. The royal peace commission might come.

The next day he tried something else. Throughout Pennsylvania, counties had formed committees to nominate delegates for the upcoming provincial convention to replace the government. Dickinson now moved to have the assembly, as the elected, chartered body, take over the nominating and delegating process for that convention. He would subsume the crowd's convention in a legitimate process. He would render the convention a creature of the assembly.

But now the Committee of Privates stepped in to stifle, by militia authority, Dickinson's seemingly endless ability to keep acting. The day Dickinson proposed taking over the convention, the minority in the assembly stayed home after lunch, and the Privates voted to poll each battalion in Philadelphia regarding support for the State House yard proceedings. Those proceedings had called for a convention on the people's authority—not the assembly's, as Dickinson was now proposing. The Committee of Privates scheduled the muster for June 10. On that day, militia rank and file would announce their intentions for Pennsylvania. Given their relationships to the City Committee, and their role in security for the province and in the upcoming invasion, the Privates' intentions would be decisive.

John Dickinson commanded the first Philadelphia battalion, so he would have to attend the muster. In the meantime, he kept trying to preserve the authority of the elected assembly.

~

It was June 6 when the Privates announced the battalion muster. That evening, Samuel Adams wrote home to say the moment was at hand. On June 7, Richard Henry Lee brought his resolution into the Congress.

Lee moved that the Congress resolve:

That these united colonies are, and of right ought to be, free and independent states, that they are absolved from all allegiance to the British Crown, and that all political connection between them and the state of Great Britain is, and ought to be, totally dissolved.

That it is expedient forthwith to take the most effectual measures for forming foreign alliances.

That a plan of confederation be prepared and transmitted to the respective colonies for their consideration and approbation.

John Adams seconded the motion. Everybody in Congress had known this was coming. John Dickinson's protégé James Wilson moved quickly to put off voting on the resolution for at least a few weeks. The Pennsylvania assembly's only real hope now lay in postponement, and Wilson tried to exploit, not deny, the political suspense in the province. He invoked the upcoming provincial convention. The people of his province ought to be allowed to consider the matter then, he said, since there weren't yet new instructions from the assembly (the body had agreed to revise them but hadn't done so yet). He assured the independents in the Congress that the people of Pennsylvania would ultimately be in favor of independence. Waiting to find out could only help their cause, he implied.

Despite his pleas, debate was postponed only until the next day. On Saturday the 8th, the Congress formed itself into a committee of the whole. It sat until seven in the evening, facing almost exclusively the stark subject of independence. Wilson kept up the steady argument for delay. He was joined by Edward Rutledge of South Carolina, at twenty-six the youngest member. Rutledge insisted that confederating and seeking treaties should be pursued, as Lee had proposed, but without calling the colonies independent. He argued that independence might prevent rather than encourage alliances with other countries, and he argued for putting off the ultimate question indefinitely. His real concern was that in declaring independence, Congress would become a creature of the North and begin to interfere with southern planters like him.

Dickinson went up and down the stairs that day. In the Congress, he supported Wilson's arguments. In the hall above, he was performing some last-resort sleight of hand. He did revise the instructions to Pennsylvania's delegates below. Late in the day, Wilson got word from upstairs that Pennsylvania's new instructions were complete.

They showed how hard Dickinson was still working. The language was vague. The assembly now allowed Pennsylvania's delegates to concur in forming treaties and compacts and taking other measures necessary to American liberty, safety, and interest. The instructions didn't commit Pennsylvania's delegation to going along with independence; nevertheless, they might be taken by independents in the Congress as a sign of eventual acquiescence, relaxing any sense of urgency and making delay appear innocuous.

Wilson even promised the other delegates that if the question were put now, he might vote for independence. But he again urged a delay until after the provincial convention met—just to get a good reading from the people, he said.

The early summer evening was falling. The committee of the whole decided to reconvene after the Sunday break to continue discussion.

On Monday, June 10, things grew dire. There was the sense of an impending showdown, a vote today that might end anywhere. John Adams, Lee, and others argued hotly, openly now, that the people were for independence, that only congressmen and representatives in home governments were against it. They called America already independent, the only question being whether the Congress would publicly admit it. They mocked as naïve young Rutledge's idea that the Congress could seek foreign alliances without first resolving for independence. They attacked Pennsylvania's and Maryland's governments directly. There was no perfect unanimity possible, they argued. The stragglers would be left behind, they threatened, when the bold risk takers moved forward.

The reconciliationists weren't intimidated. Under the independents' direct assault, they pointed out that New Jersey's and Delaware's legislative conventions were about to meet, and that Pennsylvania's assembly and New York's convention were sitting now. While it seemed as if some might be inclined to change instructions, they hadn't done so yet (Pennsylvania's new instructions were leaked to the papers but hadn't been formally given to the delegates). So if the vote were taken today, these delegations would not be permitted to violate their current instructions. They would have no choice but to walk out of the Congress.

Here was the showdown. An invasion was coming from Britain. There was everything to lose by splitting the colonies. The middle-colony bloc held, and even South Carolina, as Rutledge's arguments showed, wouldn't go for a break with England today.

So the decision of June 10 was to postpone debate on Lee's resolution until July 1. Rutledge and others wanted to postpone it indefinitely. John Adams had expected an epochal vote today. July 1 was a compromise achieved under terrible pressure.

⌒

Dickinson's government was almost destroyed, but his bloc had held. Postponing the vote meant that if peace commissioners arrived soon enough, America might still escape the final break.

But on June 10, the Committee of Privates, as scheduled, mustered all five Philadelphia battalions. Two thousand men assembled on the common. They were in ranks and in arms. Dickinson was present as a battalion commander.

A formal question was put to the men by their officers. The question wasn't about American independence. It was about the two issues facing government in Pennsylvania: forming a military union with the other colonies, and preventing Dickinson's assembly from taking over the upcoming provincial convention. Linking the two issues, the Privates brought the war to John Dickinson.

As commander, Dickinson had to put the question to his battalion. He had to stand and hear his own men vote nearly overwhelmingly against his authority.

Daniel Roberdeau, who had boomed out the resolutions from

the stage in the rainy State House yard, was a battalion commander. He put the question to his battalion. It was nearly unanimous for the same position.

McKean and Matlack, also commanders, put the question to their men, to unanimous affirmation. But John Cadwalader, the man jeered into silence in the State House yard, refused to put the question to his troops. The men hissed and insulted him, along with anybody who voted against the majority.

So the question was resolved. James Cannon's organizing had triumphed. The armed working class took charge of policy. The officers followed the men. Dickinson's resilience was astonishing, but it was organized laborers, not he, who decided the immediate future of Pennsylvania.

The Pennsylvania assembly did manage to meet one more time under the old charter. On Tuesday and Wednesday there was no quorum, but on Thursday, June 13, the assembly met and broke down at last.

Dickinson had nothing left to work with. The Privates had control of Pennsylvania. Their political arm, the City Committee and local committee radicals throughout the countryside, would run the provincial convention on June 18. Even some independents in the assembly were frightened now by the populism they'd enabled in their quest for a break with England. Today—very late in the game—these worried independents moved not to take over the provincial convention but to supplant it, by overseeing the constitutional convention that would arise from it. Other independents reminded them that the Congress had forbidden this assembly from having any part in setting up new government. Nothing cogent could now be established among these suspicious, mutually beaten assemblymen.

On Friday, June 14, there was no quorum. The few assembly members who showed up did some final housekeeping. They paid the clerk's salary. They had the new instructions to the delegates signed. The assemblymen went down the staircase and adjourned— supposedly until August 26.

There would be no reconvening. The militia slammed the door. The Committee of Privates and their officers sent a document to the nonexistent assembly. The officers addressed the body as the assembly, but pointed out that they were using a title "heretofore used" for politeness only.

Neither officers nor men would follow assembly dictates. The Privates themselves explained why. "Because many of the associators have been excluded by this very house from voting for the members now composing it," they said, ". . . and therefore they are not represented in this house."

In ensuing weeks that condemnation of the assembly, advancing a new idea about representation, would be read at militia musters all over Pennsylvania. Militia privates in every town were invited to come to Lancaster on July 4 to take over a former piece of assembly business, the appointment of generals. The men would elect the generals now.

In 1647, at Putney, a dashing Colonel Rainsborough, the highest-ranking officer to support the Levellers, had argued for allowing unpropertied soldiers to vote. "For really," he said, "I think the poorest he that is in England hath a life to live, as the greatest he . . . that every man who live under a government ought first by his own consent to put himself under the government." Oliver Cromwell rejected the plea. He cited the sanctity of property. At Putney, a radical argument about rights in government had failed.

It took almost 150 years, but in Pennsylvania in 1776, Colonel

Rainsborough's hopes were fulfilled. Militia privates stopped arguing and took the franchise.

⁓

Two days before the Privates polled the militiamen, and on the same day he revised the assembly's instructions to the delegates, John Dickinson attended a meeting of battalion commanders. An officer there made a hostile speech about Dickinson's opposition to independence. In the course of the diatribe, he predicted that Dickinson would soon find he'd lost the confidence and affection of Pennsylvanians.

Dickinson responded. "These threats we have just now heard might have been spared," he said. "I defy them, I regard them not—I stand as unmoved by them as the rock among the waves that dash against it.—I can defy the *world*, sir, but—I defy not heaven, nor will I ever barter my conscience for the esteem of mankind. So let my country treat me as she pleases, still I will act as my conscience directs."

10

~

Independence Days

June 14–July 4

On June 18, the first day of Pennsylvania's provincial convention to replace the chartered government, Christopher Marshall and other radicals arrived early at Carpenters' Hall. They wanted to mingle with the out-of-town delegates and make them comfortable in the city's artisan headquarters. While far less grand than the State House, the hall represented the ultimate degree of workmanship, and it was bigger than any building some of these visitors might have stepped inside before.

The floor was loud and crowded that day with 108 small farmers and middle and lower artisans, chosen, not elected, by town committees across Pennsylvania. Only two years earlier to the day, John Dickinson had chaired the City Committee here. The committee was the radicals' now, including names, from the German Graf and Lutz to the Scots-Irish Colhoon, unfamiliar in upscale Philadelphia politics.

Their high-Whig ally Thomas McKean presided. As the one delegate present with any experience in province-scale politics, formerly in the assembly, and now with his seat in the Congress up the street, he linked the Whig independents to the working-class insurgents. But he was growing uncomfortable in the role. The haughty Pennsylvanian wanted American independence, not working-class democracy. With the Adamses, he'd made common cause with the radicals. Now he worried about how far his allies were being encouraged to take matters in Pennsylvania. Once independence was achieved, he meant to encourage them no further.

There were other discomforts. Opening this convention marked an astounding success for the Philadelphia radicals. Once rank outsiders, with Samuel Adams's help they'd overturned one of the oldest legislative bodies in the English-speaking world. They'd organized the working class of the keystone American province in a way that Levellers, Ranters, and Diggers had only dreamed of back in England. They were bringing bold ideas about rights and equality to life here in Carpenters' Hall.

Now their differences began clanging. The alliance with gentlemen like the Adamses, McKean, and Lee was an unlikely one, but their alliance with one another involved unlikely matches, too. Marshall was a questing universalist Christian, Young a loud, sardonic rationalist. James Cannon was evangelical, as was Benjamin Rush, but both took liberal positions on freedom of religious conscience, and Rush was becoming friends with John Adams, who was busy expunging, from an emergent life story, his decisive collaboration with these men. Timothy Matlack was a charismatic tavern rowdy. Thomas

Paine was, among other things, a celebrated author now, a transatlantic personality with book sales like none seen before.

The dissonances resonated even as the convention fulfilled the radicals' shared hopes. The convention named July 8 election day throughout the province. On that day, delegates would be chosen for a provincial constitutional convention, here at Carpenters' Hall, where Pennsylvania's new government would be created. Each county, the convention decided, would send eight delegates to the constitutional convention, and Philadelphia would send eight. That gave more equal representation than had ever been attempted under the old charter. The convention went beyond that. The members decreed that any militia associator over twenty-one who had been assessed for any tax at all could vote on July 8. The point was to represent all adult white males in writing the new constitution, and the effect was to raise suffrage from around half the white male population to 90 percent or more. The old meaning of representative consent in government, based on security in private property, with lines of precedent that Whigs traced to Magna Carta and before, was overturned.

The convention also established an oath. Judges and inspectors running the election could require any voter to swear to support government on the authority of the people alone. That would prevent any voter's trying to bring back the old charter. And in keeping with the evangelical spirit of Pennsylvania's working-class radicalism, with its roots in the Great Awakening, the convention required anyone standing for election as a delegate to profess faith in God, Jesus Christ, and the Holy Spirit, and to acknowledge the divine inspiration of the scriptures.

That religious test, however, split the radical leadership. Christopher Marshall, lapsed Quaker fundamentalist and mystic, decided he was all for it. Rush and Cannon, also evangelicals, wanted tolerance, for skeptic comrades like Thomas Young and Thomas Paine, without whose contributions this convention would never have occurred.

The disagreement felt painfully abrupt. Marshall and Rush, as official members of the convention at Carpenters' Hall, were looking at one another with a shock of mutual disillusionment. Marshall had always believed Rush was, as Marshall put it, a sincere believer, that they'd been bringing about the redemption of society as preparation for the millennium. How could Rush oppose a religious qualification for public service? And Rush was surprised to learn that while Marshall had worked with and even befriended Young and Paine, now in the moment of success he hoped to bar them from government.

Marshall took things like this to heart. He felt left out and let down. James Cannon told him his position on the religious test was held by "fools, blockheads, self-righteous and zealous bigots."

Yet even as the alliance began fracturing, Samuel Adams's reason for connecting himself to the group was fulfilled. The day before the convention adjourned, it adopted a statement, written by Rush, McKean, and a farmer named Thomas Smith from York, with help from Adams himself. The statement committed the provincial convention, and by implication any new government of Pennsylvania, to a break with England. The keystone province was claimed for American independence.

$$\sim$$

John Dickinson remained a delegate in the Congress. The commitment to independence by the provincial convention didn't give Pennsylvania any new delegates or provide the existing delegates with instructions to support Lee's resolution for independence. That change awaited a new Pennsylvania constitution, or at least new appointments by the convention.

Dickinson had no assembly now. He no longer controlled the middle colonies, his own delegation, or even his protégé James Wilson. In the chamber at the State House, the members of the Congress took on more work than ever. Sure to be replaced as a delegate soon, Dickinson remained committed to serving the war effort.

Richard Henry Lee had put everybody on the spot. As the July 1 vote on independence neared, delegates were bringing or sending Lee's proposal for independence to their home governments, along with the May 10 resolution and the May 15 preamble. They sought instructions from those back home, and in some cases they sought freedom to act in favor of a break.

British maneuvers, as always, confirmed the independents' position. News came on June 9 that a fleet of 132 British ships had left Halifax. The fleet was sure to arrive in New York in about ten days. British strategy would be to occupy New York City and command the Hudson River, New York Bay, and Long Island Sound. That would cut New England off from the other colonies.

The Congress responded by calling various militias to New York. American citizen-soldiers were about to confront the greatest military deployment ever seen in the new world, a bigger fleet than the one that had beat back the Spanish Armada in Elizabeth's day. The grim contest was about to begin.

New England firmed up quickly and fairly predictably for independence. On June 14, Connecticut copied language from Lee's resolution, calling the united colonies "free and independent states." When New Hampshire delegates told their home government that independence was necessary, New Hampshire instructed them to support it. As the delegates nervously projected and reprojected outcomes for the July 1 vote on Lee's resolution, they could count all of New England as a yes.

Less predictably, Delaware changed instructions, too. Thomas McKean brought the government there the May preamble and resolution. Delaware adopted Pennsylvania's language, not instructing delegates to vote for independence, but permitting them to do so. New Jersey also gave its delegates power to join with others in independence—but like Delaware and Pennsylvania, it clearly hoped royal peace commissioners might make such a move unnecessary. Reconciliationism persisted. Maryland and New York still prohibited their delegates from joining any majority for independence, and delegations with looser instructions were still divided. Those members were permitted to vote their consciences, and some would certainly vote against Lee's resolution.

John Adams kept predicting overwhelming victory. In the weeks since the passage of his May 15 preamble, he'd been swept into a state of unrelieved optimism. No fact could seem to shake it. On May 15, Adams gloried in what he'd somehow come to imagine was Dickinson's submission to the cause of independence—submission, even, to John Adams. "What do you think must be my reflections," Adams wrote James Warren, "when I see the Farmer J. himself now confessing the falsehood of all his prophecies, and the truth of mine. . . . Yet I dare not hint at these things," he said, "for I hate to give pain to gentlemen whom I believe sufficiently punished by their own reflections." The ultimate moment was always just about to occur. Before any definite news arrived from Virginia, Adams assured everyone that Virginia was solid. Despite his worries about Massachusetts, he was thrilled by southern adoption of his ideas on government. After the State House yard meeting, he thought Pennsylvania's instructions would be changed overnight. Then he was sure the vote would be put to the Congress on June 10 and would be for independence, and he was sure nothing like it had ever happened before in all of history. "Objects of the most stupendous magnitude," he wrote, "and measures in which the lives and liberties of millions yet unborn are intimately interested, are now before us. We are in the very midst of a revolution the most complete, unexpected, and remarkable of any in the history of nations." He wrote that on the evening of June 9. Then the vote was postponed till July.

With undiminished brio he was now working with Samuel Chase, a delegate from Maryland, prodding Chase to get Maryland's position on independence changed. "Maryland now stands alone," he told Chase with grand indifference (again optimistically; New York hadn't changed its instructions, either). "I presume she will soon join company; if not she must be left alone." To another correspondent he wrote that in the Congress it was "universally acknowledged that we are independent, but there is a fear of declaring it." And to his wife: "Great things are on the tapis [i.e., under consideration]."

He assured her, with some amazement, that his health was good. It would fail soon, he predicted. But for the moment he felt well.

Adams's exuberance seemed more than justified when on June 28, nearly the eve of the scheduled vote in the Congress, Maryland finally did change instructions to its delegates. Chase had gone to Maryland, corresponded constantly with John Adams, and worked on every Maryland politician he knew. The shift was sudden and extreme, as Adams had predicted it would be. Maryland's delegates went overnight from a strict prohibition against even debating resolutions related to independence to strict orders to vote for it. Suddenly Maryland could be counted on for a yes, thanks to Adams's work with Chase.

Amid all that activity, Adams had also been appointed to one of the less important committees, with Benjamin Franklin, the Virginia delegate Thomas Jefferson, Roger Sherman of Connecticut, and Robert Livingston of New York. After the compromise delay of June 10, the Congress had assigned that committee of five to write, in case Lee's resolution should pass on July 1, a document giving the reasons for passing it. It was a practical idea. Should a unanimous break with England actually be voted on July 1, and the colonies begin confederating, the Congress would need a statement to announce the break and justify it to the world. Other nations would need to know that the colonies were forming a stable entity that could make reliable alliances. Separation and confederation must be seen to rest on deep, broad traditions of law, liberty, property, and sovereignty, and to have come about in response to repeated, criminal imbalances of royal authority.

Thomas Jefferson was selected to do the actual drafting. Franklin wouldn't have been a realistic choice for the job. He'd hardly been in the Congress all spring. He'd traveled to Quebec on the Congress's business in winter, then had had to recover from illness and exhaustion. Then he'd been struck by gout. He was barely keeping up with what was going on at the State House.

Adams, for his part, was too busy on the far more important committee to write a proposed treaty with France. While less versed in diplomacy than other members of that committee, he was pushing very hard to take the lead in drafting the treaty, which was potentially earth-shaking. A document to publicize and explain a resolution for independence was important, but drafting it wasn't important work to do. Getting Lee's resolution actually passed was the important work. So were working on the Congress's Board of War and taking up negotiation with empires in the likely ensuing transatlantic conflict. So, for that matter, was writing a constitution for Massachusetts. Adams was eagerly pursuing all of those projects. Sherman and Livingston were on other committees, too.

So the drafting fell to Jefferson, who was regarded as a strong and elegant writer. He'd collaborated with John Dickinson in 1775 on "A Declaration of the Causes and Necessity for Taking Up Arms." In Virginia in 1774 he'd written an adventurous "Summary View of the Rights of British America." A tall squire like the other Virginians, he was thirty-two, attended by slaves, and less gregarious than some. In Virginia, he didn't merely look and think west, like the Lees. He was building his mansion, Monticello, on a hilltop in the wilderness. In Philadelphia he roomed alone on the western outskirts, away from the Delaware and near the State House. He'd joined Richard Henry Lee in supporting independence, but he'd just returned from Virginia and had missed most of the wrangling of May.

He'd returned, in fact, just at the wrong time for his real ambitions. They didn't lie with jobs like drafting a justification for adopting a resolution. Jefferson wanted to take part in actual government-making. He'd written a draft constitution for Virginia. But his colleagues had left for Williamsburg to work on creating the new government there, and as the most recently returned delegate, Jefferson found himself stuck in Philadelphia while they wrote a constitution without him.

He was frustrated. Yet in his rented second-story room—the designer and master of Monticello inhabited a hot, cramped box—he began drafting the kind of document that Englishmen had always called declarations.

Early on July 1, John Adams reported: "This morning is assigned for the greatest debate of all. May Heaven prosper the new-born republic, and make it more glorious than any former republics have been." On July 2, Samuel Adams saw the realization of all he'd been doing in Philadelphia. The Continental Congress voted to make the American colonies independent of England. July 1 and 2 thus became climactic days in what John Adams had begun to call the epoch.

Nobody who was there on those days, let alone those who weren't, could ever agree on all that happened during them. Samuel Adams, in putting together the secret coalition that he used to bring down Pennsylvania, burned and tore up papers because he wanted no reconstruction of the secret events. But the July 1 and 2 sessions of the Congress could never be perfectly reconstructed for an opposite reason. The participants entered history. The two days lived deeper and longer in imagination and memory than any two real days ever could. The men of the Congress would recall them, volubly, for years to come. In the process, memories failed and wish became indistinguishable from fact. Versions developed, clashed, blurred. Those who came later, hoping to recapture the days' events, took up one version or another, or took up more than one version at once, and they, too, invented. The most celebrated of Philadelphia events of 1776 became the least commensurable.

A frightening moment came at the end of the session on July 1. The Congress had been acting almost all day long as a committee of the whole to consider Lee's resolution for independence. There had at first appeared to be little suspense. Maryland's new instructions for independence were presented during the session, making New York now the only delegation expressly prohibited from voting for independence, and even New York's home government was considering new instructions. News arrived of more than fifty British ships at Sandy Hook, the Jersey side of the great entrance to the lower New York Bay, with many more ships arriving there and fifty-three British ships off Charleston, South Carolina, too. Congressmen on both sides of the issue believed Lee's resolution was likely to pass easily.

Debate had really concluded on June 10. Much had changed since then to push the vote toward independence.

Yet early in the day John Dickinson took his last chance to speak. Some later said that he resembled a shadow, and even seemed near death. He spoke from notes, and evinced no confidence that he would persuade the members to slow down now. But silence, he said, would make him guilty of acquiescing in a fatal error. He predicted that foreign powers would make attempts on North American soil, and noted that the many differences among the colonies themselves hadn't yet been addressed or resolved. The independents' long denial that they'd been seeking independence made Lee's resolution in favor of independence especially disturbing, he said. And he predicted an American civil war. Then he sat down, ending a phase of his life unimaginable when in this same room, thirteen years earlier, he'd spoken as an upstart against Franklin, Galloway, and "royal liberty" for Pennsylvania.

It was hot and humid outside, and stifling in the chamber. John Adams became frustrated. The optimism on which he'd lived for weeks began to desert him. He rose to speak in response to Dickinson, with no notes, merely reiterating, he felt, everything he'd already said in debates of June 8 and 10, and in other sessions when he'd pushed measures tending to independence.

He'd been counting on an immediate vote today. Then, when he was finished speaking, newly appointed delegates from New Jersey arrived, late. Having missed it, they asked to hear his argument again. Adams repeated the whole thing, fed up and embarrassed.

When at last it was time to poll the committee of the whole, the result was surprising. In Pennsylvania, Dickinson, the wealthy merchant Robert Morris, and two others voted no. James Wilson did go against his former boss, as he'd promised the independents he might, and voted yes, and Franklin of course voted yes, too. A mixture of vagueness and creativity would later make it hard to know how another Dickinson protégé, John Morton, voted on July 1, but it didn't matter: a majority in the Pennsylvania delegation voted against independence. Pennsylvania was holding out, futilely now, since the provincial convention had promised support for independence, and these delegates would soon be replaced.

Delaware's vote was split 1–1, McKean of course voting yes and George Read no. So Delaware didn't count. South Carolina voted no, behind young Edward Rutledge's continuing opposition to empowering Massachusetts and the north. New York abstained. Its delegation announced that with new instructions under consideration at home, and current instructions forbidding a vote for independence, it couldn't take part.

So in committee, only nine of thirteen delegations voted for independence. That was frightening to everybody in the room.

~

At four that afternoon, heat gave way to a two-hour thunderstorm. The rain would play a strange part in the memories of the men in the room and in the recountings of later generations.

Thomas Jefferson's thermometer recorded the temperature. The radical Christopher Marshall, in his diary, noted the time and described the quality of the storm. Yet during a pause earlier that day between Dickinson's speech and Adam's rejoinder there was a long silence in the chamber (as Adams himself said), which one writer has filled with the sound of rain just starting to hit the windows, another with roaring thunder. Others say that as heat and humidity mounted, the storm held off till late afternoon (as Marshall recorded), and one writer therefore describes the sky darkening just as the committee reaches its divided result. Candles are lit in the chamber. Heat lightning flashes beyond the tall south windows. The sky murmurs and barks before a howling wind starts sweeping the windows with rain.

And the next day, according to one writer, the city was bathed in gentle summer showers all day. It saw a hard, steady rain, and also a sudden cloudburst, according to others. In tradition and in history, the rain goes on and off at will.

Considered simply as a poll result, the vote of the committee of the whole was strongly in favor of the resolution for independence. So the chairman of the committee of the whole, Benjamin Harrison, reported to the president of the Congress, Hancock, that the resolution was endorsed in committee, which of course everybody knew.

But this vote also meant that a vote by the actual Congress—as opposed to the committee of the whole—wouldn't be unanimous in favor of independence. The independents had argued that waiting for unanimity was pointless. Yet it was starkly obvious now that to adopt independence on a mere majority would leave these men staring at each other in bewilderment. An assertion of independence, binding on all yet dissented by some, augured civil war among the governments represented in the room.

So the mechanism of the committee of the whole had served one of its purposes. Without having made a formal commitment, everybody could see where things stood. There was an overwhelming majority for independence. Even delegations voting against it contained members voting for it. Realistically, what could a minority of states, voting for what now amounted only to a brief delay, do with its dissent?

Rutledge solved the immediate problem. He gave the country a gift by requesting that the vote by the Congress be postponed until the next morning. His delegation opposed independence, but it might, he said, go along with a majority for the sake of unity, if given the night for consideration.

New York was considered likely to change instructions to go along with a majority. That left two questions that the members had to live with overnight. Could Delaware somehow break its tie? And with a British fleet at the mouth of New York Bay, would John Dickinson stick to principle, soon to be overridden anyway by Pennsylvania's provincial convention, and cost America its unity?

As business was about to begin the next morning, Caesar Rodney, a delegate from Delaware, arrived in his spurs. When the session had ended the day before, McKean had hired an express rider to gallop to Delaware to alert Rodney. Rodney had been delayed by a thunderstorm, and he was seriously ill with a cancer that disfigured his face. But he'd ridden all night and made it to the State House in time to break Delaware's tie in favor of independence. McKean met the sick, exhausted rider at the State House door.

At any rate, nearly forty years later McKean recalled that he had. Rodney was still in boots and spurs, McKean remembered, and the two men walked together into the chamber. Rodney later said that he'd been detained, during his nighttime ride, by thunder and rain.

So some traditions cover Caesar Rodney with mud. Others just make him dusty. Some say that just as he arrived, the doors to the chamber were about to be closed: he barely made it. One writer has all the delegates gathered in the chamber, listening in silence for the horse and then rising as one to greet Rodney.

McKean said only that when he and Rodney came into the assembly room they were "among the latest; proceedings immediately commenced." General Washington's latest report was read—110 British ships were at Sandy Hook now, with more coming in. That news had been sent two days earlier. Soon those ships would start landing troops.

It was time for the final vote.

Around ten, rain began again.

~~~

A second important event occurred on July 2. John Dickinson stayed home. The moment had come when holding to the principles on which he'd based his career could only hurt America. He wouldn't vote for independence, but however badly he'd been wronged, his assembly undermined and thrown out, his chartered government destroyed with the help of outside schemers, he couldn't obstruct an American union, either. He and Robert Morris ended their opposition by removing themselves from the Congress.

So when the vote was taken, Delaware was 2–1 in favor, Pennsylvania 3–2 in favor. As Rutledge had offered, South Carolina went along for unity. The other delegations voted as they had in committee the day before. The official vote was twelve delegations in favor, with New York still obligated to abstain.

Close enough to unanimous, the Congress adopted the resolution. The American colonies were united and independent.

~~~

The next day the British were landing troops on Staten Island in New York Harbor. The Congress had achieved American independence just in time to oppose the invasion from Great Britain.

Also on July 3, the congressmen began editing Jefferson's draft declaration. They needed only the day and then a few hours on the 4th to wrap up work on the document. Unlike the resolution adopted on July 2, which actually made the colonies independent, this document had no legal force. What it did was clarify certain agreed-upon positions for the American public and the world, without straying too far in any counterproductive direction. Getting a statement out the door was the priority, and as Josiah Bartlett of New Hampshire said, the draft the Congress had to work with was already "pretty good."

They wanted it to be very good. Jefferson had completed his draft in about two days, and the others on the committee had lightly revised it before submitting it to the Congress on June 28. The Congress had tabled it pending the vote on independence. Now the members formed a committee of the whole to work on it.

Its two opening paragraphs announced a momentous event, and then rendered beautifully, in language appropriate for both public speaking and private reading, a summary of the conventional political ideas of the age. Those paragraphs linked the novelty of American independence to the oldest Whig ideas about the natural right of revolution against arbitrary tyranny.

Then came twenty-one charges against the king, casting him both as a tyrant and as personally immoral. Those charges justified the colonies' July 2 break with the empire.

Most of the men in the Congress considered themselves masters of grammar and rhetoric. They made changes big and small in Jefferson's draft. The members deleted Jefferson's assertion that the American colonies had planted themselves with no help from Britain. They deleted his startling diatribe against the slave trade, which claimed the king had forced the trade on the colonists. On a smaller scale they changed "inalienable rights" to "unalienable rights," changed "expunge their former systems of government" to the less extreme "alter their former systems of government," and even changed "neglected utterly" to "utterly neglected." They added some mentions of God, whom Jefferson had played down, and they inserted in the conclusion Richard Henry Lee's resolution that had actually made the colonies independent.

While his colleagues mutilated his work, as he experienced it, Jefferson sat in tense silence. That night he started writing out his original version, spending hours on that project. He sent the copies to friends. Believing his version superior, he had it printed. Throughout his life he would present the two versions side by side to show what had happened to his document.

From the Congress's point of view, the edited version did the job more smoothly and authoritatively than the draft, without advancing any theories that called for clarification or raising any awkward questions. Foreign powers would be able to imagine allying themselves with the United States. The members adopted their edited version unanimously, except for New York, which still awaited instructions.

They ordered the document printed and sent throughout the states to be published and read aloud. It had no official title. Nobody had signed it, and usually nobody signed such documents, except perhaps John Hancock as president of the Congress. The text began running in newspapers on July 6.

When on July 19 New York did make independence unanimous, Timothy Matlack, as clerk, hand-lettered a large parchment copy of the declaration for the Congress itself. He finished it on August 2. That version had an official title: "The Unanimous Declaration of the Thirteen United States," under the header "In Congress, July 4, 1776."

By then, people had started calling the document "the Declaration of Independence." So in August, members of the Congress began signing Matlack's hand-lettered copy, which lay on the table in the chamber. Signing made the document historic, placing it in the tradition of the Magna Carta, despite its having—unlike the Magna Carta, which the king too had signed—no legal force. The document lay there, and for six months members would sign when they came to the Congress. They signed whether or not they'd been in the room when Lee's resolution had passed on July 2, or when the Declaration had passed on the 4th.

Robert Morris of Pennsylvania, for example, signed as soon as the document was ready on August 2, placing his name ostentatiously at the top of the list of Pennsylvania delegates. He'd opposed independence, which had passed only because he'd joined Dickinson in abstaining from voting. One of the richest merchants in America, Morris operated trade networks from the West Indies to China. An independent America, he'd decided, offered advantages. He would became the Congress's Superintendent of Finance. Mingling private and public money and profiteering during the war with England soon made him richer than ever.

Benjamin Rush signed, too. By August the provincial convention had made him a delegate to the Congress. Signing was something the delegates wanted to do.

Royal peace commissioners landed on Staten Island on July 12. They came, as Samuel Adams had always predicted, with an overwhelming force. General William Howe, commander of British troops, planned to hold New York and cut off New England, and his brother, Admiral Lord Richard Howe, would lead negotiations for peace.

Richard Howe's instructions from the king were strictly limited.

He was to accept submissions from the colonies and possibly offer some pardons. He had no official permission to negotiate the navigation and trade acts and other matters that had inspired more than a decade of American resistance, or to push back to the relationship of empire and colonies that had existed before 1764.

But the Howe brothers were American sympathizers. They knew Americans wouldn't consider a mere submission and pardon. Richard Howe stepped onshore in high hopes that he could somehow work the negotiation back and forth and develop unofficial channels at home, where he and his brother were influential. He might repair the break on good terms for America while saving the king's face. If he did that, he would also save the empire and achieve greatness. He came prepared to take risks to avoid carnage and gain real reconciliation.

But the admiral was dismayed to find he'd arrived days late. America had declared independence. The Congress had "changed the ground," in his bleak interpretation of the July 2 adoption of Lee's resolution. Howe gave negotiating his best efforts anyway, but there was no way back.

The Declaration of Independence, in words that echoed the past and would become famous in the future, held it to be self-evident that all men are created equal. The Continental Congress was by no means suggesting with those words that fostering equality is a responsibility of government. The men it referred to were lacking government, which when instituted had the purpose of ensuring their unalienable, God-given rights. In any case, the Declaration wasn't a governing document. It established no laws or procedures. It didn't act on anyone. It would have a long life as something other than the Congress intended, but that life hadn't been imagined yet. In the immediate future, the document would be largely forgotten.

But Philadelphia stayed busy that first week of July. On July 3, Philadelphia's Committee of Privates met to pick candidates for Pennsylvania's constitutional convention. In the spirit of Carpenters' Hall, they meant to give equality legal force in Pennsylvania. James Cannon, Thomas Young, and Timothy Matlack addressed the crowd. Young harangued the people hard. He echoed a broadside written by Cannon and published by the Privates themselves. The Privates advised the people not to allow anyone rich to represent them. Education, too, the Privates warned, was a privilege often used to mislead ordinary people: plain understanding was best. Young now encouraged the Privates, in turn, not to lapse into old ways of deference to wealth, and to choose candidates who would be sure to represent their rights.

Cannon and Matlack were then nominated as delegates to the constitutional convention. Other nominees included Benjamin Franklin in absentia—and in direct contradiction to Young's advice regarding men of wealth and fame. But artisans, mechanics, and militiamen had long supported Franklin. They venerated him as not only world-famous but also a former printer, one of their own. His presence in any Pennsylvania effort that wanted prestige was now almost mandatory.

Christopher Marshall attended the Privates' caucus. But he was no longer one of the coalition. Now he thought of his old friend Young as "a noisy blunder." Cannon, Matlack, and Rush, he believed, had become an anti-Christian triumvirate to rule Pennsylvania, a new tyranny. Marshall abstained from approving Young and Matlack as delegates.

Rush, for all of Marshall's fears about him, was also pulling away from the others. When the provincial convention made him a delegate to the Congress, he happily took his seat in the chamber at the State House. Having become especially impressed by John Adams, Rush made himself an Adams protégé, and Adams, beginning as a mentor, found a friend. Both men were strivers, not genteel by birth, wanting to move up. Rush had always been nervous about the radicals' uncompromising populism. Adams's skeptical republicanism was starting to make sense to him. Rush was leaving Paine behind. He wanted to help the poor, but he was thinking about social reform now, not fundamental change. He was unradicalized.

The crew that had come seemingly out of nowhere, and changed both Pennsylvania and America, was falling apart.

Their work, however, survived their alliance. On July 8, two great events occurred in Philadelphia. The Congress's declaration was read aloud to a crowd outside the State House. In attendance was the whole City Committee, which had marched over from Carpenters' Hall in force. Bells pealed. The people cheered, and they shouted "God bless the free states of North America!" three times. Then nine privates removed the king's coat of arms from the State House.

Inside the State House that day, an election took place. Nine weeks after the Mayday election, people in Philadelphia and across Pennsylvania voted, with the broadest suffrage ever seen, for the delegates who would create a new constitution for their state. That afternoon, the five militia battalions paraded on the commons and wasted precious gunpowder in celebratory volleys. Night fell, and at a coffeehouse a big pile of wooden casks was set on fire. The king's arms were thrown on top.

In September, when the state constitutional convention met at Carpenters' Hall, working-class radicals from all over Pennsylvania convened to write equality into law, for the first meaningful time anywhere. But Benjamin Rush now called the group and its work a "mobocracy." He even praised the old Pennsylvania charter he'd helped overturn. He was soon to become chief doctor of the Continental Army, friends not only with John Adams but also with General Washington, and later, if unofficially, the first surgeon general of the United States. He would be concerned to improve diet and reduce drinking among the American poor, to help them rise from squalor by bettering themselves. A constitution to give them power scandalized him now.

Thomas McKean was out, too. Never a natural ally of the sort gathered at Carpenters' Hall, he scorned the constitution that his assault on Dickinson had helped bring about. Soon he began trying to pull Pennsylvania back to traditional forms of government. Within fifteen years McKean, Rush, the financier Robert Morris, and others in a new alliance would succeed.

But not today. Benjamin Franklin himself endorsed Pennsylvania's radical constitutional convention by serving as its president. Twenty years after he'd ended the strict-Quaker oligarchy in Pennsylvania politics, Franklin sat in the chair at Carpenters' Hall and oversaw replacement of a government he'd once dominated and had then tried to end another way, with royal power. With the overthrow of the old charter, the proprietor was gone for good, and Dickinson gone for now; the empire that had humiliated Franklin was shaken. Artisans and mechanics were building a kind of government that Franklin couldn't have imagined when he'd petitioned to bring the king into the province. Soon he was credited throughout the state with having written the radical constitution.

It actually wasn't clear to some of the convention delegates that Franklin was paying attention to the proceedings. Some later said he never read the constitution itself. Even while chairman he was taking time off to go up the street to the State House. There he worked on the Congress's diplomacy with France. Soon he would sail away again. Living in foreign capitals and discussing state matters with the mighty, not struggling in Pennsylvania politics, was what Franklin planned to do.

He wasn't the author of the state constitution and wouldn't have been. James Cannon was, aided by Young and Matlack, by a farmer from Cumberland County named Robert Whitehill, and by the writings of Thomas Paine. The new constitution followed Cannon's own writings on behalf of the Committee of Privates, as well as Paine's proposals, in *Common Sense* and elsewhere, for a radically democratic republic. It made Pennsylvania's executive branch a committee, appointed by and dependent on the legislative branch. That legislative branch had only one chamber, lacking any check by an upper house. It was elected in proportion to population. Judges were elected locally.

And there was no property requirement for the franchise. Ordinary workers and the poor could not only vote in Pennsylvania but also hold office.

Cannon and Young wanted to go further. They proposed a clause that would allow the legislature to limit the amount of property anyone in Pennsylvania could own. Dictating equality to that degree was too radical even for the radical convention, and the clause was not approved. But assemblies elected under the new constitution passed laws against concentrating wealth. They regulated monopolies. They refused to charter a bank they believed served the rich at the expense of the poor. They pushed back against predatory credit and foreclosure, forcing the lending class to accept discounted payments, the depreciating paper currencies used by ordinary people.

Whitehill, the farmer from Cumberland, served in the assembly.

William Findley, a weaver from the headwaters of the Ohio, served as well. Herman Husband, a preacher from forbidding mountains in Bedford County, served in the assembly in 1776, and his ideas were so extreme that he became known as "the madman of the Alleghenies." Husband proposed going off the gold standard and centrally regulating paper-currency inflation. He wanted taxes on income and wealth, and he wanted them to be progressive. He wanted a public program to make old people financially secure.

———

"Good God!" John Adams said when he read Pennsylvania's constitution. "The people of Pennsylvania," he asserted, "in two years will be glad to petition the crown of England for reconciliation to be delivered from the tyranny of their Constitution."

It was as if Adams didn't know he'd been instrumental in bringing down the old government of Pennsylvania. It was as if the Pennsylvania constitution's radical authors hadn't been his allies. He was busy working on Massachusetts. He wanted above all to prevent democratic populism there. He hoped for a constitution that would follow his *Thoughts on Government.*

It was a struggle. The populists pushed back. But while his constitution wouldn't be perfected until 1780, in the end Adams succeeded. The new Massachusetts government stood in opposition to Pennsylvania's. The right to vote was limited to propertied white men over twenty-one. The new government moved to subdue the insurgent western countries. It suggested that an army might be sent to occupy the region, and it threatened to deny the Berkshires any representation in the assembly at all. The Berkshire towns threatened secession, and they noted that denial of representation was listed in the Declaration of Independence as a grievance against the king and Parliament.

In the spring of 1779, a crowd closed the court at Great Barrington by force. The government responded by passing laws permitting prior restraint of crowds. Along the way, Pope's Day was banned.

⁓

Samuel Adams always expressed quiet pleasure in America's declaring independence. He reflected on it, as ever, from a seeming distance. "The Congress has at length declared the colonies free and independent states," he wrote a friend in July 1776. "Upon this I congratulate you, for I know your heart has long been set upon it." With satisfaction he wrote another, "Was there ever a Revolution brought about, especially so important as this, without great internal tumults and violent convulsions!"

Later, when he served as a councilor of the new Massachusetts government, the question came before the legislature of what to do about people who had destroyed property and committed other crimes during the period of resistance to England. The legislature proposed indemnifying any such crimes from January 1766 to the end of 1779. Adams objected. He wanted the house to set the end date at July 4, 1776. Any rioting after that, he said, occurred after the people had become sovereign, and the people could not legitimately riot against themselves. Rioting now undermined unity and even gave aid and comfort to the enemy, treason in the Christian Sparta.

In the late 1780s, when people in western Massachusetts, destroyed by state finance policies that favored creditors and investors, seized and tried to hold the armory at Springfield, Adams worked on a riot act and a resolution to suspend habeas corpus for the rebels, and he called for their execution.

⟀

Few would remember Samuel Adams. That was how he wanted it. John, not Samuel, became known as the architect of independence. In the summer of 1776, Samuel's greatest work, hidden anyway, was done. John's career on the great stage began.

As an old man, John worried over the Declaration of Independence. By then the document had been retrieved from obscurity and become the object of a patriotic cult. People believed that July 4, not July 2, was the day America became independent. They thought the Declaration had been signed on that day, and that signing it had been a collaborative act of courage and integrity in the Congress. They'd started celebrating the date with fireworks, parades, and speeches. They treated the Declaration as a legal document, a means to, not merely an explanation of, independence. They made Thomas Jefferson its sole author and thus a force of divine providence in world history. The aging Jefferson encouraged that impression.

The aging Adams flailed in his perennial envy. He dismissed the document's importance even as he tried to take credit for it. He called the Declaration a piece of stage business that Jefferson had run away with, and he mischaracterized the process by which Jefferson had been assigned to draft it. The job had really been his, Adams said; he'd passed it to Jefferson as an act of humility and political discretion.

He never got over it, and Jefferson never did, either. Well before they died, the men had been cast as twinned, rival authors of independence.

Yet they both kept thinking about Samuel Adams. John Adams, insistent on being remembered forever as the man who made America independent, nevertheless feared that future generations would not know what had happened during those weeks he called an epoch. "Without the character of Samuel Adams," he fretted, "the true history of the American Revolution can never be written." Jefferson always gave John Adams due credit for tireless work in debate. But when it came to the man who steered the Congress toward independence, he was forthright. "Samuel Adams was the man," he said.

So the episode that began in Samuel Adams's rented Philadelphia rooms early in May came to an end early in July. Nine weeks after voters defeated American independence, in the nearest thing to a referendum on the issue that the country ever had, America declared independence anyway. It declared independence not in unified response to a galvanizing idea, or by yielding to inevitability, but because of an assertive action. Much of that action had to be secret to be effective.

In the process, men in the grip of ideas about law, liberty, and property boldly challenged an empire; and men in the grip of ideas about social equality for laboring people overturned a duly elected government and made a new kind of constitution. The forces of liberty and the forces of equality combined that spring and summer to achieve their separate ends, but they were always fundamentally and even violently at odds. The Pennsylvania radicals demolished, for a short time, and in one place, the basic assumption of Whig politics, sacred to men like the Adamses: property as the basis of representation, bulwark against tyranny. The radicals put in practice a competing idea: government must restrain property, in order to foster fairness and liberate ordinary people. When the action was over, the Adamses and others like them devoted their energies to ensuring that political power in America remained in the hands of elites. They and their intellectual descendents suceeded in erasing the radical contribution—even the names of most of the radicals themselves—from the American founding.

One thing the two sides of the alliance had in common was a commitment to force. Consensus wasn't their goal. Together and separately, they worked not openly, in debate, to change opponents' minds but in complicated back-room networks. Their weapons included theater, caucus, and guns. They rendered opponents powerless. Together they defeated the forces of reconciliation.

So America declared independence, but it didn't declare, at its founding moment, an idea that might reconcile and bring to light the clashing moods and desires that had come together to push the country into breaking with England. Most Americans didn't know what had happened. Many never would. A union of former colonies entered history in confusion about the nature and purpose of its independence.

John Dickinson and Thomas Paine, however, at opposite extremes of the conflict—and despised more or less equally by John Adams—responded to independence without confusion. Dickinson never signed the declaration. He acted, as usual, consistently with his principles. Late in July, the provincial convention got around to dismissing him as a delegate to the Congress, but Dickinson had already left town. When he received news of his dismissal, which offended him deeply, he was in camp in Elizabethtown, New Jersey. Virtually the moment he'd failed in his last effort to stop independence, he'd led his militia to fight the British. Later, when brigadier generals were elected by the men to outrank him, Dickinson resigned his commission. He volunteered as a private and carried a musket in the Battle of Brandywine.

Thomas Paine also left Philadelphia as soon as independence

was declared. Like Dickinson, whom he'd worked so hard to remove, he went to serve in New Jersey, having attached himself to a militia unit. In the grim late fall of 1776, Paine took part in the retreat from Fort Lee.

That winter he wrote dispatches from the field with cold fingers. When prospects for America looked the bleakest, he challenged Americans to stand their ground and to believe.

"Not a place upon earth might be so happy as America," Paine said. And when things were at their worst, he said, "I thank God that I fear not."

Notes

These notes describe both my research and my thinking. I therefore mix source citations with discussion of the historiography, under topics that come up in each chapter. I've drawn on a number of primary sources, and I don't think the story I tell has been told before, in this kind of unified narrative. But synthesis of and contention with the secondary record provide support for the story. My inspiration in a wide range of work by other writers will become evident in these notes, as will those writers' reliance on and contests with one another and mine with them.

I classify as "common knowledge" anything noncontroversially factual that appears in most standard sources. Samuel Adams grew up in his father's house on Purchase Street in Boston. The Second Continental Congress met in the Pennsylvania assembly room on the ground floor of the State House. Most writers on the subjects say so, in words close to those, and I don't try to prove, credit, or expand on such statements.

I use notes to show sources for the wealth of less well-known information; explain interpretations; give credit to writers whose language I quote and paraphrase, and whose narratives and interpretations I follow; identify discrepancies in the primary and secondary records; air conflicting conclusions; admit interpretations other than those I advance; and suggest further reading on matters I hope readers will find interesting.

References are given by authors' last names (sometimes with first names, to clarify), with page numbers or chapter references where appropriate. Full bibliographical information is provided in the Sources section, which is limited to works I actually cite here. Where an author has more than one work in Sources, a note will give the abbreviated title of the work referred to. Where a note refers to a book not directly used in researching (*The Road to Wigan Pier*, for example), the full citation is given in the note, not in Sources.

Epigraphs

Page

ix "Who shall write": John Adams to Thomas Jefferson, July 30, 1815, in Adams, *Adams-Jefferson Letters*.

ix "All politics is local": Tip O'Neill, *Man of the House: The Life and Political Memoirs of Speaker Tip O'Neill*, with William Novak (New York: Random House, 1987), p. 26. O'Neill is quoting his father.

1. Cold Wind, Warm Election

Page

1 *May 1, 1776:* Weather: Marshall's diary entry, also cited by Hawke, *In the Midst*. Poll-opening time: Hawke, *In the Midst*,

p. 29, citing the *Pennsylvania Packet*. "The warmest election":
Caesar Rodney to Thomas Rodney, May 1, 1776, in Smith, also
cited by Hawke, *In the Midst.*

3 *Now that pause was over:* Standard sources on the period cover
the British naval threat. For detail on the withdrawal from Boston, see Allen, chapter 3. Chidsey, pp. 135–36, shows that the
British fleet of 1776 was the biggest sent from England. On
transports at sea, see James Warren to John Adams, April 30,
1776, in Adams, *Papers*, also cited by Allen. The British army's
reputation for musket fire and bayonet charge is well documented, for example in H. T. Dickinson, p. 479.

4 *"reconciliationists" opposed the "independents":* "Independents" was
the term used by contemporaries, with Hawke, *In the Midst*,
p. 112, giving a typical example; Jensen in particular uses "reconciliationists." Some writers use "radicals" versus "moderates." I
use "radical" only for those who wanted fundamental change in
society and government (see especially chapter 2)—by no means
all who wanted American independence, as this story shows.

4 *Already called the keystone:* Jensen, p. 682, sums up Pennsylvania's pivotal role as leader of a middle-colony bloc against independence. Montross, pp. 149–50, actually says "as Pennsylvania
goes, so goes the nation," placing that observation as late as June
1776. For delegates' references to the province as an obstacle to
independence: New Hampshire Delegates to the President of
New Hampshire, May 28, 1775; Richard Henry Lee to Charles
Lee, April 22 and May 11, 1776; John Adams to Horatio Gates,
March 23, 1776; all in Smith. In seeing the Mayday election as

a kind of colonial referendum on independence, I largely follow Hawke, *In the Midst*, pp. 24, 30.

6 *Samuel Adams of Boston:* All biographers cover Adams's vital statistics and tremor, arrival in town for the second Congress, rooming arrangements, quick trip to Boston, etc. His view of moral conditions in Pennsylvania and the middle colonies can be seen in letters of December 4 and 19, 1776, in Smith. For an example of his sense of the moral condition of Boston, and for the famous line "We cannot make events": Adams to John Scollay, June 30, 1776, in Smith. Samuel Adams as a rider: John Adams to James Warren, September 17, 1775, in Smith. Rakove, pp. 91–92, supports my sense of Samuel's outward confidence and steadiness under urgent pressure. For more on his activities in Boston, see chapter 7.

6 *cousin John, his top deputy:* Wills, pp. 21–22, 23–25. For more, see chapter 7.

10 *Closing the polls:* I follow Hawke's account, *In the Midst*, pp. 15–17.

10 *The election results:* Hawke and Rosswurm draw opposing conclusions from the results. Rosswurm, p. 92, denies that the turnout was heavy (although his footnote 69 does not, to me, dispel Ryerson's demonstration, pp. 173–74, that it probably was), and he thinks many nonqualified voters were turned away. To him, the result shows no victory for reconciliation but a last-ditch effort to stem a rising tide.

Hawke, *In The Midst*, pp. 33–34, emphasizes the failure of

the independence ticket as evidence that upscale voters had been turned off by radicals' association of independence with social change. He couples that shrewd reading with the idea, illogical to me, that a majority of the population, especially in the countryside, was anti-independence on May 1 and then pro-independence after May 20, solely as a result of an aggressive minority's manipulating lower-class Pennsylvania opinion during those weeks (Hawke, chapter 4).

My conclusion is that Pennsylvania's electorate, including the legally enfranchised and at least some of the legally unenfranchised, who misrepresented their credentials (Hawke, *In the Midst*, quoting Paine, p. 34), voted at least 50 percent against independence on May 1, no doubt partly to avoid radical change in the franchise itself; and a majority of the less enfranchised were no doubt already in full support of independence by May 1, as a condition and corollary of their hope for gaining legal access to the franchise (see chapter 2). Presumably because representation had been expanded for the election (as discussed in chapter 2), Wills calls the majority-reconciliationist assembly "the last and most democratically elected lower house on the continent" (p. 30). It doesn't follow that any effort to overturn that house could have occurred only through sudden manipulation of an otherwise complacent lower class, as Hawke has it. Rosswurm's work helps show that, and Rosswurm puts succinctly his thesis regarding the radicals I introduce in chapter 2: "They didn't stage a revolution, they led one" (p. 94).

2. Samuel Adams and the Secret Meeting

Page

11 *Two days after the independents' failure:* Day, time, and weather: Marshall's diary entry. I think Hawke was the first to show that Marshall made many entries documenting radical cohort meetings with Samuel and John Adams throughout the crucial period. Those meetings went unrecorded by both Samuel Adams (characteristically) and John Adams (uncharacteristically, and so revealingly, as later chapters explore). Whether Young was with Marshall and Cannon through all their rounds on May 3 the diary entry leaves ambiguous, but Hawke *In the Midst*, p. 131, is sure Young was in the Adamses' rooms that evening.

14 *Thomas Young:* The story is mainly drawn from Maier, "Reason and Revolution," and Hawke, "Dr. Thomas Young." Both rely on and expand Edes. Hawke notes that Young was radical before the Stamp Act. Maier offers much fascinating detail on Young as an innovative doctor and suggestively connects his medical theory and practice to his politics. Nash, pp. 355–65, discusses Young's role in Boston organizing. For Young's influence on Ethan Allen: Pell, pp. 13–19. Anderson shows that contrary to Allen's claim (and Vermont tradition), Young was the author of *Oracles of Reason,* known colloquially as *Ethan Allen's Bible.*

15 *Those leaders called themselves "Whigs":* The high-Whig ideology of the famous American resistance leaders is well documented and widely known. It was put well by William Pitt, Lord

Chatham, to the House of Lords on May 27, 1774, quoting a Massachusetts circular letter of 1768: "... it is an essential, unalterable right in nature, ingrafted into the British Constitution as a fundamental law, and ever held sacred and irrevocable by the subjects within this realm, that what a man has honestly acquired is absolutely his own, which he may freely give, but which can not be taken from him without his consent." Pitt's point to the Lords was that this was "no new doctrine," and he took it all the way, connecting natural rights to ultimate truth: "the appeal" of Massachusetts, he told them, "is to heaven." "The Speeches of Lord Chatham," www.classicpersuasion.org/cbo/chatham/index .htm#NC.

Bernard Bailyn's *The Ideological Origins of the American Revolution* (Cambridge, Mass.: Harvard University Press, 1967), is the definitive source for long-standing Whig and "country party" ideas—and fantasies—in the American resistance leadership, and those ideas' connection to republicanism. Maier, *From Resistance*, chapter 2, traces the American resistance's connections to the "Real Whig" and "Commonwealthman" traditions. Everdell's chapters 7 and 8 connect American republicanism to the English Civil War in a learned, illuminating, and especially exciting way.

Because I think readers have been given ample reason to mistake an upper-class Whig drive toward American independence and republicanism for a drive toward American democracy, and to miss connections between actual American desires for democracy and eighteenth-century working-class radicalism, I take care to distinguish Whig from democrat. John Adams the republican was concerned to distinguish them, too, abominating radical democracy. Thomas Young and James Cannon, the radical democrats, abominated elite privilege and learning (even as they and Adams collaborated distrustfully in 1776).

Thompson's chapter 4, with its discussion of the "Norman yoke" reading of English history, shows how the working class was able to connect its aspirations with high-Whig iconography and why radicals like Young and Paine, railing against inequities based on Whig privilege, nevertheless drew on Whig language to frame radical efforts for equality. Rosswurm discusses the issue as well, pp. 86–88, and Foner notes, p. 76, that Paine's radical denunciation of the English constitution was made "in the familiar language of the Commonwealthmen." George Orwell may be responding to that tradition when, in *The Road to Wigan Pier* (New York: Harcourt Brace, 1958), he advises English socialists to improve public receptiveness to their ideas by framing them less in terms of equality than in terms of liberty, a more broadly acceptable concept.

16 *did not qualify to vote:* Nobody denies the definitive force of the property qualification. The Pitt citation above shows how long and how reflexively rights had been connected to ownership. Examples range from Wood, *The Radicalism of the American Revolution* (New York: Knopf, 1992), pp. 178–79, explaining the perceived connection between property and independent political judgment, to John Adams in "Thoughts on Government" (discussed in chapters 7 and 9), making related points.

On the other hand, Robert E. Brown, in *Middle-Class Democracy and the Revolution in Massachusetts* (Ithaca, N.Y.: American Historical Association and Cornell University Press, 1955), presented evidence to show that in Massachusetts, and by implication also elsewhere in America, virtually all white male adults could vote legally, and that those who couldn't vote legally voted anyway. To historians ruling out social class as a significant element in the revolutionary period, that study seemed to come as a relief almost palpable in their pages; see Edmund Morgan, *The Birth of the Republic* (Chicago: University of Chicago Press, 1992), p. 8, and notes to pp. 186–87. Brown's work has been adopted without much reflection in circles where a founding American consensus is emphasized over founding American class conflict.

Jesse Lemisch, in Bernstein, pp. 3–29, wittily and persuasively demolishes Brown's methodology and interpretation, as well as the context in which Brown's conclusions have been embraced (he cites a study that uses the same statistical approach to arrive at the conclusion that nobody was enfranchised at all). From an entirely different point of view, Hawke also rejects Brown's conclusions and cites reliable sources suggesting that about 90 percent of the taxable male population in Philadelphia was unenfranchised (p. 34, footnote 5). Historians who present broad suffrage as the norm routinely ignore higher property qualifications for standing for office (Lemisch makes that point as well).

The story I tell in this book shows that many thousands of Pennsylvanians rallied so fervently to suffrage and officeholding for the unpropertied that they overturned a government. Almost all of the new American constitutions took care, for articulate reasons, to impose property qualifications. As discussed in later chapters, John Adams reacted with horror to the openness of the franchise in the Pennsylvania constitution of

1776 (despite, or perhaps because of, having secretly helped enable it), as well as the push by western Massachusetts for what radical democrats called "manhood suffrage," with no property qualification.

Given the origins of Whig ideas about rights, liberty, and the nature of constitutional law itself, how could any eighteenth-century American have imagined disconnecting property from voting rights *except* by a radical break from the past represented by Magna Carta? Paine, as discussed in chapter 5, rejected virtually the whole history of British constitutionalism, making the break in Pennsylvania, if painful, intellectually clean.

17 *Sons of Liberty:* Hoerder calls the Boston Sons a "middle class dining club after 1768" (p. 139) and emphasizes the club's non-artisan standing throughout its existence. Maier, *From Resistance*, gives probing study to the Sons, especially in chapters 3 and 4. I'm using "Sons of Liberty" as shorthand for a more complex and developing set, including the Loyal Nine. See Maier, *From Resistance*.

17 *Pope's Day:* On Pope's Day, see William Pencak, in Pencak, Dennis, and Newman, pp. 133–35; Hoerder, pp. 72–73, 75, 94–95, 97–101. For engaging and important work on relationships among elite leaders, Boston laborers, and gang members, and people in western Massachusetts, see all of Hoerder; also see Alfred Young, *The Shoemaker and the Tea Party* (Boston: Beacon, 1999).

19 *"committees of correspondence":* I closely follow Brown, pp. 133–41.

19 *James Cannon:* The story is drawn from Foner, p. 115; Ross-wurm, pp. 94, 102; Ryerson, pp. 112–15; Nash, p. 381; Hawke, *In the Midst*, pp. 105, 170. On the Bettering House: Nash, pp. 327–32, Foner, p. 46–47. Nash makes clear that poor relief in Philadelphia had formerly been a responsibility of city government. Because Marshall's many diary entries on meetings at the factory tail off when radicals start leading the City Committee, I think the factory was the first headquarters for radical planning.

In contrast to the writers cited above, Hawke, *In the Midst*, sees Cannon as an embittered loser, a conclusion unsupported by any fact he presents. Inspired by the work of Eric Hoffer, as well as his own skepticism about the oppression of the lower classes, Hawke takes it as axiomatic that all of the Philadelphia radical leaders were sociopaths (pp. 103, 106), and his speculations about Cannon's supposed resentment, presented as fact, are a prime example (p. 105). I concur in Hawke's description of Cannon as the quietest of the radicals, and in some ways the most able.

20 *many of the rest were impoverished:* Foner, pp. 23, 47.

22 *often rioted:* I draw on the wealth of literature on long traditions of crowd actions in Europe and America, referred to very briefly in this chapter. Hoerder's introduction and chapter 1 break down styles and purposes of crowd action to a degree possibly found nowhere else. Pencak, Dennis, and Newman offer a compelling set of essays on American rioting. For a larger context, spanning village regulation in Europe and political and labor protest in Europe and America, good places to start include

Alfred Young's "English Plebian Culture," in Margaret Jacob and James Jacob, eds., *Origins of Anglo-American Radicalism* (Boston: Allen & Unwin, 1984); Edward Countryman's *The American Revolution* (New York: Hill & Wang, 2003); Georges Rudé's *The Crowd in History* (London: Lawrence & Wishart, 1981); and E.P. Thompson's *Customs in Common* (New York: New Press, 1993).

22 *Philadelphia artisans and mechanics:* "Artisan" and "mechanic" were common terms with complex definitions. For nuance and detail lacking in my account, Foner is illuminating on both the terminology and the classes themselves, relying in part on figures supplied by Nash, clarifying differences among higher and lower self-employed craftsmen (pp. 28–29), tracing the developing connections between artisans and the poorer laborers, and calling the politicization of the mass of citizens the most important development in Philadelphia's politics from 1766 to 1776 (pp. 56–57). Nash, p. 377, describes the artisan march on the Whig committee, as well as the rise of working-class demands from 1770 on (pp. 374–82). In 1774 and 1775, middle-class artisans seeking a voice in politics became increasingly involved in the patriot city committees; by 1776, unenfranchised lower-class artisans and laborers with similar goals had become organized via militias (as discussed below); the various groups were powerfully allied and integrated through the leadership of Marshall, Cannon, Young, and their cohort. For more on the city committees in particular, see the next note.

22 *Pennsylvania's patriot committees:* I use the simplifying term "City Committee" to cover all phases of the extralegal Philadelphia

groups that began as the Committee of Forty-Three, became the Sixty-Six, then the First One Hundred, then the Second One Hundred. Ryerson details all iterations of them in his chapters 3–5, delineating class shifts in membership from prosperous politicians to the radicals (Ryerson supports his argument with exhaustive tables, charts, and statistics), as well as the committees' impact on both local and larger events in Philadelphia. Ryerson also uses "city committee" at times for the Second One Hundred.

24 *Committee of Privates:* I closely paraphrase Nash, p. 379, in describing the Committee of Privates as a school of labor politics and a folk echo of the New Model Army. Foner, pp. 62–66, notes that while artisan interest was motivated to enter the committees in 1774, laboring interest was motivated via the militia in 1775–76. Hawke, *In the Midst*, takes a characteristically dimmer view of the Privates (pp. 147–50), describing what Nash and Foner see as a vastly successful organizing effort as mere propaganda to manufacture aggrievement in young men who would, if left alone by the radicals, have been having "the time of their lives" (p. 149) in militia service.

24 *soldiers known as Levellers:* For the debates, see Wootton, pp. 285–317. Nash, p. 343, discusses the folk tradition of a Cromwell-era democratic working-class movement, and of the story of Cornet George Joyce. Thompson, pp. 22–25, is indispensable on the Putney debates as a foundation for English working-class consciousness. I think the Pennsylvania story of 1776, which Thompson lacks, provides an essential supplement to Thompson's first four chapters. The transatlantic link is Paine,

man of both Pennsylvania revolution and Thompson's "Radical London." For more on that, see chapter 5.

25   *now, in Pennsylvania in 1776:* Rosswurm's chapter 2 explores in detail the militia's call for radical democracy; his chapter 3 discusses the explosion of radicalism leading up to the May 1 election. Concurring with Rosswurm, Nash, p. 380, emphasizes the Privates' and artisans' focus on expanding suffrage and removing the property qualification.

26   *Christopher Marshall:* The story is drawn from Hawke, *In the Midst,* p. 103; Foner, pp. 109–11; and Marshall himself. For pharmacy as a less-than-reputable, only recently regulated business, see Kremers and Sonnedecker, pp. 155–62. Tolles, *Meeting House,* pp. 79–80, shows that Marshall's expulsion from the meeting occurred in 1751, long before he endorsed fighting the British, to which some writers have incorrectly ascribed his break with the Quaker establishment. For Marshall in the Free Quaker Meeting, see England and Kramer, p. 348. Marshall expresses the fervency of his faith in a diary entry for June 14, 1775, and his interest in universalism in entries for May 9, 1775, and March 18, 1776.

27   *And other religious groups joined:* For nudity in early Quaker, Ranter, and "Adamite" enthusiasms, see Cressey's chapter 15. For early Quaker intensity about politics, and the move in English Quakerism toward "quietism": Tolles, "Quakerism." Objections to "the ranting spirit" and the urging of discipline can be found in late-seventeenth-century Quaker tracts, as discussed by Weddle, pp. 34–36. For the Diggers: Rexroth's chapter 10.

For thorough, accessible discussions of a host of English non-conformist sects, see "English Dissenters," http://exlibris.org/nonconform/engdis/index.html.

Nash, pp. 342–47, gives texture to the urban, eighteenth-century American evangelical left. On the Great Awakening's social and economic radicalism and resistance to England: Heimert, passim, showing liberal theology as more naturally allied with upper-class Whig values than with democracy, and evangelical fervor more closely allied with working-class consciousness; see especially his chapter 10 for the democratic opposition of evangelicals to John Adams's Massachusetts constitution of 1780.

Natural connections between social and religious radicalism in the eighteenth century are explored in Thompson's chapter 2—and Thompson brings to light the alliance, counterintuitive today, between Deist skepticism and religious evangelicalism in English radical dissent at the close of the eighteenth century. The group in the Adamses' rooms on May 3 bears out an American version of that alliance. In chapter 10 herein, the same group bears out the diminishment of radical energy that Thompson discerns in the opposition of reason and religion in the nineteenth century.

29 *Marshall's shop:* Philadelphia College of Pharmacy, England and Kramer, p. 348.

30 *They'd drunk a lot of coffee:* Marshall notes with precision many times and places of coffee drinking. In the late winter and spring of 1775, those notations become so constant and pronounced that it is tempting to read "drank coffee with" as code

for "schemed with"—but too many of the occasions seem purely social and domestic.

30 *Thomas McKean's house:* For McKean's rising law practice, commitment to republicanism, and gravitation toward independence: Rowe's chapters 2–5. Rowe refers to McKean's brashness, p. 18, and discusses the relationship with the Adamses, pp. 57–58. Coleman, pp. 27, 52, describes McKean's physical intensity, domineering personality, pride, and ostentation, and mentions McKean's "hand in glove" work with local radicals and his lifelong secrecy about it (pp. 143–44), following Hawke, *In the Midst,* on the secret coalition's plans (p. 153).

31 *Thus advised and coordinated:* My discussion of Samuel Adams's and the City Committee's ploys are drawn from Hawke, *In the Midst,* pp. 19–22; Ryerson, p. 162; Jacobson, pp. 107–8.

32 *Samuel Adams was genial:* The most famous description of Adams is "eats little, drinks less, thinks much," in Galloway, *Reflections,* p. 67. John Adams, for one, saw Samuel as genteel and urbane, with an easy manner (Ferling, p. 45) and polished and refined (Adams to Morse, December 5, 1815, Adams, *Papers*). Samuel Adams's managing his own impatience: Samuel Adams to Joseph Hawley, April 15, 1776; Samuel Adams to James Warren, April 16, 1776, both in Smith. Good discussions of his attitudes about working-class crowds and his efforts to blur class differences and maintain traditional unity in Boston can be found in Hoerder, pp. 22, 218; and Nash, pp. 356–77, 361–62, 381–82.

Adams's religion, his theories of government, and the purposes of his organizing have been the subject of much discussion, with wildly varied conclusions. Some biographers see Adams as a complete Puritan throwback, others as a radically democratic populist, others as a ruthless, manipulative egomaniac. The best historiographical overview is Maier, "Coming to Terms," usefully skeptical about the construction of a populist "Sam" Adams, and also about his supposed control of all things revolutionary as single cause of the American resistance. That critique dovetails intriguingly with Alexander, the only biographer to address a salient issue in Samuel Adams studies, the degree to which the crowds that Adams supposedly controlled had what scholars call "agency" of their own. Biography has generally not served exploration of that or other questions that Adams's activities raise. For more on him, and on those issues, see chapter 7 herein; also see notes to chapter 8 on Massachusetts' western radicalism.

33 *overthrow the keystone province:* On the existence of the local radicals' plan to void the May 1 election and extralegally replace the government, in coordination with the independents in the Congress: Hawke, *In the Midst* (pp. 112–17, 130–31, and passim), Ryerson (pp. 208–16), Rosswurm (pp. 93–100), Wills (pp. 29–31), and Jensen (pp. 682–87). Rosswurm, p. 94, dates the beginning of the effort specifically to May 3. Regarding Samuel Adams's coordination of that effort, Wills points out that Adams covered his tracks and bluntly calls the events in Pennsylvania of 1776 "Samuel Adams's revolution" (p. 22). Hawke, describing John Adams's efforts in the Congress, pp. 112–14, notes that Samuel would actually have been the driving force. Maier, *Scripture,* inveterately skeptical about any effort to make Samuel Adams the explanation for everything otherwise hard to explain, nevertheless concedes, p. 68, that regarding the Phila-

delphia situation, evidence supports Adams's hidden centrality. Adams's contemporaries, who agreed on little else, agreed on his primacy in bringing about independence from behind the scenes: Jefferson, quoted (secondhand, at least) by Wells, pp. 423–24; John Adams, *Political Writings*, p. 695; Galloway, "Reflections," pp. 67, 109.

3. The Revolution Is Now Begun

Page

35 *The Revolution Is Now Begun:* Ryerson's title.

35 *royal peace commission:* For examples of reconciliationists' hopes and independents' fears of a commission: Joseph Reed to George Washington, March 3 and 15, 1776; James Warren to John Adams, March 7, 1776; James Duane to Robert Livingston, March 20, 1776; all in Smith. John Adams mocks the very idea of commissioners in letters to Abigail Adams, April 15, 1776, and Mercy Warren, April 16, 1776, as does Samuel Adams to Joseph Hawley, April 15, 1776, all in Smith. On the colonies' having plausible ways to negotiate a separate peace in the absence of a declaration and union: Wills, pp. 49–52. On foreign alliance as a major purpose of adopting independence: Wills, pp. 325–29 (Wills calls it *the* major purpose).

37 *mercenary troops:* The May 6 confirmation of the rumors as supporting independents: Ryerson, pp. 208–9. (Jensen, p. 670, notes that the treaties were not actually published in Philadelphia until May 21.) On the horror of foreign troops: Jensen, pp. 669–70;

Hawke, *In the Midst*, pp. 92–93; Montross, pp. 140–41; Declaration of Independence. Samuel Adams's Hessian calculation: Jensen, p. 669.

38 *Down the Delaware River:* I closely follow Shomette's chapter 3. Ryerson, p. 209, presents the *Roebuck*'s approach and repulsion as lending credence to independents' arguments.

41 *"There is reason that would induce":* Samuel Adams to Samuel Cooper, April 30, 1776, in Smith.

42 *at the State House:* The Second Continental Congress is merely glimpsed here in spring 1776. For its activities throughout this story, I've used Jensen's later chapters in detail. Rakove offers a strong modern study of the body, showing clearly that even late in the process independence still seemed remote. He also focuses on consensus, seeing independence emerging "as a logical conclusion" from a set of developing factors, and noting that the Adams-Lee alliance could not have controlled everything that happened in the Congress (Samuel Adams said that, too). That there was an Adams-Lee alliance, and that it tried to control as much as it could, Rakove concedes, and he concurs with other scholars in seeing the May 15 preamble as an effort to overthrow Pennsylvania. He lacks the story of the local radical coalition with the Adamses, which others whom I cite see as throwing a different light on the "logical conclusion" reading.

Burnett remains an important source for all of the Congress's activities, with Montross developing Burnett entertainingly; both write in strikingly old-fashioned styles. I base my estimates of number of delegates on Montross's lists, pp. 426–31.

For the period covered by this book, Hazelton is a great source, old-fashioned in a different way, funny, skeptical, astonishingly comprehensive. I've also relied heavily on the delegates themselves, in Smith.

Many of those writers describe the pressures and minutiae facing the congressmen. On the bad mood: Wills, p. 37; John Adams to Abigail Adams, September 25, 1774, saying "skittish," in Smith; Burnett, p. 147, quoting Hewes of North Carolina.

43 *Members held a variety of opinions:* Jensen, pp. 641–45, surveys the status of instructions. Head provides much background and theory on why and how various colonies went pro- or anti-independence. On Hancock in the Congress: Adams, *Autobiography*, sheet 20, sheet 33; Jensen, p. 652; Wills, p. 24. Samuel Adams and Hancock had fallen out temporarily in Boston, too, in the early 1770s. On Hancock's sartorial style: Hawke, *Honorable*. On lobbying out of doors: Wills, pp. 20–21 (referring to 1774, when instructions had been looser). On the need for Virginia and Massachusetts to step up: Jensen, pp. 670–71.

46 *On big issues, they sought delay:* Adams, *Autobiography*, sheets 31, 32, 35.

46 *committee of the whole:* On the history of the mechanism: Schneider, pp. 1–2, quoting De Alva Stanwood Alexander. For the uses of the committee in the Congress: Burnett's chapter 9.

48 *The resolution's existence:* See the *Journal*, week of June 6, 1776, for my tracking the resolution's progress through committee, starting Tuesday the 7th. Note that Robert Taylor, editor of John Adams's *Papers*, rightly says that other matters may also have

been discussed in the committee of the whole that week, and we therefore can't absolutely know how debate progressed before the resolution's adoption May 10 (Adams, *Papers*, vol. 4, pp. 11–12, footnote 1). I think my narration takes the caveat into account, and I also rely on John Adams, *Autobiography*, sheet 35, where he complains, with precise reminiscence of May 6, about the opposition's use of small matters in the committee of the whole to block consideration of big matters such as his resolution. Adams's knowledge that objecting to wasting time only wasted more time (referred to later in the chapter): sheet 35.

My presenting the resolution's real nature as an attack on Pennsylvania represents the consensus of Hawke, Wills, Jensen, Ryerson, Ferling, and Foner, who view both the resolution and its preamble (regarding which, see chapter 6) as "unquestionably aimed" at Pennsylvania (Hawke on the preamble, p. 120; see also Jensen, pp. 683–84; Foner, pp. 127–28). Ferling calls it a "thinly veiled ploy" (p. 146). Hawke describes Dickinson as having "enervated" the resolution with his response, and John Adams as refusing to be "outmaneuvered" when bringing in the preamble on May 15 (p. 120); Wills says the Adams faction was "stymied" by Dickinson's interpretation of the resolution and that the preamble was a comeback (p. 32); Ryerson calls Pennsylvania the resolution's "prime target" and says that Dickinson's move "forced" Adams to write the preamble (p. 212). Jensen implies that Dickinson merely assumed the resolution didn't apply, yet joins the others in saying Dickinson "underestimated" Adams when leaving town, which Jensen also deems an error in tactics (p. 684).

4. The Farmer Immovable

51 *John Adams had an explanation for Dickinson's:* Adams's calling Dickinson's assembly a Quaker and proprietary interest: in Smith, Adams to Benjamin Hitchborn, May 29, 1776, and Adams to Horatio Gates, March 23, 1776; Adams, *Autobiography*, sheets 18, 19, 39; Adams, *Diary*, September 24, 1775. Adams's view of Dickinson's temperament and family: Adams, *Autobiography*, sheets 19–20; Adams, *Diary*, October 24, 1774. According to Flower, Joseph Reed was the source of the story about the excessive influence of Dickinson's wife and mother-in-law.

52 *John Dickinson knew only:* The most reliable biographer is Flower, correcting older work by Charles Stillé (which also see). I follow Flower, pp. 1–30, on the family and upbringing, the time in London, the developing attitudes about England, the law practice in Philadelphia, and identification with Whig ideals. See also Bregman on Dickinson and Tacitus. Like John Adams, but with greater sympathy, Flower sees Dickinson as temperamentally cautious. Jacobson, focusing on the revolutionary period, disagrees. I follow Jacobson's arguments in understanding Dickinson's principles and temperament. Jacobson also clarifies Dickinson's politics as defending not the proprietary interest but the charter. For greater specificity, see notes below.

55 *Benjamin Franklin:* The exhaustive day-to-day source is Lemay—but only through the 1750s. Lemay's third volume

was published while I was concluding research, and I haven't contended with it here; Lemay's death in 2008 leaves us in suspense as to how his deeply Americanist Franklin squares with the Franklin who courted royal government in the 1760s, and I hope notes or other portions of his volume 4 will be published as well. Wood believably presents a Franklin who until his humiliation at the hands of British government was a committed, ambitious British imperialist. Franklin's electrical experiments, international fame, and amazing range of lasting discoveries and inventions have been widely documented, as have details on the kite experiment. For the electrical rigging of his home, Franklin, *Works*, p. 435.

59 *Paxton Boys:* Along with Newcomb, pp. 71–79, I follow Hindle, still the standard source on the Paxtons' activities. Also see my "Early American Insurrections," in *A Blackwell Companion to American Military History*, ed. James Bradford (Malden, Mass.: Wiley-Blackwell, 2009), p. 624.

60 *Benjamin Franklin wanted royal government:* Newcomb says Franklin's hope for royal government went back to the 1750s, and he explains Franklin's petitioning for it on the basis of proprietary incompetence, certainty that rights in the 1701 charter would be left intact, and confidence in his influence with the Board of Trade (pp. 79–82). Wood explains the move in light of what he presents as Franklin's naturally imperial mind-set. But Franklin's focus on the evils of the proprietor, to the exclusion of almost all else, has not been satisfactorily explained to me. In all of Franklin's varied schemes of government, the one element for which there is no place is the proprietor. His

political life pre-1776 is often reduced in popular narratives to his authorship of the Albany plan of union, sometimes loosely seen as presaging American independence. That plan, like all of Franklin's efforts—until they were drowned in the American resistance that he failed to see coming, and then failed to understand—may reasonably be considered as yet another tactic for rendering proprietary government irrelevant in Pennsylvania. In the end, Franklin swung all the way around from royalism to the independence that ended the proprietary government, defeated his enemy Dickinson, and harried the ministry that had rejected him. See chapter 10 herein.

61 *Hence his fury with Franklin's plan:* I largely follow Newcomb's narrative, pp. 82–100.

61 *American charters:* The sacredness, to the high-Whig mind, of charters relates to the discussion of property rights in notes to chapter 2. Even before the signing of the Magna Carta, documentation of natural rights—usually a list of specific restraints on government, not an assertion of rights of individuals or groups—was considered necessary to guaranteeing liberty. The Americans focused on their colonies' founding (sometimes revised) charters, which established their colonial governments. "Several acts of the British parliament, tending to the entire subversion of our natural and charter rights": that and very similar language appears in hundreds of revolutionary-era public documents produced by towns, counties, militias, committees, and colonial assemblies. (Internet-searching "natural and charter rights" in itself returns a fairly overwhelming array.) Henry I's promise not to quarter his household by force, in the 1130–33

London charter of self-government, has been widely seen as an ancestor of the Third Amendment to the Constitution of the United States, which forbids housing soldiers in private homes without the owner's consent.

61 *instructions to:* Newcomb, p. 50. It was Lord Granville, the Prime Minister, who told Franklin that royal governors' instructions were ironclad; Newcomb says that Granville was wrong, and that Franklin knew it, but that Franklin also knew he'd have trouble convincing the ministry of that. I take the point that the quest for royal government was unlikely to result in greater practical latitude for the representative branch—especially in the 1760s. Franklin's real attitude about that fact I find mysterious.

61 *wouldn't have a lightning rod:* The assertion appears, weakly sourced, in multiple popular Franklin biographies.

62 *Joseph Galloway:* My main source is Newcomb, who probes deeply, yet is notably partisan for his two subjects. Long-standing assembly-proprietary tensions in Pennsylvania government: Newcomb, pp. 17–19. The rise of Franklin's party in the context of the militia bills, and the involvement of Galloway: Newcomb, pp. 34–36. Tolles, pp. 24–28, adds nuance to the story of a do-nothing assembly, saying the assembly did in fact pass militia bills, couching them in vague language; he also sees the shift from strict-Quaker hegemony as less solely a result of Franklin's effort than Newcomb does, and provides much interesting detail on the Quakers' Indian relations, in the context of global-imperial politics. Franklin in London, Galloway

in Pennsylvania, their party's hegemony, and grievances against the proprietor: Newcomb, pp. 41–47, 50–68.

62 *Together they'd fended off:* Newcomb, pp. 41–45.

63 *Dickinson firmly asserted all the arguments: Writings*, pp. 21–49. In the Bonsal & Niles 1801 edition, "armed force" is capitalized; in some other editions it is italicized.

64 *Joseph Galloway stood at once to rebut:* Galloway, "Speech."

64 *the Philadelphia pamphlet war:* I follow Flower, pp. 40–41, on the unedifying back-and-forth in the pamphlet war. Where Newcomb routinely calls Dickinson's new party "the proprietary party" (e.g., p. 90), Jacobson argues persuasively that Dickinson was at odds with the proprietor, yet stood on a belief that power must be "limited by fundamental or constitutional principles" and that order, as desired by Franklin, was less important to Dickinson than liberty and law (p. 19). Jacobson also presents Dickinson as more sensitive than Franklin to London's tendency to remove liberty (p. 20)—undeniably, it seems to me. On Dickinson and Penn in London: Flower, p. 15.

65 *In the election:* Newcomb, pp. 82–100.

66 *a circular letter:* Flower, p. 40.

67 *Dickinson sought new ways:* On Dickinson's rise in the countrywide resistance, his ups and downs at home, and his uniquely

consistent parsings of the trade laws and how to resist them, I am influenced by Jacobson's chapters 3 and 4. For more on Franklin's battle in London, and his return to America, see Newcomb, chapters 4–9.

67 Letters from a Farmer: Dickinson, *Writings* (and see the fine summary in Jacobson, pp. 45–55). On the "slippery slope": *Farmer* 7 and 11. On the absence of an internal/external distinction and the right of Parliament to regulate trade: *Farmer* 6. On the duty to resist tyranny, *Farmer* 12.

69 *Dickinson was the most important:* Also see notes to chapter 2. There is much detail in Jacobson's chapter 5 on Dickinson in City Committee ploys with Thomas Mifflin, Charles Thomson, and other high-Whig Pennsylvania patriots—many of whom would soon, unlike him, become independents—and on the work of all those patriots with the Adamses. Also in that chapter, Jacobson covers Dickinson's growing discomfort with the artisan membership, his withdrawal from the committee, and ultimately his opposition to it.

In this context, readers may be interested in considering John Adams's much-quoted recollection, from 1822, of the Massachusetts delegation's being met, on its way into Philadelphia for the first Congress, by local patriots who warned the Adamses not to openly espouse independence, as that position was unpopular and the Massachusetts men were feared and disdained in the middle colonies (Adams, *Works*, vol. 2, p. 512). The letter containing the recollection is tendentious, glossing over compromised activities Adams engaged in, taking credit for other people's achievements, and depicting Adams himself as unfairly persecuted. It is unsupported in certain key details by Adams's own diary entry for the same scene (Adams, *Diary*, number 21).

Regardless of accuracy, however, Adams would have been referring to secret collaborations with the City Committee when that committee was led by upscale men he admired, including, at that point, Dickinson. In 1774, the Adamses were still conspiring with Dickinson, McKean, and others against Galloway, not yet conspiring against Dickinson with the independents in the Congress and the committee radicals.

The salient issue to me is that John Adams referred in writing to collaborating secretly with famous men like Mifflin, Thomson, and Richard Henry Lee (and Rush, when he had joined that company). He did not mention by name (except, in other contexts, to excoriate them) the radicals with whom he and Samuel collaborated so closely in overthrowing an elected government in Pennsylvania. Even while events unfolded during the second Congress, Adams was blurring the distinction between the earlier, more gentlemanly committee, whose names he had enjoyed dropping in 1774, and the scruffy radical core he worked with closely but didn't name in 1776. See his letter to James Warren, March 21, 1776 (in Smith), where Adams can't help revealing his back-channel role, with Samuel Adams, in getting representation expanded for the May 1 Pennsylvania election. There he mentions secret connections with members of the City Committee. He doesn't name them, and Warren might have been inclined to assume that Adams was still referring to the likes of upscale men like Thomas Mifflin and Joseph Reed, not Matlack, Paine, Marshall, and Cannon, whom Adams later dismissed (*Autobiography*, sheet 23) as irresponsible democrats.

On the end of Galloway in Pennsylvania (and the end of the Franklin-Galloway partnership): Newcomb, pp. 278–98. On Dickinson as the leader of the powerful middle-colony bloc: Jensen, 617; and Jacobson, pp. 87–88, discussing the collaboration of Dickinson and James Duane of New York, and p. 100, calling July 1775 the peak of Dickinson's influence in America.

5. The State House and the Street

Page

73 *He was forty-four and still sickly:* Flower, p. 23; Adams, *Diary*, number 21.

73 *Their mutual sympathy was unfounded:* However, the early admiration of the Adamses for Dickinson is attested by the letter from Samuel Adams to James Warren, September 25, 1774, where Adams calls Dickinson "a true Bostonian" (the highest praise Adams could imagine bestowing), in Smith; and by John Adams's admiring description of Dickinson after an early meeting, Adams, *Diary*, September 12, 1774.

74 *"Our towns":* Dickinson to Arthur Lee, April 29, 1775, in Smith.

74 *"A Declaration of the Causes":* As adopted, it is often presented as Dickinson's toning down of Jefferson's more confrontational language. Julian Boyd, editor of Jefferson's papers, shows how Dickinson's draft actually made the document more confrontational than Jefferson's draft (Jefferson, *Papers*, pp. 187–92).

74 *"a measure of imbecility":* Adams, *Autobiography*, sheet 20.

74 *"a piddling genius":* John Adams to James Warren, July 24, 1774, in Smith. On the fallout: Adams, *Diary*, number 24.

75 *turned against him:* See notes to chapters 2 and 4, and Wills, pp. 30–31.

77 *Benjamin Franklin was back:* The Hutchinson letter episode is covered most fully by Bailyn, pp. 231–59, chapter 7, and succinctly by Wood, pp. 139–51. Bailyn quotes Franklin on "scapegoat," p. 238. The return to America is covered in all standard sources. For Franklin's early caginess and his commitment to independence: Wood, pp. 154–58. Adams, *Autobiography*, sheet 24, says of Franklin, "he was commonly as silent on committees as in Congress."

78 *Dickinson made a surprise move:* For Dickinson's argument, see Thomas Rodney to Caesar Rodney, May 19, 1776, quoted in Smith, pp. 62–63; cited and developed by Hawke, *In the Midst*, pp. 119–20. Also see notes to chapter 3 herein on the resolution and Dickinson's response. What we can't know is whether Dickinson embraced the resolution during debate in the committee of the whole or waited until debate was over and sprang the trap after the report was read. Writers have avoided the question by setting the whole event on the 10th, when the measure passed, as if it were brought in that day, too (Jensen does say the resolution had been brought in "a few days earlier"). That approach tends to blur relationships within the body and the measure's effect.

80 *Thomas Paine:* Hawke delineates Paine's role in the coalition, pp. 26, 33–35, 131–32, as does Foner's chapter 4. Paine's background, arrival, rise, and later activities are covered in all standard biographies. I rely mainly on Foner, whose focus is the revolutionary period, and Fruchtman, who places the whole life in the context of Paine's vision of liberty. Thompson's chapter 4, though lacking the Philadelphia story, is the great source for Paine's importance to pre-Owenite English radicalism, and for connections with Blake and Wollstonecraft. For Paine and Washington: Fruchtman, pp. 350–54. For Paine in prison: Fruchtman's chapter 15. "Mad Tom": caption to Cruikshank engraving, Fruchtman, illustrations. Foner, pp. 4–5, notes the degree of squalor Paine had seen, compared to that known by his American comrades.

83 *Paine had done some writing:* Paine, *Writings*. See especially "African Slavery in America," "An Occasional Letter on the Female Sex," and "A Serious Thought."

84 *Benjamin Rush:* Hawke, *In the Midst*, p. 104; Fruchtman, pp. 60–62; Foner, pp. 109–15, 119; Nash, pp. 308, 321.

85 *a long and remarkable pamphlet:* I mingle Paine's thinking in *Common Sense* with some ideas shown even more clearly in *Rights of Man.*

For the American republican sense of the British constitution: Everdell, pp. 151–55.

Many writers hold that Paine said nothing new in *Common Sense,* but only said it in a new way. I disagree, and the unprecedented 1776 working-class revolution in Pennsylvania illuminates for me the freshness of Paine's vision, as first fully expressed in the pamphlet. Thompson, p. 92, writing mainly on *Rights of Man*, shows Paine departing from classic Whig ideology to find the right of revolution in the present and the future, not in Pitt's ancient past, and Thompson describes that attack on English constitutionalism as shocking. It was at least as shocking in the context of *Common Sense*.

Some historians have ignored or patronized the ideas about government in *Common Sense*, focusing almost exclusively on the call for independence and republicanism, at the expense of Paine's advocacy of democracy. John Adams, by contrast, focused much disconcerted attention on the pamphlet's proposed government (as discussed in chapter 7 herein), seeing the importance of the pamphlet in its call for democratic populism, not its call for American independence. Foner, p. 142, points out that in *Common Sense* Paine calls only for "broad," not manhood suffrage; it is in letters supporting the 1776 Pennsylvania constitution that Paine pushes hard for opening the franchise and against the property qualification.

88 *the May 8 Forester article:* Forester 4, "To the People," Paine, *Writings*, vol. 1.

6. *Der Alarm*

Page

91 *what made Dickinson leave:* Hawke, *In the Midst*, p. 121, takes it that Dickinson assumed Adams was now silenced and indepen-

dence forestalled, so it was time for a vacation; he cites the letter from Thomas Rodney to Caesar Rodney, *Rodney Letters*, p. 82. Jacobson says Dickinson "sensed no danger" (p. 110). No explanation is very satisfying. Coleman notes suggestively, p. 155, that Galloway had retired in similar fashion at a moment of crisis with Dickinson.

92 *John Adams's preamble: Journals*, May 15, 1776. Adams's sole authorship: Adams, *Autobiography*, sheet 24; Taylor in Adams, *Papers*, p. 11, footnote 1, and p. 187, footnote 2. See also notes on the resolution, chapter 5 herein.

94 *But Congress's business wasn't secret:* Ryerson, p. 212, notes with some amazement that on May 15 the radical committee discussed the resolution that the Congress had passed only hours earlier. Measures for secrecy are discussed by Montross, pp. 38, 98.

94 *Timothy Matlack:* Foner, pp. 109–11; Hawke, *In the Midst*, 103–4.

95 *The radicals hoped:* I don't think the day-to-day, hour-by-hour coordination between independents in the Congress and radicals in the committee, from May 6 to May 20, has been delineated so fully elsewhere, although it has all been documented, and other writers have referred to parts of it in detail. See Wills, p. 32; Hawke, *In the Midst*, chapter 5; and Rosswurm, pp. 94–95, closely tying actions of the radical movement to the support of the Congress through the resolution (and noting that Delaware and other states kept their governments even while

complying with the resolution). Ryerson, however, says only that Adams's preamble "solved the problem" facing the radicals (p. 212).

Another form of coordination, if looser, may be found in a petition to the Congress from the local chapter of the Committee of the Privates, coinciding with the week's other events. The *Journals* show that on the 11th, right after adoption of the resolution itself, a petition came in from the Privates, along with resolves of the officers (who by now were always concurring with the Privates). Only John Adams also mentions this May 11 petition, and I haven't been able to determine what it said. It probably addressed the Privates' demand to elect their own officers, even up to the rank of brigadier general. The petition was postponed and ignored by the committee, to Adams's specific frustration in *Autobiography*, sheet 35. On the 15th, with the preamble's passing, the Privates' petition disappears.

95 *First to speak:* Carter Braxton refers to the debate's ensuing for two to three days after the first reading (Braxton to Landon Carter, May 17, 1776, in Smith). The *Journal* says that on Monday discussion was postponed until Tuesday. In any event, the measure must have caused intense informal discussion from Monday through Wednesday, when it was officially debated and passed. On what was said and by whom: John Adams, *Diary*, "Notes of Debates," May 13–15.

101 *It was time:* My tally is the standard one, based on Carter Braxton's letter to Landon Carter, May 17, 1776, in Smith. But Smith, p. 20, footnote 3, observes that James Allen called the vote at 7–4. If Braxton is right, says Smith, Pennsylvania and

Maryland indeed abstained, but if Allen is right, North Carolina voted yes and Pennsylvania voted no. Maryland's walkout is also in Braxton's letter.

102 *the city was in turmoil:* I follow Hawke, *In the Midst,* chapter 6; Rosswurm, pp. 94–95; and Ryerson, pp. 211–16. The location of "Philosophical Hall" is not yet clear to me: the organization didn't yet have its building and often met at Christ Church School and at Carpenters' Hall. Hawke calls the gathering of May 15 and 16 a scheduled City Committee meeting; Ryerson corrects that, calling it an unofficial meeting, though initiated by committee members and the other radicals, specifically to give an impression of the committee's being subjected to spontaneous popular pressure (pp. 212–13 and related footnote 25). Hawke also states that the intention of the committee for the May 20 mass meeting was to prevent the assembly from sitting at all, citing Marshall's entry for May 16. Ryerson disagrees, saying the idea came up only in the unofficial meetings and may have been Marshall's alone, referring to the language of the protest as it was adopted by the crowd on May 20. Ryerson, p. 213, footnote 28, calls "quite plausible" Hawke's speculation, p. 135, that Paine was author of "The Alarm."

7. Blind Eyes

Page

105 *Of all the people John Adams hated:* Adams, *Autobiography,* sheets 9, 23; Adams to Jefferson, June 22, 1819, Adams, *Adams-Jefferson Letters.*

106 *Adams believed fervently:* "Thoughts on Government," in *Adams, Papers,* vol. 4. For more on the exclusion from the franchise of women and the unpropertied: Adams to James Sullivan, May 26, 1776. Breen traces Adams's development on these issues from "Novanglus" to "Thoughts." "Government of laws": in "Thoughts" (as "empire of laws"), quoting James Harrington.

107 *As a youth, he'd discovered:* Shaw, pp. 11–24, 35–36, 44–45, focusing on struggles in Adams's early Diary entries (which also see), citing the Tacitus quotation. Ferling draws on Shaw's emphasis on Adams's persistent struggle with vanity, self-recrimination, defiance, and envy (pp. 17–19). "The love of fame . . .": Adams's earliest Diary (June 1753–April 1754, September 1758–January 1759). "Oh!": Adams's earliest diary. "Pettifoggers": Shaw, p. 43, quoting Adams. Shaw discusses Adams as a "Yankee" evolution of the Puritan archetype (p. 11).

108 *Yet he faced frustration:* Shaw discusses the problematic relationship to Braintree politics and business, and Adams's irritable mood, pp. 47–48. See also Ferling, pp. 26–27. On circuit riding: Adams, Diary, number 15.

110 *were investors in the Hancock business:* The relationship with the Hancocks is drawn from Lewis, p. 3. On the Hancocks as smugglers: Wills, p. 39.

110 *Unlike John, Samuel knew:* Also see notes to chapters 1 and 2. Wells, the nineteenth-century hagiographer, is still a good source. Overshooting by constantly asserting New England primacy in all things revolutionary and Samuel Adams primacy

(especially over James Otis) in all things New England, Wells nevertheless makes an overwhelming case for Adams's central role in organizing Boston politics from well before election to the Massachusetts assembly, and he has a firm understanding of the harmony of Adams's resistance and the conservative values of Adams's father. That understanding, coming from a highly romanticized, upper-middle-class point of view, tracks intriguingly with Hoerder's "bottom-up" analysis, pp. 92–97, 139, which emphasizes elite Boston's commitment to traditional corporate unity in New England, in opposition to the egalitarian goals of the crowd. Where Wells is at pains to deny Adams's involvement in any popular protest that became unjustifiably violent, Hoerder shows that the Sons wanted to control and deploy, not empower, ordinary people's political action. They thus agree in dissenting from those like Miller, who makes Adams "Sam" and a democrat, his father a populist opposed to wealth.

111 *"Help, Lord":* Many sources quote the eulogy from the *Independent Advertiser* and note that Adams did most of the writing for that paper; only Alexander, p. 9, suggests that the obituary might as well have been written by Samuel Adams *fils*. I think it was, and that Adams *fils* was also its main audience and subject.

111 *inherited his father's public life:* Lewis, p. 10, emphasizing the connection of Adams Sr. to wealth, not populism, says the family lost a third of its wealth in the land-bank debacle. Fowler emphasizes the weakness of Boston's economy after the 1720s. Wells, pp. 7–10, 25–30, gives detail on the legal struggles. All sources discuss the caucus and Adams's rise through the town meeting. Fowler has a poor understanding of the meeting as a

concentration of elite power—instead see Hoerder, pp. 23–29—but is lively on the roles played by Adams Sr. and Elisha Cooke, Jr., in building the caucus.

112 *his friend William Billings:* "The Music of William Billings," article excerpts, Amaranth Publishing, www.amaranthpublishing .com/billings.htm.

115 *Yet he vacillated:* Shaw, pp. 53–54, emphasizing resentment in the election loss; Ferling, pp. 53–54., emphasizing Adams's jealousy. Adams, Diary and Autobiography, for this period, are critical to tracking his troubled relationship to Samuel and the Sons. Ferling uses an entry from 1768 to support a description of John's mood in 1766; he also states that Samuel communicated whispers in the town about John's lack of firmness in the cause, citing the Diary's chaise ride and dinner scene, where that issue doesn't in fact come up. In his entry on the Sons of Liberty picnic (which Ferling presents as resulting from the chaise ride scene, although it occurred a year earlier), John does mention being accused of weakness in the cause.

115 *Christian Sparta:* Adams uses the expression more than once, in disappointment at a falling off; for example, Adams to John Scollay, December 30, 1780, quoted in Wells, pp. 114–15.

116 *"What a blessing":* Samuel Adams to Christopher Gadsen, December 11, 1766, Adams, *Writings.*

116 *And in the end:* Ferling clarifies the importance of Samuel's operation to John's rise, and John's subservience to Samuel (pp. 46,

62, 67–68). Yet Ferling's chronology of the development of their relationship and of John's chronically mixed feelings, pp. 62–63, doesn't track ideally with Adams's *Diary*, the only really illuminating source for understanding John's mood and thought when taking up the court-closing cases and his relationship with Samuel and Boston politics.

Admirers have sometimes gone along with John himself in suggesting that Samuel's Boston Resolves were based on John's Braintree Resolves, not the other way round, but Wells makes clear that the Braintree Resolves were written only after John had conferred with Samuel; Samuel's Resolves were published in the Boston *Gazette* on September 19, 1764, and John's Resolves are dated September 24 (p. 66, footnote). As Wills says, with reference to 1774–76, John "moved in his cousin's wake" (p. 21), and being a member of Samuel's faction was "his principal claim to importance in the resistance movement" (p. 23).

119 *Boston Massacre trials:* Facts in the shootings themselves are covered in detail in many standard sources. It is the overwhelming consensus of historians that John Adams, far from acting in defiance of the Sons of Liberty, was approached by the Sons and assigned the role of Preston's lawyer, in exchange for election to the house. Zobel details the story (pp. 219–22, 331), basing it on the political situation in Boston, the failure of the loyalist Forrest to support John's version, and a smoking-gun letter from Josiah Quincy, Jr., clearly explaining to Quincy Sr. the Sons' role in approving defense attorneys; Zobel also discusses Samuel Adams's reasoning, which I follow closely. Wills (p. 23) fully endorses Zobel's analysis (he also notes John F. Kennedy's retelling John's version in *Profiles in Courage*). Ferling calls

the evidence provided by the Quincy letter "incontrovertible" (p. 67), and places the issue in the context of John's subservient relationship to Samuel and burning ambition to get into the house. Shaw, lacking the Quincy evidence but possessing insight into John Adams, hears the dissonances in John's own account and raises the matter of election to the house to wonder how badly John suffered as a result of the defense (pp. 58–59). Hoerder (p. 239) takes nearly for granted that John and Quincy were doing Samuel's and the Sons' bidding.

Interestingly, Lemisch dissents from Zobel's case for John Adams's complicity with the Sons in defending Preston. While everywhere else in his essay, Lemisch demonstrates Zobel's tendentious Toryism, I don't think he does so with respect to John Adams's role in the trials.

For trial scheduling and preparation: Zobel, pp. 219–30. For John Adams's lawyering: Zobel, chapters 18 and 19, also distilled by Ferling.

121 *He had a breakdown:* Shaw, pp. 64–68; Ferling, pp. 72–73, referring to both overwork and the pressures of carrying out Samuel Adams's plans. For the crowd's terrorism, I follow Zobel, pp. 232–34. "They call me": quoted by Zobel, p. 215. For the bad night, diary gap, mockery in Braintree, and the trip to the springs: Adams, *Diary*, number 17. "I believe there is no man": number 17.

124 *At first, after the nightmare:* Shaw uses Adams's diary and autobiography to show the withdrawal from politics in fall of 1772, and sees the Port Act as the turning point for a full commitment.

Ferling details the refusals and hesitations, pp. 78–80. Adams's mood swings are notable throughout his diary and letters from 1774 through 1776. The first Congress was clearly intensely exciting. His description to Warren of Samuel's learning to ride (September 17, 1775, in Smith), is full of high-spirited, non-acerbic, self-effacing humor, rare for this period. "We have been obliged": John Adams to William Tudor, September 29, 1774, in Smith. Superseding Hancock: Wills, pp. 23–24.

Adams's misery in the second Congress (after having become frustrated in the first), emphasized by both Shaw and Ferling, is equally clear. "Blind eyes": to Abigail, May 29, 1776, in Adams Family Papers. "Always unwell": to James Warren, May 12, 1776, in Smith. "Not one creature": to Abigail, May 22, 1776, in *Correspondence*. (For a startling list of Adams's symptoms and illnesses, see "The Health and Medical History of President John Adams," www.doctorzebra.com/Prez/g02.htm.)

After May 10, 1776, the mood changes again (see notes to chapter 10). "This day the Congress": to James Warren, May 10, 1776, in Smith. "Who am I": Adams to Abigail Adams, May 17, 1776, in *Correspondence*.

128 *"entertaining maneuver"*: John Adams to James Warren, May 20, 1776, in Smith. Rosswurm, p. 96, notes in that context that Adams's concern was "ends rather than means."

8. Black Silk

129 *John Dickinson came back:* See first note to chapter 9.

130 *Certain governments had loosened up:* Jensen, pp. 638–40, 677–79, closely traces changes in instructions during the spring of 1776; he notes, p. 679, that only North Carolina had used the word *independence.*

131 *Richard Henry Lee dressed:* I've mostly used Hendrick, supplemented by the sometimes fanciful Fiske on the old Virginia families. Wills describes Lee's personal demeanor, pp. 3–4; my description of the Virginian's size and charisma follows Wills's chapter 1 closely. The hunting accident and black silk appear, not surprisingly, in virtually every source that mentions Lee. "Very high": Adams, *Diary*, number 21, and widely quoted. My brief background on the Lee family blends Hendrick's realism on the family's actual origins (pp. 3–4) with the romanticism exhibited by Virginia families themselves, in Fiske, chapter 10. Greene, chapter 10, discusses Lee's persona in the Burgesses and the nuances of his roles in Virginia politics. John Adams, *Autobiography*, describes Lee's rhetoric and voice, and Greene, p. 214, cites Edmund Randolph to the same effect, and on the idea that Lee practiced in front of a mirror; he also describes Lee, for all the sportsmanship, as a serious worker (p. 216). Detail on internecine Virginia politics, including the Lees' taking up leadership of Shenandoah and Piedmont representation, may be gleaned

from Hendrick, as well as from McCaughey's chapters 2 and 3, as may the Lee brothers' growing attachment to the Adamses, New England, and republicanism. Lee's movement toward a more northern sensibility, attested by McCaughey, is revealed by Lee's endorsement of and involvement in "Thoughts on Government." For John Adams and the history of New England town meetings, see Breen.

133 *found a partner in Patrick Henry:* Wills discusses the Henry-Lee partnership and the relationship with Samuel Adams, pp. 7–10, 22–26. "Lee-Adams junto": Jensen, p. 477.

136 *people in the western towns and counties:* Jensen, pp. 671–77, bases his account of the upheaval in Massachusetts on Stephen Patterson's *Political Parties in Revolutionary Massachusetts* (Madison: University of Wisconsin Press, 1973); he describes John Adams as "anguished" by the problem. I see a swing away from anguish in Adams after May 15, all the more pronounced for occurring in spite of the fact that Massachusetts had come no closer to taking the lead (discussed in chapter 10 herein). Raphael tells how radicalism developed in the western part of the state, discerning a shift, upon passage of the Massachusetts Government Act, from a Boston-led resistance against British authority to a rural movement for independence and democracy. Hoerder seems to concur, pp. 373–75, suggesting that by 1774, rural crowds saw themselves not as rioting but as holding open-air town meetings, with votes and resolves more important than violence. In earlier years, Hoerder says, rioters came in blackface at night; after 1774, they came by daylight, unmasked.

Thomas Young's letter to Samuel Adams: Samuel Adams, *Papers*, also cited by Raphael. The Vermont declaration of independence: Pell, p. 135.

137 *John Adams goaded Warren:* Jensen presents the struggle clearly, pp. 671–72, 675–76. In Smith: John Adams to James Warren, April 16, 1776; Adams to Warren, April 20, 1776; Warren to Adams, April 2, 1776.

138 Thoughts on Government: The premises are discussed in chapter 7. My history of the pamphlet is drawn from Smith, p. 405, footnote 1.

139 *When writing home:* Samuel Adams to Joseph Warren, September 24 and 25, 1774, in Smith. For Samuel Adams on *Common Sense:* Samuel Adams to James Warren, January 10, 1776, in Smith.

139 *matters started moving quickly in Virginia:* Lee to Henry, April 20, 1776, in Smith. "Democrat": Henry quoted by Jensen, p. 681. I follow Beeman on Henry's effort for independence and the role of the convention. Beeman calls the Virginia elite "reconciled to independence" (pp. 78–79) when the convention opened. (But Jefferson's discussion of the convention, in *Notes on the State of Virginia,* in *Papers,* seems to claim that independence was still barely thought of in April 1776.) Like all others on the subject, Beeman relies on Edmund Randolph's notes on the debates, and he also follows Henry's original biographer, William Wirt Henry. My discussion of the presentation of resolutions at the convention is drawn from Beeman, pp. 80–85.

141 *Information usually took:* Henry to John Adams, May 20, 1776, John Adams, *Papers*; Henry to Lee, May 20, 1776, and John Adams to Richard Lee, June 4, 1776, in Smith. According to Taylor, editor of John Adams's *Papers*, it took about ten days for news to travel from Williamsburg to Philadelphia. When on May 20, John Adams famously said that news from Virginia was firm, he was referring not to the Virginia resolution of May 15 but to newspaper reports of various Virginia counties' instructions to their delegates to that convention (as clarified by Burnett, regarding a letter from Elbridge Gerry, *Letters*, p. 459). In addition, a letter from Charles Lee regarding the likelihood of the Virginia convention's supporting independence was sent May 10 and read to the Congress on May 20.

142 *On May 20, the day of the mass meeting:* I follow Hawke, *In the Midst*, chapter 6. Hawke cites James Clitherall on the intimidation of the grocer and the silencing of Cadwalader, whom Ryerson, p. 214, thinks was the John Cadwalader who had sat on the City Committee. Rosswurm, p. 96, supports my sense that the event was not a town meeting but rather "a demonstration."

9. "They are not represented in this house"

Page

143 *And his assembly was operating:* I draw on Ryerson, pp. 219–28, and Hawke, *In the Midst*, chapters 7, 8, and 9, with support from *The Pennsylvania Archives*, series 8, vol. 8. Those sources trace the request for clarification; the end of oath-taking and the controversies it sparked; the role of the Remonstrance; the effect

of the Virginia instructions; denial of quorum; the loosening of Pennsylvania's instructions; and the effort to take over the provincial convention. Rosswurm, pp. 94–95, notes that Delaware and other states kept their existing governments while complying with the resolution.

Rush's note to Lee: Hawke, *In the Midst*, p. 156. Smith reports that the note was handwritten and came with papers to be circulated among the southern delegates, which Smith takes as another sign of collaboration between the radicals and independents in the Congress (p. 91, footnote 4).

Hawke sees the provision for keeping the assembly operating until the convention as illogical, possibly because he overstates, according to Ryerson, the committee's intention to keep the assembly from operating at all (see the note on radical planning in chapter 6 herein). Hawke also emphasizes a tendency in Dickinson's decisions to bring the assembly fully in line with the resolves of the Congress, and the likelihood that if Dickinson had had a few more weeks, he might have actually done it (p. 159). Ryerson emphasizes a sense of chaos (pp. 219–28) and even "despair" (p. 226) in the assembly, with focus lost on all sides. Both writers note that some independents in the assembly were now in favor of retaining the charter, a fact that only adds to the fragmentation Ryerson points to.

145 *The secret coalition:* Hawke, *In the Midst*, chapters 7, 8, and 9, discusses the coordinated efforts of the City Committee, the Committee of Privates, the independents in the assembly, and the Adamses. On the move to stop clarification of the resolution: Hawke, pp. 156–57, citing Marshall on the meetings with the Adamses. On the dissemination of the State House yard protests,

and opposition to the Remonstrance: Hawke, pp. 145–50, with Ryerson, p. 210, noting the militias' hostile attitudes, by summer of 1776, about anyone pro-assembly and pro-reconciliation. Rosswurm, p. 97, describes county militia musters adopting the May 20 resolutions.

Hawke says that in propaganda sent to the countryside against the Remonstrance there was no mention of lowering suffrage requirements, as there had been in the city (p. 147). His implication is that gaining access to the franchise was not a main consideration in the countryside. The implication clashes with his presenting the entire move against the Remonstrance as a response to Cannon's letters to the Privates, which Hawke shows specifically emphasized the voting-rights issue, beginning in February, and that "every communiqué" hinted at "the kind of government it planned" (p. 184).

148 *In the Congress's chamber:* For main events, I draw on Jensen, pp. 687–91, and Burnett, pp. 170–77. For the military minutiae with which the Congress now began to cope, see *Journals* for June; for a mood of urgency about independence caused by the impending invasion, see Maier, *Scripture*, p. 44. The Adamses' collaboration with Lee on the timing and substance of his resolution is evident in Samuel Adams's letter to James Warren, June 6, 1776, in Smith.

149 *He planned to introduce it:* For the debate and postponement in the Congress: Jefferson's "Notes on Debates and Proceedings," *Papers.* For Dickinson's work on the instructions: Hawke *In the Midst*, pp. 160–61; Ryerson, p. 223. For Rutledge's motivations in opposing a declaration: Powell, "The Debate."

154 *A formal question was put to the men:* The call for and exercise of the Privates' poll against the assembly was clearly planned to coincide with the introduction of Lee's resolution in the Congress, as Hawke says, *In the Midst*, p. 171 (and Lee's introduction may have been planned to coincide with the poll).

At least as important, however—and not unrelated to Lee's resolution—is the militia muster as a response to Dickinson's effort to take over the provincial convention. Had Dickinson's move been successful, it would have recommitted Pennsylvania to its old charter and possibly to shoring up the middle-colony bloc against independence. See Ryerson, pp. 227–28, for the Pennsylvania focus. In footnote 93 to p. 227, Ryerson notes that the first few battalions weren't asked about independence but about change in society, in the context of defense.

In Ryerson's view, the most important cause of the final shutdown of the assembly was the militia's taking "intense measures" to stop Dickinson and the assembly by fiat (p. 227), which, as Rosswurm reminds us, pp. 97–100, was a fiat not of the officer class but of the Privates. And Hazelton, writing in 1906, may have been the first to recognize the battalion muster as a use of decisive military force against the assembly (pp. 188–89). Rosswurm, p. 97, quotes Clitherall on the militia muster's abuse of a majority position to pressure and intimidate dissenters.

Ryerson names the officer refusing to put the question as John Cadwalader, the same man silenced by the May 20 crowd; Hawke thinks it was Lambert Cadwalader.

156 *There would be no reconvening:* For the last days of the Pennsylvania assembly as a viable body under the 1701 charter: Ryerson, pp. 226–28. Later, the body did in fact try to reconvene, with

quorum difficulties, but delegates to the constitutional convention had been elected and the charter was a dead letter. Protests of the Board of Officers and the Committee of Privates: Pennsylvania Archives, series 8, vol. 8, pp. 7546–48. For protests being read in the form of a circular letter at militia musters, along with the July 4 invitation to elect officers: Rupp and Hamilton, pp. 395–401.

156 *"For really":* Wootton, pp. 285–317.

157 *"These threats":* Hawke, *In the Midst,* pp. 166–67, quoting the diary of William Bradford, later the second attorney general of the United States, and instrumental in suppressing western Pennsylvania during the Whiskey Rebellion of the 1790s. In 1776 Bradford was a young Philadelphia independent and militia officer who attended the meeting. The punctuation is his. Hawke and others quote the youth as noting that Dickinson's speech "appeared to me to be the unpremeditated effusions of the heart.... He was clearly wrong, yet I believed him right. Such are the effects of oratory."

10. Independence Days

Page

159 *Pennsylvania's provincial convention:* I follow Hawke, *In the Midst,* pp. 171–77, and Ryerson, pp. 228–37. Ryerson notes that it was two years to the day since Dickinson had chaired the committee at the hall; states that the effect of the election franchise was to expand suffrage by as much as 90 percent; and describes

representation for the constitutional convention as making backcountry counties as powerful as eastern ones. Hawke, pp. 175–76, notes that the Adamses met with Cannon and Marshall yet again on June 23.

160 *Their high-Whig ally:* As McKean's activities in response to the new constitution make clear (see notes below), he was entirely out of sympathy with the convention he chaired. Marshall versus Rush: Hawke, *In the Midst,* p. 175. Cannon on Marshall's position: Ryerson, p. 240. I follow Foner, pp. 136–38, on the shift in Rush from radical to reformer.

163 *They sought instructions:* Jensen, pp. 691–93. A growing expectation that by July 1, all delegations would support independence may be traced in Smith: e.g., Barlett and Whipple to New Hampshire, June 11, 1776; and Gerry to Massachusetts, June 11, 1776.

164 *John Adams kept predicting:* In Smith: John Adams to James Warren, May 15, 1776; Adams to Cushing, May 9, 1776; Adams to Chase, June 24, 1776; Adams to John Winthrop, June 23, 1776. In Adams family *Correspondence:* Adams to Abigail Adams, June 16, 1776.

165 *Maryland finally did change:* For detail lacking in my account: Jensen, pp. 693–96.

167 *So the drafting fell to Jefferson:* I follow Wills, pp. 348–51, and Maier, *Scripture,* pp. 102–3. Both dissent from John Adams's famous description of the committee process in his *Autobiography,*

sheet 24. I also draw on Maier's succinct and compelling discussion of Jefferson's position in Philadelphia in June 1776 (pp. 47–48). On Franklin's dissociation from activity in the Congress: Franklin to Washington, June 21, 1776, in Smith. Both Maier and Wills emphasize the Declaration as an explanation of an action, not the action itself, and Wills's chapter 25 traces the development of public confusion between the two. For the English history of declarations: Maier, pp. 50–59; Wills, pp. 334–37.

168 *July 1 and 2 thus became climactic days:* Jefferson, "Notes on Debates in Congress," *Papers*; John Adams to Bullock, July 1, 1776; Adams to Chase, July 1, 1776. Hazelton, chapter 7, does a fascinating job of deconstructing and elaborating various accounts of the days' activities. Powell lays out some scenarios, discounting Benjamin Rush's secondhand account of the speeches of July 1, calling all accounts "imperfect" and even doubting John Adams on giving a second speech. Wills, chapters 25 and 26, reviews the faulty later memories of Jefferson and other signers.

169 *John Dickinson took his last chance:* For Dickinson's speech: Powell, "A Speech." Dickinson looked "gaunt" and even "near death," says Ferling—believably enough but I think recycling Adams's first impression from 1774 (*Diary*, number 21). Jacobson, p. 113, insists that Dickinson no longer believed in reconciliation but merely wanted to delay a declaration (p. 116); Dickinson later suggested that, too (his "Vindication," Stillé, p. 364). I think the policy of delay—in the sense of delaying the Congress from declaring independence—is fairly obvious, but I don't see Dickinson coming in June and July to any heartfelt support for declaring independence at a more prudent date. Adams's atti-

tude and speech: Adams to Chase, July 1, 1776; Adams, *Autobiography*, sheet 38; Adams to Mercy Warren, quoted by Hazelton, p. 159.

170 *At four that afternoon:* Hazelton cites Jefferson's thermometer reading and Marshall's diary. On July 1, they show a very hot day, with a thunderstorm starting about four in the afternoon and ending by six; on July 2, they show a cloudy morning, with a heavy rain starting before ten and clearing at five that afternoon. Powell, "The Debate," states that after Dickinson stopped speaking on July 1, thunder roared and rain began falling. David McCullough, *John Adams* (New York: Simon & Schuster, 2001), says that in the silence between Dickinson's and Adams's speeches came the sound of rain, which had started hitting the windows while Dickinson was speaking. Chidsey has the rain coming only after Adams's speech, preceding it with heat lightning and accompanying it by violent winds and candles being lit in the chamber. Rowe calls the arriving congressmen of July 2 wet, presumably because (as also noted by Ferling) it started raining that morning at about ten. Ferling makes the July 2 rain gentle and quenching and all-day, Hawke makes it heavy, and McCullough describes a cloudburst.

172 *Caesar Rodney:* Many authors describe Rodney as muddy, others as dusty; some state that just as he arrived, the doors to the chamber were about to be closed; and Chidsey has all the delegates gathered in the chamber, listening in silence for the horse, then rising as one to greet Rodney. Others have all the delegates arriving at the State House as usual, with Rodney simply join-

ing them; others get the session going inside and leave McKean standing outside waiting.

For McKean's recollections: Burnett, *Letters*, p. 534. For Rodney's: Caesar Rodney to Thomas Rodney, July 4, 1776, in Smith.

173 *John Dickinson stayed home:* All writers on the subject report it, supported ultimately, I think, by McKean's later recollection; McKean to Rodney, September 22, 1813, Burnett, *Letters*. Jefferson's memory of the arrival of new Pennsylvania delegates on July 2 has been widely discounted.

174 *editing Jefferson's draft declaration:* The scene, and Jefferson's discomfiture, are documented in standard sources. "Mutilations": Jefferson, quoted by Hazelton, p. 178. "Pretty good": from Bartlett's "a pretty good one," quoted by Maier, *Scripture*, p. 144. I follow Maier, pp. 143–50, very closely in examples of alterations, and I distill Maier's discussion, pp. 149–50, on Jefferson's attachment to and promotion of his own draft.

There is of course much to be said about the two versions, and Wills and Maier say it. They agree that the purpose of the document was immediate and tactical, far from the most important thing the Congress had on its plate, its cultural importance attaching only later, an unintended consequence. Wills's book delves into a reading of Jefferson's inspirations and sources, largely in the Scottish Enlightenment. Maier, skeptical about much of Wills's discussion (as is Everdell, p. 334), places Jefferson's and the Congress's versions in a variety of revealing contexts. I've found both authors indispensable for matters well beyond the scope of this book. For more, see the note below on equality.

175 *They ordered the document printed:* I follow Wills, pp. 339–44, on steps in publishing the document and on the later signing. Wills relies in part on Hazelton. Yet Wills, Hazelton, and Maier have not dispelled the image of men standing around the table—on July 4—and signing together. Dissenting from the tradition of the signing as a daring compact, Wills sees the act as highly ceremonial; he draws the distinction between the Magna Carta and the Declaration as legal documents. Maier takes more seriously the mutual pledge evinced in the signing, and notes that it was nevertheless not until the American victories at Princeton and Trenton in 1777 that the Congress sent the document to the states with names inscribed (*Scripture*, pp. 152–53). For more on Robert Morris, see my *The Whiskey Rebellion*, and the sources on Morris I cite there.

176 *Benjamin Rush signed:* Hawke, *In the Midst*, p. 194.

177 *the Howe brothers:* Fleming discusses the potential for negotiations and Richard Howe's possible hopes. In Smith, pp. 137–44, see "Henry Strachey's Notes on Lord Howe's Meeting," with "changed the ground," p. 138.

177 *The Declaration of Independence, in words:* I repeat Maier's point, p. 192, on the thrust of "created equal." Maier says that the document was at first "all but forgotten" (p. 160). Wills's chapter 27 reviews and dissents from the progressive-history tradition of the Declaration as a radically egalitarian document and the

U.S. Constitution as a conservative one. On the document's later metamorphosis and cultural emergence, and its service as a beacon to democratic equality, both Maier and Wills are again indispensable.

178 *On July 3:* Ryerson, pp. 239–40. "Noisy blunder": quoted by Ryerson from Marshall's letter book. On the Privates' broadside: Rosswurm, pp. 101–2. As Ryerson reports, Marshall, while saying that Young was especially assertive with the crowd, also claims Young called for delegates with independent fortunes. This claim is hard to square with anything else both Cannon and Young had been saying or kept saying, as Ryerson points out (p. 239, footnote 138). Cannon and Matlack were nominated by the caucus; and neither had fortunes. I think Marshall was flailing. Hawke discusses Cannon's June 16 broadside, pp. 176–77.

179 *Rush was leaving Paine behind:* Rush became surgeon general of a department of the Continental Army and is widely seen as the first unofficial one of the United States. He was certainly among the first busy American health reformers. His later efforts involved limiting alcohol in army rations and lecturing the public on the unhealthy effects of smoking tobacco.

179 *On July 8:* Hawke, p. 181. Events of that day are widely covered in standard sources.

180 *"mobocracy":* Rush to John Adams, quoted in Hawke, p. 178.

180 *Pennsylvania's radical constitutional convention:* I follow Selsam's description, pp. 146–59.

180 *It actually wasn't clear:* Selsam, p. 149, quoting Alexander Graydon's memoirs. Everdell, by contrast, sees Franklin as the first democratic republican in American history (p. 161). As my narrative probably makes clear, I'm dubious about ascribing to Franklin any consistent point of view on government.

181 *He wasn't the author:* Ryerson (p. 241), Hawke (*In the Midst*, pp. 186–88), John Adams (*Diary*, number 29), and Selsam agree that Cannon wrote the Pennsylvania constitution, with Young's help. Paine's influence is attested by Hawke, p. 184, and Adams, *Autobiography*, sheet 23. Radical features of the constitution are discussed by Selsam. Read the document itself at the Avalon Project, http://avalon.law.yale.edu/18th_century/pa08 .asp. Foner, p. 133, notes the failure of the clause restricting property.

Rowe discusses McKean's opposition to the constitution (pp. 93–95) and his adopting John Adams's defense of balance in the late 1780s (pp. 242–44). For McKean, Rush, the Pennsylvania anti-constitutionalists, and the post-1776 story: Robert Brunhouse, *The Counter-Revolution in Pennsylvania* (Harrisburg: Pennsylvania Historical Commission, 1942); Harry Marlin Tinkcom, *The Republicans and Federalists in Pennsylvania, 1790–1801* (Harrisburg: Pennsylvania Historical and Museum Commission, 1950); Terry Bouton, *Taming Democracy* (New York: Oxford University Press, 2007). For Whitehill, Findley, and Husband, again see Bouton, as well as my *The Whiskey Rebellion* (New York: Scribner, 2006), and the sources I cite there.

182 *"Good God!":* Adams according to Rush, and quoted widely.

182 *busy working on Massachusetts:* I follow Hoerder, pp. 377–83, in tracing the pushback against radicalism and describing the constitution of 1780 as evincing Adams's "Thoughts on Government." Everdell, pp. 164–66, analyzes Adams's constitution pithily in the context of the whole history of republics.

Samuel Adams on gaining independence: Samuel Adams to Hawley, July 9, 1776; Adams to Kent, July 27, 1776. On the indemnification of rioters: Hoerder, pp. 383–89, connecting Adams's preferred indemnification end date to the subduing of the western counties. Adam's reaction to the seizing of the armory—the action known as Shays's Rebellion—is documented in most biographies. Only writers who see the 1776 Adams as a populist democrat find that response contradictory.

186 *Dickinson never signed:* In "Vindication," in Stillé, p. 384, Dickinson recalls bitterly the news of his dismissal. See also Dickinson's letters to Thomson, quoted in Stillé, pp. 203–4, for his mood in the field. Jacobson, pp. 117–19, drawing largely on "Vindication," notes that with Dickinson's support, the Congress sent Pennsylvania forces to the New Jersey theater, where Dickinson served as a militia colonel; when the Pennsylvania convention appointed brigadier generals that would outrank him, he resigned and later volunteered to serve as a private. Jacobson calls it unsupported tradition that Dickinson served as a private in the Delaware militia (pp. 121–22), but Flanders, in his review of Stillé, says that Dickinson carried a musket at Brandywine, and Dickinson himself, in "Vindication," says that he carried a musket as a private (Stillé, p. 394).

187 *"Not a place upon earth":* Paine, *Crisis* 1, *Writings.*

Sources

Adams, John. *Autobiography.* "Adams Family Papers: An Electronic Archive," Massachusetts Historical Society, www.masshist.org/digitaladams/aea.

———. *Diary.* "Adams Family Papers: An Electronic Archive," Massachusetts Historical Society, www.masshist.org/digitaladams/aea.

———. *Papers.* Ed. Robert J. Taylor; Mary-Jo Kline, associate editor; Gregg L. Lint, assistant editor. Cambridge, Mass.: Belknap Press of Harvard University Press, 1977.

———. *Works.* Ed. Charles Francis Adams. Freeport, N.Y.: Books for Libraries Press, 1969.

Adams, John, and Abigail Adams. *Correspondence.* "Adams Family Papers: An Electronic Archive," Massachusetts Historical Society, www.masshist.org/digitaladams/aea/.

Adams, John, Abigail Adams, and Thomas Jefferson. *The Adams-Jefferson Letters: The Complete Correspondence between Thomas Jefferson and Abigail and John Adams.* Ed. Lester J. Cappon. Chapel Hill: University of North Carolina Press, 1988.

Adams, Samuel. *Papers*. Manuscripts Collection, New York Public Library.

———. *The Writings of Samuel Adams*. Ed. Harry Alonzo Cushing. New York: Octagon, 1968.

Alexander, John K. *Samuel Adams: America's Revolutionary Politician*. Lanham, Md.: Rowman & Littlefield, 2002.

Allen, Gardner Weld. *A Naval History of the American Revolution*. Boston: Houghton Mifflin, 1913.

Anderson, George Pomeroy. "Who Wrote 'Ethan Allen's Bible'?" *New England Quarterly* 10, no. 4 (December 1937).

Bailyn, Bernard. *The Ordeal of Thomas Hutchinson*. Cambridge, Mass. Belknap Press of Harvard University Press, 1974.

Beeman, Richard R. *Patrick Henry*. New York: McGraw-Hill, 1974.

Bernstein, Barton, ed. *Towards a New Past: Dissenting Essays in American History*. New York: Pantheon, 1968.

Breen, Timothy Hall. "John Adams's Fight against Innovation in the New England Constitution, 1776." *New England Quarterly* 40, no. 4 (December 1967).

Bregman, Alexander. "Reading under the Folds: John Dickinson, Gordon's Tacitus, and the American Revolution." Unpublished senior honors thesis, University of Pennsylvania, 2008, http://reposi tory.upenn.edu/hist_honors/16/.

Brown, Richard D. *Revolutionary Politics in Massachusetts: The Boston Committee of Correspondence and the Towns, 1772–1774*. Cambridge, Mass.: Harvard University Press, 1970.

Burnett, Edmund C. *The Continental Congress.* New York: Macmillan, 1941.

Burnett, Edmund C., ed. *Letters of Members of the Continental Congress.* Gloucester, Mass.: P. Smith, 1963.

Chidsey, Donald Barr. *July 4, 1776: The Dramatic Story of the First Four Days of July, 1776.* New York: Crown, 1958.

Coleman, John M. *Thomas McKean, Forgotten Leader of the Revolution.* Rockaway, N.J.: American Faculty Press, 1975.

"Constitution of Pennsylvania, September 28, 1776." Avalon Project, http://avalon.law.yale.edu/18th_century/pa08.asp.

Cressey, David. *Travesties and Transgressions in Tudor and Stuart England: Tales of Discord and Dissension.* Oxford: Oxford University Press, 2000.

Dickinson, H. T. *A Companion to Eighteenth-Century Britain.* Malden, Mass.: Wiley-Blackwell, 2002.

Dickinson, John. "A Reply to a Piece Called the Speech of Joseph Galloway, Esq." J. Whiston and B. White, 1765.

———. *Writings.* Vol. 1, "Political Writings, 1764–1774." Ed. Paul Leicester Ford. Historical Society of Pennsylvania, 1895.

Edes, Henry H. "Memoir of Dr. Thomas Young, 1731–1777." Colonial Society of Massachusetts, 1910.

England, Joseph Winters, and John Eicholtz Kramer. *The First Century of the Philadelphia College of Pharmacy, 1821–1921.* Philadelphia: Philadelphia College of Pharmacy and Science, 1922.

"English Dissenters," http://exlibris.org/nonconform/engdis/index .html.

Everdell, William R. *The End of Kings: A History of Republics and Republicans*. Chicago: University of Chicago Press, 2000.

Ferling, John. *John Adams: A Life*. Newtown, Conn.: American Political Biography Press, 1996.

Fiske, John. *Old Virginia and Her Neighbours*. Boston: Houghton Mifflin, 1902.

Flanders, Henry. "The Life and Times of John Dickinson, 1732–1808, by Charles J. Stillé, LL.D." *Pennsylvania Magazine of History and Biography* 15, no. 1 (1891).

Fleming, Thomas J. "The Enigma of General Howe." *American Heritage* 15, no. 2 (February 1964).

Flower, Milton E. *John Dickinson, Conservative Revolutionary*. Charlottesville: Friends of the John Dickinson Mansion and University Press of Virginia, 1983.

Foner, Eric. *Tom Paine and Revolutionary America*. New York: Oxford University Press, 2005.

Fowler, William M. *Samuel Adams: Radical Puritan*. New York: Longman, 1997.

Franklin, Benjamin. *Works*. Vol. 5. Ed. Jared Sparks. T. MacCoun, 1882.

Fruchtman, Jack. *Thomas Paine: Apostle of Freedom*. New York: Four Walls Eight Windows, 1994.

Galloway, Joseph. *Historical and Political Reflections on the Rise and Progress of the American Rebellion.* Johnson Reprint Corp., 1972.

————. "The Speech of Joseph Galloway, Esq., One of the Members for Philadelphia County, in Answer to the Speech of John Dickinson, Esq., Delivered in the House of Assembly of the Province of Pennsylvania, May 24, 1764, on Occasion of a Petition Drawn up by Order, and Then Under the Consideration of the House, Praying His Majesty for a Royal in Lieu of a Proprietary Government." Early American Imprints, First Series, No. 9671.

Greene, Jack P. *Understanding the American Revolution: Issues and Actors.* Charlottesville: University Press of Virginia, 1995.

Hawke, David Freeman. "Dr. Thomas Young—'Eternal Fisher in Troubled Waters': Notes for a Biography." *New-York Historical Society Quarterly* 64, no. 1 (January 1970).

————. *Honorable Treason: The Declaration of Independence and the Men Who Signed It.* New York: Viking, 1976.

————. *In the Midst of a Revolution.* Philadelphia: University of Pennsylvania Press, 1961.

Hazelton, John H. *The Declaration of Independence: Its History.* New York: Dodd Mead, 1906.

Head, John M. *A Time to Rend: An Essay on the Decision for American Independence.* Madison: State Historical Society of Wisconsin, 1968.

Heimert, Alan. *Religion and the American Mind, from the Great Awakening to the Revolution.* Cambridge, Mass.: Harvard University Press, 1966.

Hendrick, Burton J. *The Lees of Virginia: Biography of a Family*. Boston: Little, Brown, 1935.

Hindle, Brooke. "The March of the Paxton Boys." *William & Mary Quarterly*, 3rd series, vol. 3, no. 4 (October 1946).

Hoerder, Dirk. *Crowd Action in Revolutionary Massachusetts, 1765–1780*. New York: Academic Press, 1977.

Hutchinson, Thomas. *The History of the Province of Massachusetts Bay, from the Year 1750 until June, 1774*. John Murray, 1828.

Jacobson, David L. *John Dickinson and the Revolution in Pennsylvania, 1764–1776*. Berkeley: University of California Press, 1965.

Jefferson, Thomas. *Papers*. Ed. Julian P. Boyd. Princeton, N.J.: Princeton University Press, 1950.

Jensen, Merrill. *The Founding of a Nation: A History of the American Revolution, 1763–1776*. Oxford: Oxford University Press, 1968.

Journals of the Continental Congress, 1774–1789. Ed. Worthington C. Ford et al., http://memory.loc.gov/ammem/amlaw/lwjc.html.

Kremers, Edward, and Glenn Sonnedecker. *Kremers and Urdang's History of Pharmacy*. Philadelphia: Lippincott, 1976.

Lemay, J. A. Leo. *The Life of Benjamin Franklin*. Vols. 1 and 2. Philadelphia: University of Pennsylvania Press, 2005.

Lemisch, Jesse. "Radical Plot in Boston (1770): A Study in the Use of Evidence." *Harvard Law Review* 84, no. 2 (December 1970).

Lewis, Paul. *The Grand Incendiary: A Biography of Samuel Adams*. New York: Dial, 1973.

Sources

Maier, Pauline. *American Scripture: Making the Declaration of Independence*. New York: Random House, 1998.

———. "Coming to Terms with Samuel Adams." *American Historical Review* 81, no. 1 (February 1976).

———. *From Resistance to Revolution: Colonial Radicals and the Development of American Opposition to Britain, 1765–1776*. New York: Knopf, 1972.

Marshall, Christopher. *Diaries*. Christopher Marshall Papers, Historical Society of Pennsylvania.

McGaughy, J. Kent. *Richard Henry Lee of Virginia: A Portrait of an American Revolutionary*. Lanham, Md.: Rowman & Littlefield, 2004.

Miller, John C. *Sam Adams: Pioneer in Propaganda*. Boston: Little, Brown, 1936.

Montross, Lynn. *The Reluctant Rebels: The Story of the Continental Congress, 1774–1789*. New York: Harper, 1950.

"The Music of William Billings," Amaranth Publishing, www.amaranthpublishing.com/billings.htm.

Nash, Gary B. *The Urban Crucible: The Northern Seaports and the Origins of the American Revolution*. Cambridge, Mass.: Harvard University Press, 1986.

Newcomb, Benjamin H. *Franklin and Galloway: A Political Partnership*. New Haven, Conn.: Yale University Press, 1972.

O'Neill, Tip, with William Novak. *Man of the House: The Life and Political Memoirs of Speaker Tip O'Neill*. New York: Random House, 1987.

Paine, Thomas. *Writings.* Ed. Moncure Daniel Conway. Putnam, 1894. Online Library of Liberty, http://oll.libertyfund.org/?option=com_staticxt&staticfile=show.php%3Ftitle=1743&Itemid=27.

Pell, John. *Ethan Allen.* Freeport, N.Y.: Books for Libraries Press, 1972.

Pencak, William, Matthew Dennis, and Simon P. Newman, eds. *Riot and Revelry in Early America.* University Park: Pennsylvania State University Press, 2002.

Pennsylvania Archives. Series 8, vol. 8. J. Severns, 1852–56.

Powell, J. H. "The Debate on American Independence, July 1, 1776." http://dspace.udel.edu:8080/dspace/bitstream/19716/4601/1/article3.pdf.

Powell, J. H. "Speech of John Dickinson Opposing the Declaration of Independence, 1 July, 1776." *Pennsylvania Magazine of History and Biography* 65, no. 4 (October 1941).

Rakove, Jack N. *The Beginnings of National Politics: An Interpretive History of the Continental Congress.* New York: Knopf, 1979.

Raphael, Ray. *The First American Revolution: Before Lexington and Concord.* New York: New Press, 2002.

Rexroth, Kenneth. *Communalism: From Its Origins to the Twentieth Century.* New York: The Seabury Press, 1974.

Rodney, Caesar. *Letters to and from Caesar Rodney, 1756–1784.* Ed. George Herbert Ryden. Philadelphia: Historical Society of Delaware and University of Pennsylvania Press, 1933.

Sources

Rosswurm, Steven. *Arms, Country, and Class: The Philadelphia Militia and "Lower Sort" during the American Revolution, 1775–1783*. New Brunswick, N.J.: Rutgers University Press, 1987.

Rowe, G. S. *Thomas McKean: The Shaping of an American Republicanism*. Boulder: Colorado Associated University Press, 1978.

Rupp, Israel Daniel, and Von Gail Hamilton. *History of the Countries of Berks and Lebanon*. G. Hills, 1844.

Ryerson, Richard. *The Revolution Is Now Begun: The Radical Committee of Philadelphia, 1765–1776*. Philadelphia: University of Pennsylvania Press, 1978.

Schneider, Judy. "Committee of the Whole: An Introduction." Congressional Research Service, 2003, http://lugar.senate.gov/services/pdf_crs/Committee_of_the_whole_An_Introduction.pdf.

Selsam, J. Paul. *The Pennsylvania Constitution of 1776: A Study in Revolutionary Democracy*. Philadelphia: University of Pennsylvania Press, 1936.

Shaw, Peter. *The Character of John Adams*. Williamsburg, Va.: Institute of Early American History and Culture and University of North Carolina Press, 1976.

Shomette, Donald. *Shipwrecks, Sea Raiders, and Maritime Disasters along the Delmarva Coast, 1632–2004*. Baltimore: Johns Hopkins University Press, 2007.

Smith, Paul, ed. *Letters of Delegates to Congress, 1774–1789*. Washington, D.C.: Library of Congress, 1976.

Sources

Stillé, Charles J. *The Life and Times of John Dickinson, 1732–1808*. Historical Society of Pennsylvania, 1891.

Thompson, E.P. *The Making of the English Working Class*. London: V. Gollancz, 1963.

———. "Quakerism and Politics." Quaker Pamphlets, www.quaker.org/pamphlets/ward1956a.html.

Tolles, Frederick B. *Meeting House and Counting House: The Quaker Merchants of Colonial Philadelphia, 1682–1763*. Chapel Hill: Institute of Early American History and Culture and University of North Carolina Press, 1948.

"The Unanimous Declaration of the Thirteen United States of America." American Memory, Library of Congress, http://memory.loc.gov/cgi-bin/query/h?ammem/bdsbib:@field(NUMBER+@od1(bdsdcc+02101)).

Weddle, Meredith Baldwin. *Walking in the Way of Peace: Quaker Pacifism in the Seventeenth Century*. New York: Oxford University Press, 2001.

Wells, William V. *The Life and Public Service of Samuel Adams: Being a Narrative of His Acts and Opinions, and of His Agency in Producing and Forwarding the American Revolution*. Little, Brown, 1866.

Wills, Garry. *Inventing America: Jefferson's Declaration of Independence*. New York: Doubleday, 1978.

Wood, Gordon S. *The Americanization of Benjamin Franklin*. New York: Penguin, 2004.

Sources

Wootton, David, ed. *Divine Right and Democracy: An Anthology of Political Writing in Stuart England.* Indianapolis: Hackett, 2003.

Zobel, Hiller B. *The Boston Massacre.* New York: Norton, 1970.

Acknowledgments

I'm grateful to Eric Lupfer, who gave this book tireless representation; to Bob Bender, who gave it wise and scrupulous editing; to Suzanne Gluck, who first encouraged me to pursue it; to Daniel Bergner and Carol Rawlings Miller, who were generous, as always, with literary insight. Thanks to Johanna Li and everyone else at Simon & Schuster whose diligence, patience, and taste helped turn a manuscript into a book.

I've relied on collections housed in the Stephen A. Schwarzman building of the New York Public Library, especially the Milstein Division, and on collections of the Historical Society of Pennsylvania. Scholars who have been generous in responding to and encouraging my adventures in American history include Terry Bouton, William Everdell, Jesse Lemisch, Gary Nash, Gwen Wright, and Wythe Holt steered me toward sources I might otherwise have missed, but I like to publish without submitting work to prior scholarly comment (an oddball approach, in history circles), and they are blameless of anything I say in the book.

Various family members, friends, colleagues, and competitors have aided and supported my projects, spreading the word, advising in various capacities, and being encouragingly interested. They include Gerald Anders, John Antinori, Clarissa Atkinson, Holley Atkinson, Bruce Castellano, Ed Finnegan, Kyle Gann, Lorenz Glaser, John Gulla, Henrietta Hallenborg, Mary Ann Hallenborg, Matt Hallenborg, Neil Hallenborg, Jim Halverson, Brigid Hogeland, David Hogeland, Webster Hogeland, David Kamp, Jody Kantor, Aya Karpinska, Bruce Makous, Jack McShane, Rohn Jay Miller, Jim Miller, Rick Perlstein, Paul O'Rourke, Stephen Plumlee, Douglass Rushkoff, Marilyn Sande, Bernard Shakin, Eleanor Shakin, Sam Sifton, Emily Stone, and Kip Voytek.

My stepdaughter Barbara has been not only a beloved supporter but also an inspiration. Men and events in this book have made me think often of my father, William Hogeland, and my maternal grandfather, Bethuel Webster; I've dedicated *Declaration* to their memories. Above all, I thank my wife, Gail, for, among other things, helping me find the ways to tell this story and for being its first and most constant reader.

Index

Academy and College of
    Philadelphia, 20
Act of Settlement, 15
Adams, John, 6–7, 8, 11–12, 32, 42,
    44, 46, 48, 52, 63, 69, 70, 74, 78,
    80, 91, 99, 101, 105–28, 131,
    132, 137–38, 140, 151, 153, 167,
    169, 185–86
  Adams-Lee resolution and, *see*
    Adams-Lee resolution
  ambition of, 108–9, 118, 121, 138
  as architect of independence, 184
  attends Harvard, 109–10
  and "Boston Massacre" trials,
    118–20, 121, 124, 227–28
  breakdown of, 121
  checks and balances and, 106–7
  and closing of Boston courts by
    Stamp Act, 112–15
  and committee on treaty with
    France, 166
  and committee to write
    Declaration of Independence, *see*
    Declaration of Independence
  and Congress's Board of War, 166

  as delegate to First Continental
    Congress, 124–25
  diary of, 114, 122, 123, 124
  on Dickinson's reconciliationist
    attitudes, 51–52, 96, 105, 107,
    164, 186
  elected to Massachusetts assembly,
    120–21
  and friendship with Rush, 160
  frustration of, 107–8
  hatred of Hutchinson, 121–22
  hatred of Paine, 105–6, 139, 186
  health of, 107, 121, 122, 123, 124,
    125, 138, 165
  as lawyer, 107, 108–9, 113, 114,
    118–20
  loneliness of, 125
  loses Massachusetts assembly
    election, 115
  made selectman, 115
  and Massachusetts constitution,
    166, 182
  old age of, 184
  and Pennsylvania constitution,
    182

Index

Adams, John (*cont.*)
  predicts vote for independence by
    Congress, 164–65
  in secret coalition, *see* secret
    coalition
  as seen as traitor, 118
  and *Thoughts on Government*,
    138–39, 140, 142
  and use of term "independence," 86
  as "Yankee," 108
Adams, Samuel, 6–8, 8, 10, 17, 18–19,
  29, 31, 32–33, 35, 36, 37–38, 41,
  42, 46, 63, 67, 69, 70, 78, 97, 99,
  101, 109–12, 120, 122, 131, 132,
  136, 137, 148, 150, 167, 176,
  185–86, 204–5, 240
  Adams-Lee resolution and, *see*
    Adams-Lee resolution
  attends Harvard, 110
  becomes clerk of Massachusetts
    assembly, 115
  and "Boston Massacre" trials, 118,
    119
  Calvinism of, 31
  as councilor, 183–84
  delegate lobbying by, 45
  description of, 131
  family background of, 110
  and father's death, 110, 111
  Hancock's turn against, 43–44, 125
  and influence of, 112, 115
  marriage of, 112
  names "Boston Massacre," 117
  and reaching out to younger men,
    109
  and riot act, 183–84

  in secret coalition, *see* secret
    coalition
  and use of term "independence," 86
Adams, Samuel, Sr., 110, 111, 112
Adams-Lee resolution, 46–49, 73–74,
  75–76, 78–80, 81, 88, 89, 92, 95,
  96, 98, 99, 101, 125, 126, 141,
  154–55, 208–9
  debate on preamble to, 95–100
  as means to independence, 144,
    146, 147–48, 150, 163, 164
  preamble to, 92–102, 125, 126
  vote on preamble to, 101–2, 130
Age of Reason, The (Paine), 82
Aitken, Robert, 83, 84, 85
"Alarm, The" (Paine), 103
alchemy, 26
Allen, Ethan, 14, 137
Amenia, N.Y., 12–13, 14, 22, 137
American Manufactory, 21, 23, 24,
  25, 28, 30, 84, 126
American Philosophical Society, 94,
  102
American Prohibitory Act, 36
American Revolution, early defensive
  nature of, 4, 36
*American Scripture: Making the
  Declaration of Independence*
  (Maier), 241
Anglicanism, 31, 63
Army, British, 2–3, 101, 117, 136,
  173, 176
artisans, 15, 88, 94, 116, 159
  in Philadelphia, 22–23, 70, 75, 84,
  178, 200
"associators," 23–24

Bartlett, Josiah, 174
Bedford County, Pa., 182
Bellew, Mr., 47
Berkshire mountains, 136, 137
Bettering House, 20–21
Billings, William, 112
Bill of Rights, 15
Blackstone, William, 54
Blake, William, 82
Blue Ridge Mountains, 133
Bolingbroke, Henry St. John,
    Viscount, 54
Boston, Mass., 2–3, 6, 17, 38, 108,
    109, 113, 116, 135–36
  courts closed by Stamp Act in,
    112–15
  description of, 110
  occupation of, 117, 120
  port closure in, 124
  Puritan roots of, 17–18, 110–11,
    112
  riots in, 121
  siege of, 3
"Boston Massacre," 117–20,
    124
Boston Massacre, The (Zobel),
    227–28
Boston "Tea Party," 124, 136
boycotts, 22, 67, 69, 121
Braintree, Mass., 108, 109, 112
Brandywine, Battle of, 186
brewers, 110
Bunker Hill, Battle of, 135

Cadwalader, John, 127, 128, 155
Calvinism, 31

Cannon, James, 12, 19–22, 23–24, 25,
    28, 29–30, 32, 33, 70, 75, 81, 82,
    84, 88, 155, 178
  American Manufactory founded
    by, 21
  as author of Pennsylvania state
    constitution, 181
  background of, 20
  as delegate to Pennsylvania
    constitutional convention, 178
  as evangelical, 161–62
  in secret coalition, *see* secret
    coalition
Carpenters' Hall, 70, 71, 159, 160,
    162, 178, 179, 180
Carter, Landon, 133
Cato, 53
"caucus, the," *see* town meetings
Charleston, S.C., 168
Chase, Samuel, 165
Checkley, Reverend, 112
Chester, Pa., 39
Christ Church (Philadelphia), 9
Christ Church School (Philadelphia),
    102
Christian Sparta, 115, 139, 142, 183
Cicero, 108
City Committee, 22–23, 24, 25, 31,
    69–70, 71, 74–75, 76, 95, 98,
    102, 126, 129, 143, 145, 150–51,
    155, 159–60, 179
  intimidation by, 149
  and petition to Congress, 145, 146
Civil War, English, 15, 54, 110
class war, 33
clerks, 53

Club of Honest Whigs, 66, 83
coffee, 30, 83, 84, 103, 179
Coke, Edward, 54, 61
Committee of Inspection and
 Observation, *see* City
 Committee
Committee of Privates, 24, 25, 75,
 98, 99, 102, 136, 143, 147,
 150–51, 154, 155, 156, 157,
 178, 181
Committee of Safety, 22
committees of correspondence, 19
Common Sense (Paine), 85–86, 87, 88,
 89, 105–6, 138, 139, 145, 181,
 219–20
Concord, Mass., 2, 6, 7, 23, 43, 136
"Congress Sundays," 103
Connecticut, 123, 146, 163
Continental Army, 2–3, 9, 29, 44,
 180
Continental navy, 39
"Cool Thoughts" (Franklin), 62–63
Cromwell, Oliver, 24, 25, 156
Cumberland County, Pa., 181
Cushing, William, 120
Custom House (Boston), 117, 120

debt relief, 22, 137, 181, 183
Declaration of Independence,
 165–67, 174, 177–78, 179,
 183, 184, 186
 changes made by Congress to,
 174–75, 241–42
 signers of, 175–76
*Declaration of Independence, The: Its
 History* (Hazelton), 241

"Declaration of the Causes and
 Necessity of Taking Up Arms,
 A" (Jefferson), 74, 167
Delaware, 5, 30, 45, 60, 80, 91, 94,
 146, 150, 153, 164, 170, 172, 173
Delaware Bay, 38–39
Delaware Indians, 57
Delaware River, 38, 167
Dickinson, John, 49, 51–71, 80–81,
 84, 96, 107, 129, 130, 132, 139,
 142, 157, 162, 163, 164, 167,
 169, 172, 180, 186–87, 240
 absent from Philadelphia, 91, 102
 Adams-Lee resolution and, *see*
 Adams-Lee resolution
 at Battle of Brandywine, 186
 and British trade laws, 66–67
 childhood of, 52–53
 City Committee and, 69–70, 75,
 129, 159, 215–17
 as delegate to First Continental
 Congress, 69–70
 and fight to save government,
 143–47, 149–51, 152, 154–55
 "fits" of, 53, 91
 interest in law and liberty of, 54
 law practice of, 54–55
 in London, 53–54
 as militia commander, 151, 154,
 157, 186
 opposition to Franklin by, 60–61,
 63–66, 99
 petition to king by, 74
 pseudonym of, 67–69, 148, 164
 as reconciliationist, 73, 76, 79, 93,
 99, 143

removes himself from Congress, 173

returns to Philadelphia, 129

support for war of, 74

travels to Delaware plantation, 80

Diggers, 27–28, 160

Duane, James, 95–97, 98, 99

as reconciliationist, 95

Dunmore, Lord, 3, 140

electricity, 55

Elizabeth I, Queen of England, 163

Elizabethtown, N.J., 186

England, 2, 3, 4, 14–16, 27, 106

corruption in, 54

English Bohemianism, 82

Enlightenment, 27

"enthusiasms," 26

equality, 104, 177, 178, 180, 181, 185

Ethan Allen's Bible, 14

Fanueil Hall (Boston), 113

Farmer, the, *see* Dickinson, John

farmers, 136, 137, 139, 159, 162

Fifth Monarchy Men, 27

Findley, William, 182

First Continental Congress, 2, 69–70, 124, 134

foreclosures, 13, 21

Fort Lee, N.J., 187

France, 57, 59

Franklin, Benjamin, 55, 62, 65, 69, 77–78, 100, 169, 170

challenge to Penn family by, 56–59

as delegate to Pennsylvania constitutional convention, 178

as delegate to Second Continental Congress, 77, 78

and diplomacy with France, 181

kite experiment of, 55–56

and letters of introduction for Paine, 83

as liaison between America and England, 77

in London, 58, 66, 77–78, 83

as president of Pennsylvania constitutional convention, 180–81

Franklin, William, 62

free press, 62

Free Quaker Meeting, 29, 202

French and Indian War, 57

French Revolution, 82, 88

Galloway, Joseph, 62–66, 69, 70, 71, 73, 75, 84, 94, 169

General Baptists, 27

George III, King of England, 35–36, 37, 60, 61, 63, 86, 105, 126, 174, 176, 177

Georgia, 101

delegate instructions by, 45

Germans, 63, 146, 160

immigrants, 8–9

Godwin, William, 82

Great Awakening, 28, 161

Great Barrington, Mass., 183

Green Mountains, 13–14, 137

Gridley, Jeremiah, 113, 114

Guy Fawkes Night, 17–18

habeas corpus, 184

Halifax, Nova Scotia, 3, 37, 163

Hamond, Andrew, 38, 39, 40, 41

Hampden, John, 54, 61

Hancock, John, 42, 43–44, 46, 48,
    109, 112, 120, 125, 132, 171,
    175
  elected to Massachusetts assembly,
    115
  family background of, 110

Harrington, James, 15, 16, 24

Harrison, Benjamin, 44, 46, 171

Harvard University, 109–10

Henry, Patrick, 67, 138–39, 140, 141,
    142
  as Cicero of the Burgesses, 133
  as delegate to First Continental
    Congress, 134

Hessians, 37–38, 39, 96

House of Commons, British, 15, 42,
    46, 54, 86

House of Lords, British, 15, 78, 86

Howe, Richard, 176–77

Howe, William, 176

Hudson River, 163

Hunt, Isaac, 25

Husband, Herman, 182

Hutchinson, Thomas, 77, 117, 119,
    124
  and hatred of J. Adams, 121–22
  seen as traitor, 122

hypocrisy, 108

Ideological Origins of the American
    Revolution, The (Bailyn), 195

immigrants, 8–9

independence, 4–5, 8–10, 45, 74, 75,
    76, 79, 81, 83–84, 85, 88, 89,
    102, 122, 124, 125, 126, 130,
    134, 160, 162, 170, 171, 185, 186
  and the Massachusetts-Virginia
    partnership, 135–42
  and role of Adams-Lee resolution,
    144, 147–48, 150
  as term used by Adamses, 86

"independents," 4, 8, 36–37, 130, 143,
    145, 146, 149, 152, 153, 155,
    160, 163, 169, 170, 171

India, 83

Indians, 57, 59–60, 83

In the Midst of a Revolution (Hawke),
    192–93, 194, 233–34, 236

Inventing America (Wills), 256

investors, 110

Jefferson, Thomas, 74, 167, 170, 184
  and committee to write
    Declaration of Independence, see
    Declaration of Independence
  in Philadelphia, 167
  and S. Adams, 184–85

John, King of England, 15, 24

John Dickinson and the Revolution in
    Pennsylvania (Jacobson), 215

Joyce, George, 24–25

judiciary, 106–7, 181

King George's War, 57

King Lear, 114

laborers, 88, 106, 116, 155, 185

Lancaster, Pa., 59, 146, 156

"land bank," 111
land-jobbers, 13–14
landlords, 106, 133
Lee, Richard Henry, 44, 45, 46, 48,
    100, 131–35, 138, 140, 145, 148,
    153, 167
  as delegate to First Continental
    Congress, 134
  as Demosthenes of the Burgesses,
    133
  description of, 131–33, 230–31
  drunkenness of, 132
  family background of, 132–33
  family home of, 132
  and resolution for independence,
    149, 151–54, 162, 163, 164,
    166, 168, 169, 173, 174, 175,
    176, 177
Lee-Adams alliance, 134–42
Letters from a Farmer in Pennsylvania
    to the Inhabitants of the British
    Colonies (Dickinson), 67
Levellers, 24–25, 27, 33, 75, 88, 156,
    160
"Levelling spirit," 137
Lexington, Mass., 2, 6, 7, 23, 43,
    136
liberty, 16, 84, 104, 107, 111, 115,
    136, 137, 152, 166, 185
"Liberty Song, The," 67
Liverpool, HMS, 38, 39, 40
Livingstone, Robert, 165–66
London, 53–54, 55
London Coffee House, 30, 102
Long Island Sound, 163
loyalists, 8, 117–18, 120

McKean, Thomas, 30–31, 32,
    45, 94, 95, 126, 155, 160,
    164, 170, 172–73, 180
  as moderate, 97
Magna Carta, 15, 16, 24, 161, 176,
    242
marriage, 88
Marshall, Christopher, 12, 26–29,
    29–30, 33, 75, 81, 82, 84, 88,
    159, 178
  diary of, 29, 170
  as evangelical, 26, 161, 162
  pharmacy of, 26, 29
  in secret coalition, see secret
    coalition
Mary II, Queen of England, 15
Maryland, 5, 45, 153
  delegate instructions by, 101,
    130–31, 150, 164, 165, 168
  delegation walks out of Congress,
    101, 130
Massachusetts, 3, 4, 6, 19, 33, 45, 66,
    77, 96, 170
  assembly in, 109, 112, 114, 115,
    122
  constitution of, 166, 182
  courts closed by force in, 136–37,
    183
  delegate instructions by, 135, 137,
    164
  insurgents in, 182–83, 183–84
  militia in, 136, 137
  provincial convention in,
    135
  reaction to mercenary troops in,
    37

Massachusetts (*cont.*)
  shadow legislature in, 19
  Virginia partnership of, 131,
    135–42
Massachusetts State House, 113, 120
Mather, Increase, 108
Matlack, Timothy, 12, 30, 33, 94, 126,
    155, 178
  background of, 94
  and copy of Declaration of
    Independence, 175, 176
  as delegate to Pennsylvania
    constitutional convention, 178
  and Pennsylvania constitution,
    181
  in secret coalition, *see* secret
    coalition
  as tavern rowdy, 160
mechanics, 178, 200
Mennonites, 57
mercenary troops, 37–38, 96–97,
    98
merchants, 20, 110
  as landowners, 13
Merchants Coffee House, 30
*Middle-Class Democracy and the
    Revolution in Massachusetts*
    (Brown), 196
militias, 23–24, 39, 102–3, 139–40,
    147, 148, 149, 161
  intimidation by, 25
Milton, John, 15, 16, 24
mobile vulgus, 22
"mobocracy," 180
monopolies, 181
Monticello, 167

Morris, Robert, 169, 173, 176, 180
  as Congress's Superintendent of
    Finance, 176
Morton, John, 170
musters, 24
"myrmidons," *see* mercenary troops

Navy, British, 163, 168, 172, 173
New Castle, Del., 39
New England, 3, 163, 176
New Hampshire, 174
  delegate instructions by, 163
New Jersey, 5, 45, 138, 146, 150, 153,
    164, 169
New Model Army, 24
New South Church (Boston), 112
New York, 5, 13–14, 21, 45, 95, 96,
    146, 176
  delegate instructions by, 96, 98,
    150, 153, 164, 165, 168, 170,
    172, 173, 175
  1765 congress in, 67
New York, N.Y., 163
New York Bay, 163, 172
New York Harbor, 173
Norfolk, Va., 38, 140
North Carolina, 138, 139
  delegate instructions by, 45, 130

Ohio River, 182
Otis, James, 112, 113, 114, 120

pacifism, 29
Paine, Thomas, 12, 30, 33, 80–89, 128,
    160–61, 162, 186–87
  arrives in Philadelphia, 82–83

attitude toward English system of government of, 86–87
background of, 81–82, 82–83
beliefs of, 81, 83–84
calls for provincial convention in Pennsylvania, 89
and *Common Sense,* 85–86, 87, 88, 89, 105–6, 138, 139, 145, 181
as editor of *Pennsylvania Magazine,* 83
"Forester" article of, 80, 88, 89, 91, 92, 93, 98
Franklin's letters of introduction and, 83
friendship with Rush of, 84, 85
and ideal American republic, 87–88
as intellectual, 82
and kings as tyrants, 86, 88, 105
as "Mad Tom," 82
in militia, 187
and Pennsylvania constitution, 181
poverty of, 82
pseudonym of, 80, 88, 89
in secret coalition, *see* secret coalition
pardons, 177
Parliament, British, 15, 16, 17, 27, 35–36, 37, 54, 68–69, 83, 96
Boston port closure by, 124
Government Act of, 136
"land bank" declared illegal by, 111
Stamp Act repealed by, 114–15
trade laws passed by, 66–69, 109, 177
Particular Baptists, 27

paupers, 20–21
Paxton Boys, 59–60, 64
peace commissioners, 97, 101, 141, 150, 164, 176
Penn, John, 59
Penn, Thomas, 58, 61
Penn, William, 27, 56
Penn family, 51–52, 56
Franklin's challenge to, 56–59
and Quakers, 56–57
Pennsylvania, 9, 12, 32, 49, 88
assembly in, 127–28, 130, 143–49, 150, 151, 153, 155–56, 233–34
charter of, 61, 75, 76, 79–80, 98–99, 107, 129, 146, 147–48, 155, 161, 180
class war in, 33–34, 81, 161
constitutional convention in, 161, 178, 179–80
constitution of, 181–82
defense of, 56–58
delegate instructions of, 44–45, 75, 79, 99, 150, 152–53, 156, 162, 164, 173
Franklin-Galloway party in, 62–66
as haven for Quakers, 27
Paine's call for provincial convention in, 89
Penn family's control of, 56
poverty in, 82
provincial convention in, 144, 150, 150–51, 154, 155, 159–62, 170, 172, 179, 186
reaction to mercenary troops in, 37
as reconciliationist, 4–5, 100
"Remonstrance" and, 146–49

Pennsylvania (*cont.*)
  rural poverty in, 21–22
  1776 election in, 1–2, 5–6, 8–10,
    29, 31–32, 45–46, 75, 76, 79–80,
    81, 84, 88–89, 99, 102, 107, 126,
    179
  wealth and strategic importance
    of, 5
Pennsylvania Archives (Severns),
  233
Pennsylvania Magazine, 83
Pennsylvania State House, 1–2, 3–4,
    5, 10, 35, 42, 62, 63, 70, 71, 88,
    91, 101, 102, 129–30, 159, 166,
    167, 172, 179
  king's coat of arms removed from,
    179
  protests at, 102, 103–4, 126, 127,
    128, 142, 143, 149, 155, 164
"pettifogging," 109, 115, 120
Philadelphia, Pa., 1–2, 3, 4–5, 6, 12,
    20, 22, 30, 37–38, 54–55, 69,
    178
  militia in, 23–24, 57–58, 102–3,
    150–51, 154–55, 156–57, 178,
    179, 236
  pamphlet war in, 64
  Paxton's march on, 59
  Roebuck incident at, 38–41
  working-class organization in,
    22–23, 87, 95, 160, 161
Philadelphia County, Pa., 146
Philosophical Hall (Philadelphia),
  102
pirates, 36
Pitt, William, 78

Pittsfield, Mass., 136
"Plain Truth," *see Common Sense*
Pontiac's Rebellion, 59–60
Pope's Day, 17–18, 116, 135
  banning of, 183
Presbyterians, 63, 84
Preston, Thomas, 117, 118, 120
private property, 16–17, 23, 53, 76,
    87, 88, 106, 107, 166, 181, 185
  destruction of, 183
provincial convention, 31–32
Puritans, 27, 108, 110
Putney debates, 24, 88, 156

Quakers, 20, 26–29, 31, 51, 56, 59, 81,
    94, 161, 180
  as pacifists, 56–58
Quebec, 3
Queen Anne's War, 57
Quincy, Josiah, Jr., 109

radical coalition, *see* secret coalition
*Radicalism of the American Revolution,
  The* (Wood), 196
Rainsborough, Thomas, 156, 157
Randolph, Peyton, 44, 133, 142
Ranters, 160
rationalism, 27, 33
Read, George, 170
Reading, Pa., 146
reason, 84
reconciliation, 4, 32, 79, 96, 150,
    192–93
"reconciliationists," 8, 10, 36–37, 42,
    44, 47, 48, 93, 95, 99, 101, 125,
    134, 147, 150, 153–54

"Remonstrance, the," 146–49
Rhode Island, 146
  delegate instructions by, 45
Rights of Man (Paine), 88, 89
Roberdeau, Daniel, 126, 154–55
Robespierre, 82
Rodney, Caesar, 172–73, 240–41
Roebuck, HMS, 38–41
Roman Catholic church, 17–18
"royal liberty," 169
Royal Marines, 38
royal peace commission, 35–36
Royal Society, 66
Rush, Benjamin, 12, 33, 84–85, 88,
    145, 176
  background of, 84
  and Continental Army, 180
  as evangelical, 84, 161–62
  as first surgeon general, 180
  and friendship with J. Adams, 160,
    179, 180
  and friendship with Paine, 84, 85
  and "mobocracy," 180
  in secret coalition, *see* secret
    coalition
  as social thinker, 84–85
Rutledge, Edward, 152, 153, 154,
    170, 172, 173

Salisbury, Conn., 137
Sandy Hook, N.J., 168, 173
Scots-Irish, 160
Second Continental Congress, 2, 3,
    4–5, 7, 9, 10, 30–31, 33, 35–36,
    37, 42–43, 71, 137, 143–44, 146,
    167–73, 177, 181, 207–8

Adams-Lee resolution and, *see*
    Adams-Lee resolution
  as administrative body, 43
  and Board of War, 166
  committee of the whole in, 46–49,
    169–70, 171, 174
  delegate instructions in, 44–45, 96,
    98, 101, 130–31, 148, 163
  delegates to, 42–43
  J. Adams's resolution on forming
    new government in, 46–49
  and Lee resolution for
    independence, 149, 151–54, 162,
    163, 164, 166, 168, 169, 173,
    174, 175, 176, 177
  Maryland delegation walks out of,
    101, 130
  meets with Washington, 149
  middle-colony bloc in, 45–46,
    95–96, 130, 144, 154, 162
  militias sent to N.Y. by, 163
  Virginia delegation to, 44
  vote to open ports to foreign trade
    by, 37
  war powers of, 149
secret coalition, 11–12, 80–81, 92,
    105, 107, 125, 127, 144, 145,
    147, 168, 185, 194
  fracturing of, 162, 178, 179
  protest meetings organized by, 95,
    99, 102, 104, 126
  and secrets of Congress, 94, 95
  and "Thoughts on Government,"
    139, 140
sedition, 2
Seventh-Day Men, 27

Seven Years' War, 57
Sherman, Roger, 165
Sidney, Algernon, 15, 16, 24, 54
slaves, 3, 83, 85, 132, 135, 140, 167,
    174
Smith, Thomas, 162
Society of Friends, *see* Quakers
Sons of Liberty, 17, 18, 109, 116, 117,
    118, 119, 124, 135, 136
    intimidation by, 121
South Carolina, 138, 152
    delegate instructions by, 45, 150,
    153
sovereignty, 166
Spanish Armada, 163
Springfield, Mass., 183
Stafford mineral springs, 123
Stamp Act, 18, 66, 67, 68, 109
    and closing of courts in Boston,
    112–15
    Parliament's repeal of, 114–15
Staten Island, N.Y., 173, 176
Stockbridge, Mass., 136
Stratford, 132
suffrage, 87, 88, 179
Sugar Act, 66, 109
"Summary View of the Rights of
    British America" (Jefferson),
    167
Swift, Joseph, 8–9

Tacitus, 54, 108
tariffs, 68–69
tax collectors, 83
taxes, 68, 113
tea, boycott on, 30

Tea Act, 124
    see also Boston "Tea Party"
Temple and the Inns of Court, 53
tenant farmers, 12–15, 88, 106
Thoughts on Government (J. Adams),
    138–39, 140, 142, 182
thunderstorms, 170–71, 172
Tories, 16, 136
town meetings, 19, 111–12, 113, 114,
    116, 118, 119, 120, 134, 136,
    137, 139
trade, 53
tyranny, 86, 108, 185

"Unanimous Declaration of the
    Thirteen United States, The," *see*
    Declaration of Independence
unemployment, 20–21
United Company of Philadelphia
    for Promoting American
    Manufacturers, *see* American
    Manufactory
United States, 175
universalism, 31, 33

Vermont, 13–14, 137
Vindication of the Rights of Men, A
    (Wollstonecraft), 88
Vindication of the Rights of Woman, A
    (Wollstonecraft), 88
Virginia, 3, 45, 132–35, 138, 139–40
    delegate instructions of, 141, 142,
    148, 149, 164
    delegation of, 44
    House of Burgesses in, 131, 132,
    133

Massachusetts partnership of, 131,
135–42
provincial convention in, 134,
140–41, 141–42, 167
Voltaire, 13, 82
voting qualifications, 87–88, 106, 140,
146, 147, 156–57, 161, 179, 181,
182, 196–98

War of the Austrian Succession, 57
War of the Spanish Succession, 57
Warren, James, 74, 125, 128, 135,
164
Warren, Joseph, 17, 18, 109, 112, 116,
135, 137–38, 139
and "Levelling spirit," 137
Washington, George, 3, 44, 82, 142,
173
meets with Congress, 149
Whigs, 15–17, 22, 24, 30–31, 32, 55,
58, 65, 86, 88, 94, 108, 110, 113,
121, 126, 140, 160, 161, 174,
185, 194–96
Whitehill, Robert, 181
William III, King of England, 15

Williamsburg, Va., 131, 134
Wilson, James, 74, 98–100, 151–53,
169–70
as protege of Dickinson, 98, 163
Wollstonecraft, Mary, 82, 88
women's rights, 85, 88
working class, 27, 33, 88
in Boston, 17–18, 33
in Philadelphia, 22–23, 87, 95, 160,
161, 179
Wythe, George, 138

York, Pa., 146, 162
Young, Thomas, 12–15, 16–17, 18–19,
20, 25, 26, 27, 28, 29–30, 32, 33,
70, 75, 81, 84, 88, 121, 125, 137,
162, 178
background of, 12–13
blasphemy indictment of, 13
in Boston, 17
as delegate to Pennsylvania
constitutional convention, 178
poverty of, 12, 82
in secret coalition, see secret
coalition